**LAW FOR THE
SMALL BUSINESS**

Law
for the
Small
Business

The *Daily Telegraph* Guide

THIRD, REVISED EDITION

Patricia Clayton

Kogan
Page

To Dennis, Richard, Jane and Charles
With love and thanks

Copyright © 1979, 1981, 1982 Pat Clayton

First published in Great Britain in 1979 by
Marchmont Publications Ltd under the title
'Law for the Small Businessman'. Second, extensively
revised edition 1981, reprinted 1982; third extensively
revised edition 1982, reprinted 1983, both published by
Kogan Page Ltd, 120 Pentonville Road, London N1 9JN

British Library Cataloguing in Publication Data
Clayton, Patricia E.
  Law for the small business. 3rd ed
  1. Small business — Law and legislation
  — Great Britain
  i. Title
  344.106'652   KD2079

  ISBN 0-85038-606-3
  ISBN 0-85038-607-1 Pbk

Printed in Great Britain by
Whitstable Litho Ltd

Contents

Preface

This is a guide to your legal and financial responsibilities as entrepreneur and employer. But it is a 'how-to' not a 'do-it-yourself' book: how to start your business, how to keep it going and how, in doing so, to avoid the legal pitfalls that beset your path. Some areas are the province of the expert and you are forewarned and forearmed, but *not* equipped to be your own lawyer. The pile of legislation grows daily higher. Whether it is protection or interference, in too many areas of law ignorance is no defence and risking yourself and your capital in the legislative jungle without some knowledge of the terrain is a commercial risk you cannot afford.

Chapter 1 gives a broad outline of business structures, and covers sole traders, partnerships and companies. On the not unreasonable assumption that you are in business to make a profit, the company structure discussed is that of a limited liability company.

Your choice of structure affects you, your business activities and your associates and creditors. Later chapters deal with the impact of your choice on various aspects of your business dealings. Some land, tax and insurance law and relevant areas of commercial law are covered. There is also a summary of health and safety and employment legislation, about which you must have a working knowledge for your own protection.

I had hoped to keep the language straightforward but Chapter 3 (on capital structure) and Chapter 10 (on financing) assume some familiarity with the terms used. Appendix 3 defines some commonly used legal and business terms.

It is one thing to know your rights and another to enforce them. Do-it-yourself litigation is currently in style. Advocacy and legal phraseology have a certain attraction and there is even more attraction in the supposed savings in costs. If your time is less expensive than your solicitor's, you can often deal with the initial skirmishes yourself. In a clear-cut situation, if, for instance, you are owed money for goods delivered, you may be able to go it alone. But do not make threats you cannot carry out. 'Dear Sir, unless . . .' must be followed through and if you decide only a creditor has sufficient dedication efficiently to pursue a debtor, you should ascertain the legal position before you go hotfoot and in person to law. A company cannot go to the law in person and litigation must be conducted through a solicitor, but a sole trader, or a partner with his co-partner's consent, can appear on behalf of the business.

The arbitration procedure recently introduced into the county court for straightforward claims of up to £500 is specifically designed for the litigant in person and, even if you fight out your problems in open court for an amount of up to £1000 or more, you may decide you do not wish to incur additional legal fees. Court staff are invariably courteous and helpful if you fight on your own behalf. Judge and opposing counsel or solicitors will combine in their efforts to see your case is properly put, but inevitably your assessment of the strength of your claim will be biased. In addition, legally untenable and inexpert argument may lengthen the hearing unnecessarily. You should therefore prepare your case thoroughly in advance and be sure of the legal groundwork.

High Court costs for claims over £5000 and £30,000 (depending on the area of law) are far from low. And, whatever the amount of the claim and at every stage of the proceedings, you will need strong nerves, stamina and good judgement in the pursuit of a reluctant and elusive opponent.

Do not confuse your legal rights with the justice of the case. Matters of principle are seldom profitable, litigation is a last resort and legal revenge is expensive. It is often not financially worth while to pursue a claim. A quick settlement at a discount is usually preferable to pursuing the full amount as all your legal costs will not be recovered nor will you be compensated for the aggravation and emotional energy expended.

In addition, going to law is a time-consuming business. Your legal advisers work on a time basis and their time is your money. Before you make your first telephone call, put together a written summary of the facts and send it to your solicitor, so that you both have an opportunity to consider the situation in your own time. When you visit his office, do not put your bulging file on the desk and leave him to piece the story together; give him a bundle of notes and correspondence in indexed and dated order and keep copies for reference to anything he may want to discuss. Your lawyers are there to look after your interests, so make it easy for them. Take advantage of their knowledge of the law and their experience in dealing with your kind of problem.

Patricia Clayton
July 1981

Preface to the Third Edition

When the first edition went to press in 1979 small businesses were struggling for legal recognition as a special case. Since then legislation has taken a more realistic view of the peculiar problems of small businesses in various areas, including employment law and under the provisions of the Companies Act 1981 relating to accounts a new and simplified form of incorporation for the smaller business is presently being considered.* Unfortunately, however, there have been other changes, notably in the economic climate and it is now more than ever a positive advantage to have a working knowledge of business law and how to enforce your legal rights.

This edition therefore includes two additional chapters covering litigation and enforcement of court judgements and orders. Knowledge, however, does not presuppose expertise and where you face major problems, or the facts and/or the law are complicated, you should only resort to the law with the help of an expert.

Patricia Clayton
July 1982

* See Cmnd. 8171, HMSO £3.20.

1
Starting Out:
Sole Trader, Partnership
or Company

Going out into the wicked world of business can be a simple matter but the financial implications are far from simple. Independence is a heady draught but going it alone is a lonely business. Partnership, like any close and interconnected relationship, has its pitfalls, and behind the facade of many a private limited liability company is an entrepreneur as fully exposed to the slings and arrows of outrageous business misfortune as the sole trader.

Nevertheless, your choice of business structure is essential to the way you operate. It is the legal framework within which is determined your share of profits (or losses) and your responsibilities to associates, creditors and to anyone else who invests in your expertise.

Choices

You have three choices: you can operate as a sole trader, running a one-man business, join up with partners, or trade as a private limited company. The sole trader and the partnership run their own show. You put your money in and the business and its profits are yours, but so are its losses, debts and obligations. A company is everybody's business: once you give it birth and equip it for the world, it can manage quite well without you, if you have paid the price for outside investment, put in competent management and sold shares in the company's future.

This is, of course, an oversimplification but it is a reasonable basis from which to start. In this chapter the explanation of the implications of your choice is made in broad terms for the purposes of comparison, and it is dealt with in more detail in subsequent chapters.

The sole trader

The ultimate entrepreneur is the sole trader. You risk only your own neck and you are financially committed to the extent of everything you own. You chart your own course in your search for profit. You can put in and take out of the business as much money and time as you wish and only the tax inspector will question whether your business expenses are related to, and therefore properly may be deducted from, your profits before tax.

You can trade in exotic places under esoteric names but, if the business has problems, they are your problems without financial limit. If the business fails, the creditors can turn to you for payment in full, seizing and selling not only the assets of the business but also your personal possessions.

Protecting your assets
You can ensure that at least some of your personal assets are beyond the reach of business creditors. However, you may also find that you have put them beyond your own reach and control. Creation of a trust, for instance, under which you put certain assets in a relative's name, with the understanding that they invest in the business, leaves you dependent on their continuing agreement to stand by you; transferring the family home into your wife's name can be a disaster if you end up in the divorce courts.

Such devices may be prudent but they are also expensive and inevitably reduce your flexibility of financial action. In addition, you have an immediate liability for capital transfer tax and/or stamp duty. They should therefore only be undertaken after having taken legal advice, so that you are aware of the amount of control you have retained over your possessions and the cost of putting them beyond the reach of your business creditors. And there is a 10-year risk period during which the transaction can be set aside if the business goes bankrupt. If there is any intention to defraud your creditors, the risk period is unlimited.

Comparison with the limited liability company is useful here. The companies' legislation enables you legally and legitimately to go into business and make a fortune for yourself while leaving your creditors unpaid if you fail, but the sole trader and the partner cannot go into business and, immediately before doing so, deliberately put their assets beyond the reach of creditors.

Partnership

If you do not want to go it alone, you can share problems and profits with partners. Most partnerships (except in some professions) are limited by law to 20 partners but the price for sharing may be high. A partnership, unlike a company, is not (except in Scotland) a legal entity and you, your partners and your business stand or fall financially together. Partnership, in law and in fact, is based on the partners' trust and confidence in each other and in their close involvement with the management of their own business. Partnership is the tie that binds: competence and expertise do not necessarily carry with them a commitment to joint business success and the creditors of an insolvent partner can put the partnership out of business.

You should bear in mind that all partners are 'jointly' liable for all the partnership's commercial obligations. Even death does not release the partners from their joint liability and the estate of a deceased partner will, in some circumstances, remain liable (see Chapter 14). But you are only responsible for your partners' dishonest dealings if you are in some way involved, although, if fraud is alleged and the firm is sued by name, you will — initially at least — be a party to the proceedings.

Your financial responsibilities continue if you leave the partnership, unless you take public leave of your liability by notifying your business contacts and advertising your retirement in the official *London Gazette*.

Your joint venture can be based on an oral or informal understanding as to how work and profits are to be shared, but the law will put a full agreement together for you if you do not spell out all the details. A formal agreement, contained in partnership articles and executed in a deed, avoids needless problems and costly litigation. Having agreed the arrangement in principle, you should take legal advice before finalising it. Simple words conveying ostensibly simple meanings can be quite differently construed when inspected by lawyers and it is surprising how often a straightforward and agreed statement is completely misunderstood by the parties. Your agreement is an important document, upon which is based your current and future financial life, with short- and long-term implications reaching into your personal and private finances, when you may not be present to explain and to protect your interests.

Limited partnerships

If you want to put a limit on your financial commitment you can form a limited partnership but at least one of the partners must have the usual (unlimited) liability for all partnership assets. The limited partner, however, only has limited rights and can only give general business advice. Any real involvement in management means you have the unlimited liability of an ordinary (general) partner. Your position is similar to that of a lender to the partnership at a rate of interest varying with the profits, except that you are not, of course, a creditor, and you can resign only by selling out with the other partners' consent, unless you have previously agreed other arrangements.

A limited partnership must be registered by delivering a statement containing specified information to the Registrar of Joint Stock Companies (an official of the Department of Trade). He must be notified within 15 days if you sell out or change the limitation. Both the limitation and/or the change must be advertised in the *Gazette* and the details must also be sent to the Registrar of Companies (also attached to the Department of Trade) to be filed with company and business names.

The sleeping partner

Sleeping partners have the same responsibility for all the partnership debts as general partners, whether the partnership is limited or unlimited and even if they take no part at all in management and their only involvement in the business is putting up some money in return for a share of the profits.

Limited companies

From the foregoing you may well conclude, as do the great majority of people starting out in business in this country, that you should put your business together under the protection which the law affords to a private limited liability company incorporated under the Companies Acts. A company can be formed by two shareholders, one of whom must be a director, and you must appoint a company secretary, who can be one of the shareholders or an outsider such as your accountant or solicitor.

Incorporation

Incorporating your business activities literally confers life on the business as a separate legal person. Debts are the company's debts and the business continues in spite of the resignation, bankruptcy or death of its management and shareholders. (These can lead to instant dissolution of a partnership, which is dependent for capital on the partners, although you can agree in advance to continue in business while buying out the share of retiring or deceased partners.)

The easiest and quickest method of incorporation is to buy a ready-made 'off-the-shelf' company from one of the many registration agents who advertise in financial and professional journals. The Registrar of Companies will grant you a Certificate of Incorporation for a new company, but the application involves delays, extra documentation and expense and also requires advertisement of registration in the *Gazette*.

The existing shareholders of the ready-made company, usually the agent's nominees, resign in favour of your shareholders and you appoint your director and secretary. As it was taken off the shelf, it will probably have an unsuitable name, but this can be changed and the only real consideration is whether the objects clause of its Memorandum permits you to carry on business in your chosen field. The agents can be extremely helpful and the procedure is straightforward but there are technicalities and, whether you buy ready-made or custom-built, you should seek professional advice before you go shopping for your company.

The company's constitution: the Memorandum and Articles of Association

Your company will be 'limited by shares', indicating optimistically to the world at large that you are in business to make a profit and the liability of the members of the company, your shareholders, is limited to the nominal value of the shares they hold.

A partnership agreement sets out the partners' shares in the business and your company's Memorandum and Articles of Association set out the rights and obligations of the shareholders. Even if you start out with a nominal and actual investment in your company by way of share capital of £100, it is best to express the shares in comparatively small denominations, so that they are easily transferable. Issuing 100 shares at £1 each gives you more flexibility than starting off with two at £50 each and you can take in new shareholders and retain control without going through unnecessary legal convolutions.

Directors, shareholders and limited liability

Whoever is to subscribe for and hold the company's shares must pay the company for them and, because you are forming a limited liability company, each shareholder's responsibility for the company's debts is limited to the nominal (face or par) value of his shares. If they are completely paid for (fully paid up) the company cannot call on him again, even if the business is insolvent. It is the directors and management who are responsible to the company, the shareholders and the creditors, but, unlike sole traders and partners who have unlimited liability for debts and obligations, they are liable only in specified circumstances. Parliament and the courts have painstakingly defined those circumstances and the Companies Acts dictate your company's internal administration and its dealings with shareholders and outsiders. If you do not go beyond the limits of the authority given to you by the company's Memorandum and Articles and you act honestly and reasonably, ultimate responsibility rests with the company and claims by the creditors can only be made against business assets.

There are, however, some difficult areas, particularly under some provisions of the 1982 Companies Act relating to the purchase by the company of its own shares (see page 47), where expert advice is your best protection.

Unlimited companies

You can, however, form an 'unlimited' company or re-register your limited company with unlimited liability. The shareholders are then liable for all the company's debts, although the creditors cannot enforce payment against them without going to court.

But there are advantages: you do not have to file reports and accounts with the annual returns sent to the Registrar; and the company can reduce its capital without going to court. These advantages now have less attraction as the 1981 Companies Act has exempted smaller businesses from some of the more demanding accounting requirements.

The unlimited liability company is, however, comparatively rare and unlimited financial exposure in the context of the Companies Acts should only be taken on after having taken expert advice.

EEC law

Until recently our law was a purely local affair but we are now part of the EEC and our commercial legislation (including, eventually, taxation) must be brought into line with the other member States. Despite some attempts by the judiciary to hold back the tide sweeping from across the Channel, Community law applies directly in the member States and cannot be altered or amended by reference to our earlier or later legislation.* The individual can, moreover, now rely on Commission decisions requiring the abolition of national laws until the appropriate legislation has been passed by the member States,† a new departure in our law, which has not previously permitted legislative changes to be anticipated.

Community law applies generally to *all* legislation, but specific changes have been made which, for the most part, apply to public companies.

Loans

The sole trader can borrow from and lend to the business on his own terms, and the partners can make borrowing and lending arrangements as agreed between themselves, but the company director has some recent and complicated statutory provisions which stand between him and his business capital. A director can borrow up to £5000 from his company, but credit facilities and guarantees of over £50,000 (or, in some instances, of over £5000) are only available if the company is in the lending field or the transaction is for the purposes of the business and you will also need your shareholders' consent.

When the business borrows money, the sole trader's and the partners' contingent liability — that is, their ultimate responsibility for business debts — is enlarged accordingly. The same applies to a partnership merger, although the new partners share it. When a company broadens its capital base, the contingent liability of directors and shareholders does not change. Additional shareholders and debenture-holders buy a share of existing and future profits. As investors or creditors, their claim, like that of any other lender, is on the company and not on the directors.

---

* *Amministrazione delle Finanze dello Stato* v *Simmenthal SpA* (No 2) (1978) 3 CMLR 263
† *Salumficio di Cormido SpA* v *Amminstrazione delle Finanze dello Stato* (1979) 3 CMLR 561 and see also the series of European Community's Commission cases against the Italian Republic (1980) ECR 2635, 2643 and 2687 where provisions, practices and circumstances related to national legal systems do not justify failure to comply with Treaty obligations.

Retaining control

Partnership or company, the majority rules the business. Statutory protection for minority shareholders is difficult to enforce and, in practical terms, is not very effective. A junior partner is in a stronger position than a junior director or minority shareholder. He can be forced out only in the circumstances set out in the Partnership Agreement and there can be no change of partners or in your business activities without his consent. If he resigns, the partnership is automatically dissolved and in some circumstances he can insist on being bought out, although you can provide against some of these circumstances in your Partnership Agreement.

It is more difficult to put restraints on the majority shareholders of a company, who can often ride roughshod over the objections of minority shareholders and dissenting directors. If inefficient or incompetent management has the support of the majority of the shareholders, minority shareholders may be able to do nothing.

Formalities

The sole trader and the partnership can open the doors for business simply by putting their plate on the door, if they use their own names and are permitted to use the premises for business. Paperwork and administration are their own (and the VAT and tax inspectors') business and the Partnership Agreement is mainly for the protection and information of the partners.

Sole traders can, although they should not, keep accounts on the back of old envelopes but partnerships and companies have to present accounts in a prescribed form and must have an annual audit and keep certain registers. Companies must, in addition, file their accounts and annual returns, listing shareholders, directors and changes of ownership during the year, with the Registrar.

Consequently there is a certain amount of inevitable publicity that attaches to even the smallest company, as records are available on request at Companies House. You do not have to file reports or accounts if you register or re-register with unlimited liability, but you must still send in the annual return.

Under the 1981 Companies Act the small company is allowed to be rather more private. Companies are categorised according to size of turnover, their balance sheet total and the number of their employees, and two out of the three qualifying conditions are sufficient to put you into the relevant category. The small company will be permitted to file abridged accounts with the Registrar instead of a copy of their accounts prepared in accordance with the more stringent requirements of the earlier legislation. The directors must state on the accounts that they have relied on the 'exemption for individual accounts' because the company is entitled to benefit from those exemptions (ie from the requirement to file full accounts). An auditors' report must also be filed which states that, in their opinion, the company qualifies for the exemption. The report must, however, reproduce in full the text of their report on the full accounts, which are still required to be prepared in accordance with the existing legislation, even though they are not sent to the Registrar. You will not have to file a directors' report, and details of salaries of directors and certain other employees, which are at present included in the accounts, can be omitted.

Trading alone or in partnership, you can start at any time but your private company cannot trade until it receives its Certificate of Incorporation and all business must be transacted in the company's name. Formal company meetings must be held at specified intervals to keep shareholders informed of corporate activities although, since you may only have two shareholders, your formal meetings can in fact be very informal, as long as you comply with the procedure imposed by the Companies Acts.

As a sole director you can retain control even if you take on the permitted maximum of 49 shareholders in addition to yourself, but the right to sell shares is restricted and you cannot invite public participation. Provided you retain a majority shareholding or, at least, control of the sale of shares, you can retain a tight grip on company affairs. If you want to take an entirely independent line in opposition to a vociferous minority, however, you will in some circumstances require control of 75 per cent of the shares.

Nevertheless, in spite of regulation and restrictions, your private limited liability company, bought at a total cost of around £100 plus the capital duty based on your issued share capital, is an ideal vehicle for eventual propulsion into the field of big business, as its structure readily accommodates an increasingly complicated organisational structure and the injection of outside capital.

Close companies

Family and director-controlled companies have a tax disadvantage if they are what the Inland Revenue calls 'close' companies. Broadly, a close company is one which is controlled by up to five 'participants' and their 'associates'. The Revenue classify directors, lenders and anyone with a claim to the company's income or capital as participants. Your 'associates' include your family and, in some circumstances, nominee shareholders (who hold the shares in their name for someone else) and it is automatically assumed that you control the company through them, even if you fight at home or around the boardroom table. Participants are assessed to additional personal income tax on some fringe benefits and loans to participants and associates are also liable to income tax.

Taking on additional shareholders or going public to the extent of 35 per cent of your share capital takes you out of the category of close company, but your growth will have to be considerable before you are able to consider the option.

Tax comparisons

Revenue law is a complex area and cannot be dealt with in a few short paragraphs but some broad comparisons at an early stage are useful.

The sole trader, the partner, the director and the partnership pay income tax; companies pay corporation tax. Trading on your own account takes your assessment to tax from Schedule E to Schedule D, from the category of an employee to the self-employed, with implications which are dealt with in more detail in Chapter 6. The Schedule E taxpayer is taxed at source under the PAYE scheme and any concessions he may win from the tax inspector must be fought after the Revenue has taken its toll. The Schedule D taxpayer has more control over his income, his outgoings and his tax and, if well-advised, can usually retain more of his earnings.

The sole trader is personally liable, and the partners are personally and jointly — not severally — liable, to the Revenue for the tax bills of the business. When a partner dies, the surviving partners are responsible for the tax liability on his partnership income. Otherwise your tax liability is based on your agreed share of profits and, if both husband and wife work for the business, you can elect for separate taxation of earned income arising from the business. If you are the partnership's landlord, rent is received as unearned income and you may be liable to investment income surcharge. You may, therefore, be better off taking a low rent and a correspondingly larger share of the profits or an additional salary. Sleeping partners and retired partners are also assessed as being in receipt of unearned income but payment under a consultancy agreement, showing services in consideration for a share of the profits or for a salary, will put payments into the earned category for income tax purposes.

Income from the business is taxed separately from outside income but your income for tax purposes includes interest on loans to the business, as well as your salary, and a sole trader or a partner is not entitled to a redundancy payment. The tax concession on 'golden handshakes', which are tax-free to the £25,000 limit, now applies to both compensation and *ex gratia* payments.

The director remains placed firmly in the Schedule E with certain disadvantages if his salary is in what the Revenue calls the category of the 'higher-paid employee' who receives more than £8500 per annum. Interest on loans to the company and share income are included in your taxable earnings as unearned income and you can claim redundancy payments as an employee if the company goes into liquidation.

The company is taxed separately on corporation tax and, unless it is a close company (see above), the directors and shareholders are not affected. Corporation tax is currently payable at 52 per cent on all the company's taxable income, including a tax of 30 per cent on capital gains, whether or not they are distributed as dividends. 'Small' companies are taxed at a lower rate, presently 40 per cent. To qualify as small, the company's taxable profits must not exceed £80,000 and there are tapering arrangements up to £200,000, after which the full rate is payable. Capital allowances, stock relief and the newly introduced tax incentives for investment in small businesses have combined to make this country a corporate tax haven, so make sure you take advantage of the situation by seeking proper advice.

Companies make payments of advance corporation tax (ACT) during the year of three-sevenths of the value of a distribution to shareholders. The ACT goes to reduce the total amount of tax payable for the financial year and the full tax bill must be paid within nine months of the end of the company's accounting period. ACT satisfies the income tax basic rate liability of the shareholders, so that they are only liable to higher rate tax and investment income surcharge on dividends.

Partnership income is assessed to income tax on a preceding year basis, which is advantageous if your profits are climbing, and the rates are the same as your personal income tax rates.

If you incorporate your business and sell it to your company as a going concern in exchange for shares, the Inland Revenue has to wait for its slice until you sell the shares. The taxable gain (or allowable loss) is based on the difference between the price of the shares when they were first issued to you (unless they were acquired before April 1965) and the selling price. If you give them, or anything else, away you may be liable for capital transfer tax. Capital transfer tax and capital gains are personal to the sole trader and the partner and can probably be avoided on transfers of shares and goodwill between the partners, although capital transfer tax has not yet come up for consideration in this context. Expert advice may eliminate the probability where capital gains tax is concerned but educated guesswork is your only option on capital transfer tax until the courts have come up with a decision.

For the most part, unless the business is very small, a director is better off than a sole trader or partner taking out the same share of the profits from the business, but so much depends on your stake in the business and your outside income that a real comparison is only possible on specific figures and there is no substitute for personal advice.

Closing down

Winding up the business of the sole trader or the partnership can be as casual as commencement but your relationship with business creditors is far less casual. This is your business and your liability and, unless you are able to sell out on satisfactory terms, the ghost of business failure may follow you into the bankruptcy courts.

Shares in your company are more easily bought and sold and, if you can find a buyer, you can more easily sell out at a price. If the company is insolvent, business assets must be liquidated to satisfy the claims of the company's creditors but, unless fraud is alleged, the creditors have no claim on your personal assets.

Choosing a business structure

In spite of the legal restrictions imposed on companies, the difference between a partnership and a company is often only one of machinery. If you want to go into business with someone who is prepared to contribute equally with you in capital and management, the only real consideration is whether you know enough about each other to work together. A sole trader can convert to a company, but there must be at least one other shareholder, although he need have no real interest or involvement in the business. Two partners can convert themselves into a company and continue to carry on business in much the same way as before incorporation. This does not affect their existing liabilities and they remain personally liable for debts existing at registration.

It is often comfortably assumed that 'forming yourself into a limited company' is a magic formula for success. Additional shareholders and participants and further capital and loans are easily assimilated into the corporate structure and corporate ownership of business assets and liabilities ensures continuity. Most of the company legislation, however, applies at present to both public companies with outside investors and to privately owned director-controlled family businesses. The Department of Trade is currently considering a simplified form of incorporation, possibly a variation of one of the European-style 'incorporated partnerships', which has been adopted in parts of the United States. But for the present corporate life remains expensive: capital duty is payable on formation and the cost of documentation and administration of accounts is high. Although some concessions are made to the small business under the 1981 Companies Act, accounts must still be published, audit fees must be paid, and time will be spent ensuring that business is carried on in compliance with the legislation. In addition, cases dealing with the legislation have mainly been concerned with the 'up-market' version of the limited company and have emphasised the importance of majority rule and the separation of corporate functions between management and ownership of the business.

The sole trader and the partner lead a less complicated legal life and can generally choose their own route to success or failure. Conversely, in the company, unless you have attached restricted voting rights to shares, a bare majority of your company's shareholders can dictate policy, appoint and set the salary of directors, declare the dividends and, subject to certain rather unclear limitations, ratify the acts of directors.

The main effect of incorporation is to distance you from your business liabilities but limited liability is illusory* if you are called upon personally to guarantee corporate debts and the restrictions of the legislation can be extremely confining if you put yourself in a position where you can be outvoted by your shareholders.

STATUTORY REFERENCES

Companies Acts 1948 to 1980
Companies Bill 1981
European Communities Act 1972
Finance Acts 1965 and 1975

Income and Corporation Taxes Act 1970 (as amended)
Limited Partnership Act 1907
Partnership Act 1890

---

* See for instance, *Habib Bank* v *Tailor, Law Society's Gazette*, 30 June 1982, p 851 where the company's overdraft was secured by a charge on a director's house. The court could not defer an order for possession of the house, as it could have done in the case of an ordinary mortgage.

2
Establishing the Business

The way you organise the business is left to your discretion if you are a sole trader, but you should set out some ground rules in a Partnership Agreement if you go into partnership. The limited company has no choice but to comply with the rules of corporate organisation and management which are mainly contained in the Companies Act 1981. Some relaxation in the rules which apply to smaller businesses have been introduced recently and further amendments are promised to comply with the EEC Directives, which are bringing commercial law into line in the member States of the Common Market.

Business names

The sole trader and the partnership can simply put their names on the door and start trading but describing business activities through a choice of name is a cheap and effective means of advertising.

Under the Companies Act 1981, the Registry of Business Names was abolished and registration of your business name must now be effected through the Registrar of Companies. Almost any name is now acceptable provided it is not misleading or, unless you have the consent of the Minister, it implies a connection with the government or a local authority. The proprietors' names and the name of the business must appear on business letters and demands for payment, with an address at which service of documents relating to the business will be accepted. The names must also be displayed prominently in any premises where you do business. Anyone with whom you do or discuss business but who does not visit the premises must be notified in writing of the names and the address.

Existing business names properly registered under the earlier legislation can still be used and you can still start trading immediately under your own name or names or under an additional name which indicates that you have taken over from the previous owner.

Partnerships

Again you can put your name on the door and start trading and it is only the limited partnership which needs to file details with the Registrar of Companies, in which case the name must not offend the Secretary of State or be a name the use of which would, in his opinion, constitute a criminal offence; a name implying a connection with the government or a local authority can only be used with the Minister's consent.

The names of the partners and of the partnership must appear on business letters and demands for payment and an address given at which service of documents relating to the business will be accepted. Partners' names and the address for service of documents must be displayed at your place of business, and business contacts who do not visit the premises must be given written notification of the names and addresses.

Partnerships of more than 20 partners can omit details from their letterheads and demands for payment, provided that the address of the principal place of business is given on their documentation and a list of partners' names is available for inspection during office hours at that address on payment of a reasonable fee.

Corporate names

A brand new company's brand new company name costs £50 on application for incorporation to the Registrar of Companies and changing your ready-made company's name costs £40.

Unless the company is registered or re-registered with unlimited liability, the last word of a private limited company trading for profit must be 'limited'. Like the name of a limited partnership, the company name must not be offensive to the Secretary of State or one, which, if used, would constitute a criminal offence; nor, unless you have the Minister's consent, can it imply a connection with the government or local authority.

Application is made direct to the Registrar's Cardiff office. When permission is granted, the name is reserved pending the passing of a special resolution of 75 per cent of your share-holders confirming the name or agreeing to the change, a copy of which must be sent to the Registrar, together with the registration fee. Your new name must not be used and is not effective until the Registry issues a certificate and permission may be withdrawn before it is issued. You should therefore allow at least four weeks for your application for conditional approval and it may be a further four weeks before you receive the certificate permitting use of the name, which must appear on all company documentation, together with the company's registration number, the address of the registered office and the names of the directors. The company name must also be prominently displayed at your principal place of business.

An index of names is kept by the Registrar and an application to change the name takes effect on issue of an altered Certificate of Incorporation.

Trademarks

Acceptance of your business or company by the appropriate Registry does not mean that it is available for use as a trademark. You can find out if there are any trademark rights in your name from the index at the Trade Mark Registry and the relevant law is dealt with in Chapter 11.

Partnership Agreement

However close the relationship between the partners, a formal Partnership Agreement, executed in a deed, should be agreed in principle and drawn up by your solicitor to include details of the following:

1. *The partnership's name, its address and the nature of its business.* Although you do business in the partnership's name, transactions are implicitly entered into by all the partners, with a consequent direct liability on them for all business activities. Assets should be put in the partnership's name, or in the name of the partners as trustees for the business, to a permitted maximum of four, to avoid disputes as to ownership.

2. *The date of commencement and the date of termination of the partnership.* If you do not agree a fixed term and it is not defined by reference to a specific business venture, the partnership lasts only until a partner gives notice. It is therefore useful to include a clause stating that it can be terminated by 'mutual agreement only'. If you continue after the stated date, the agreement continues unchanged but a syndicate formed for a single business project lasts only until it is completed.

3. *The amount of capital contributed by the partners.* If you want to claim interest on your investment or on advances made to the partnership, this must be stated in

the Agreement and you should also specify whether interest is to be paid on the initial contribution before profits are divided.

4. *The partnership's bank account.* Details of who can sign cheques and a provision that all cheques and monies received on account of the business be paid into the partnership account on receipt should be included.

5. *How profits are to be calculated and divided.* If this is not specified the partners are entitled to equal shares of cash received, less cash paid, during the year, without any consideration of book debts or allowances for bad debts and regardless of their initial contribution to partnership capital.

An increase in the value of goodwill is added to capital and is not taken into account in computing profits, so you should provide that goodwill be disregarded in taking annual accounts.

It is advisable to specify at the outset the spheres of activity of the partners and to include this in the Partnership Agreement and you could also include the entitlement to holidays. You should state which partners are to be engaged in full-time management and whether or not partners not involved full time in the business are to draw salaries instead of taking a share of profits. Provision should be made for monthly or weekly drawings on account of future profits and state what items, such as cars, not exclusively used for the business, can be charged to partnership expenses. You may want to put a top limit on partners' expenses and you should also specify a stated figure above which no partner can enter into transactions without the consent of the other partners and you may want to include other restrictions on the partners' activities.

The Partnership Agreement can be altered with the consent of the parties but, until the agreed alteration, it is binding on the partners and should be expertly and carefully drafted, so that it shows exactly what the partners have agreed.

6. *Accounts.* You should provide for the preparation of regular accounts and an annual balance sheet on a fixed date, showing what is due to each partner in respect of capital and share of profits and what is due to him from the business.

7. *Arbitration.* It is advisable to include an arbitration clause giving you recourse to an uninvolved outsider to avoid the expense of litigation in the courts. It is often helpful if you can refer 'to the president for the time being' of your trade or professional organisation, who will nominate an arbitrator. Otherwise you can provide that disputes be referred to the principal of the Institute of Arbitrators, providing that his nominee be acceptable to the parties.

8. *Dissolution.* If you omit a clause stating what is to happen on the retirement, death or bankruptcy of a partner, the partnership is automatically dissolved. You should also specify what is to happen if the partnership is dissolved and include, if you wish, provision for the family of a deceased partner. Bankruptcy, however, cannot be completely covered as it leads to special problems in partnerships which are dealt with in Chapter 14.

Specific provision should be made as to how a retiring or deceased partner's share is to be valued and paid off, otherwise the estate is only entitled to the increase in the assets which is not attributable to profits accruing in the ordinary course of business.* It is best to base the valuation on the last balance sheet, which should be stated to be conclusive as to the amount if taken at the date specified in your Agreement. If the balance sheet has not been taken, you can provide that the necessary account be taken.

It may be more convenient to arrange to pay off the share at a fixed rate plus interest on the capital left in the business since the last balance sheet, instead of paying over a share of current profits, when you will have to prepare an interim balance sheet to the date of retirement or death. Alternatively, you could pay the retiring partner or deceased partner's spouse (or personal representatives) an annuity out of profits, or the personal representatives can take the share as sleeping partners.

Your Partnership Agreement, however, is a private document, setting out the private agreement between

* *Barclay's Bank Trust* v *Bluff* (1981) All ER 232

the partners. As far as outsiders are concerned, once you
are a partner and your name is on the letterhead you are
responsible for the firm's actions, debts and liabilities
unless they are specifically informed to the contrary.*

Taxation

Points 2 and 8 above are particularly important from the tax
point of view. Any change of partners is a discontinuance of the
old partnership and a commencement of a new one for tax
purposes, unless all the partners, both before and after the
change, choose to 'continue' the partnership.

Discontinuance for tax purposes means that the partnership
is technically dissolved and the business taxed as if you had
stopped trading and begun again at the time of the change.
Since all the partners have to consent to continue the partnership, it is simpler to write it into your initial Agreement. The
choice must be confirmed within two years of the change by
sending written notice, signed by all the partners involved in the
changeover, to your tax inspector.

Special rules apply to partnerships in which one or more of
the partners is a company and you only have to elect for
continuance if there is a change in the individual (as opposed to
any corporate) partners.

The discontinuance and commencement rules are complicated
and, if you are trading successfully, are almost bound to result
in an artificially inflated tax liability. You should, therefore,
seek advice if you are planning a change of partners: death and
bankruptcy cannot be brought into precise calculation even in
a partnership.

Insurance

If the partners are pulling their weight, the loss in management
skills and investment can be fatal to the business and it is
advisable to insure against the contingency at an early stage.

Life assurance policies can be taken out by the partners on
each other's lives, or on their own lives for each other's benefit.
These provide cash on death to enable the partnership to buy a
deceased partner's share of the business from his estate. The
amount of insurance is related to the value of the business and
you can insure for inflation or appreciation in value. Usually all

---

* *Saywell (t/a Eaton Trading Co)* v *Pope* (1979) TC 40D

the partners must be covered but not all insurance companies insist upon this.

Similar assurances can be taken out by the sole trader, to ensure that the business carries on after his death, by, for instance, providing sufficient finance to employ a manager.

Senior business executives can also be covered to compensate for the loss of their services. The amount is usually calculated on a multiple of between five and 10 times their salary, plus additional remuneration, such as bonuses or commission.

Your company's constitution

The constitution of your company is more complicated than the business organisation of partnerships. The law does not read agreements into corporate arrangements but dictates the company's administration and management's responsibilities.

On registration you will receive copies of your company's Memorandum and Articles of Association, some share transfer forms, a Minute Book, the Company Seal and the Certificate of Incorporation. The Memorandum and Articles should be handed on to your solicitor or accountant for checking and your bank manager will want to see the Certificate of Incorporation and the Memorandum and Articles before you open the company's bank account.

Memorandum of Association

The Memorandum is your company's charter. It sets out the company's basic constitution and its powers and duties as a legal person. Schedule 1, Table B of the 1948 Companies Act, available from HMSO, gives a standard form of Memorandum for a private limited liability company with a share capital of £200,000, which can be cut down to fit your purse before you apply for registration.

The Memorandum of a limited liability company must state:

1. *The company's name.* Unless it is registered or
   re-registered with unlimited liability, the last word of
   the name of a company which is trading for profit must
   be 'limited'. The restrictions on your choice of name are
   discussed earlier in this chapter and if you carry on
   business under a trading name, it must be separately
   registered. The company name must be displayed at
   your place of business, on the company seal and on
   your business letters and order forms. If it is not on

company cheques, you may be personally liable for the amount.

2. *That the registered office is in England or Wales* (reference to certain major cities is also accepted) to establish the company's domicile, which, unless you can show that management and control are elsewhere, means that you must pay British tax and that the company operates under British law.

Your registered office need not necessarily be the place at which you carry on business. It is often convenient to use your accountant's or solicitor's address, particularly if they deal with the legal and official side of the business. But you will, of course, thereby lose some control, as you will not always know whether important matters are being dealt with as they arise.

The address must be filed with the Registrar of Companies as soon as you start business or within 15 days of incorporation, whichever is the earlier date. You can change the address, provided you stay in England or Wales, and you must notify the Registrar within 15 days of the change.

The address of the registered office, place of registration and registration number of the company must also be put on your business letters and order forms.

3. *The objects for which the company is formed.* You must define the area in which you propose to do business: 'to make a profit' is implied, but every other objective must be set out in the objects clause.

If you have formed the company for a specific money-making venture, this will be its main object and, if it does not produce a profit and you have included nothing else, the company must be wound up.

You can change the objects clause but only to extend or vary your approach to your chosen business activities if you restrict or abandon them or sell out to another company. Alterations have to be approved by a special resolution of 75 per cent of the shareholders and can be cancelled by the court if a minority of your shareholders and debenture-holders make an application within 21 days of the resolution. A printed copy of your Memorandum, as altered, together with a copy of the resolution authorising the change, must be sent to the Registrar, who will announce the change in the *Gazette* and until this is done you cannot act on the alteration.

You should try to include everything which you may want to do and it is best to set out several possibilities, stating that any of them can be the main and independent object of the company, so that your search for profit can be flexible. The standard form is by inserting a clause stating that 'every object shall be considered a separate and independent main object and none of the objects specified shall be deemed to be subsidiary or auxiliary to any other'.

Directors cannot borrow or invest on behalf of the company unless they are given the power to do so in the objects clause and you should frame it so as to give them the widest possible powers. You may also want to authorise them to make charitable, political or other contributions, though excessive philanthropy and wilder speculation should be controlled by providing that no director can act without the approval of a majority of the board.

However widely you frame the objects clause, some acts and transactions will be outside the powers of the company and of senior management but, if an outsider is not specifically aware of a restriction and is acting in good faith, he can insist that the company meet its commitments. This can have far-reaching effects on the company but there are some safeguards. The transaction must be one which the company's representative would apparently have the authority to make and it must be subsequently approved by the board: no one can buy the office furniture from the caretaker after working hours and make the company hand it over.

An additional safeguard is that directors must also act in good faith and in the best interests of the company, so that, for instance a loan made by a director for purposes outside the company's objects clause and not made in good faith, may be set aside, even if all the directors have approved the transaction.*

---

* *International Sales & Agencies Ltd* and *Another* v *Marcus* and *Another* NLJ 15 April 1981

If the transaction is not approved by the board, the director or senior employee responsible may be personally liable to the company and may also be liable to the outsider. And if it should have been patently obvious that the employee could not possibly have had the authority to act as he did, the outsider has no rights against the company but can only take action against the employee who misled him.

4. *The liability of the shareholders and that the liability is limited by (their) shares.* This means that if the company goes into liquidation the shareholders are only liable to the creditors for the amount still owed on their shares. This applies to all the shareholders, including the directors, but the latter have an additional liability to the company as directors.

If the company continues trading for more than six months after the number of its shareholders is reduced, to their knowledge, to less than two, the sole shareholder is personally liable for the company's debts incurred during that period. (If the Articles of Association permit the change, a director's limited liability can be converted to unlimited by special resolution of 75 per cent of the shareholders.)

5. *The amount of initial nominal (or authorised) capital and how it is divided into shares.* The capital fixes the fees and duty (currently £1 per £100 or part of £100) payable on formation of the company. The percentage of the capital which is subscribed in cash or asset value on incorporation is called the issued share capital. Any balance remaining unpaid is the uncalled capital and the shareholders' liability is limited to this amount if the company goes into liquidation.

The capital clause can in addition deal with class rights but it is more usual to set them out in the Articles and any reference to share capital in your letterhead must quote the issued/paid-up amount and not the nominal figure.

The capital clause can be altered to increase the share capital, or to consolidate and divide all the share capital into shares of larger amounts than the existing shares or to subdivide the shares into shares of smaller amounts, by an ordinary (majority) resolution of the shareholders. Again, any alteration must be notified

to the Registrar of Companies by sending a copy of the
resolution authorising the change and a copy of the
altered Memorandum.

6. *The names of the subscribers* (or signatories) to the
Memorandum in the association clause, stating that they
want to be formed into a company and that they agree
to take out at least one share each. There must be at
least two prospective shareholders, whose names and
addresses will already be on your ready-made company's
Memorandum when you buy it off the shelf. They will
stand down in your favour on registration, when you
send the Registrar the names of your directors and
secretary, with their consent to act, on forms provided
by the registration agents. Any further changes of
director, secretary or shareholders must also be filed
with the Registrar.

Articles of Association
The Articles deal with your internal organisation, the company's
relationship with the shareholders and their relationships with
each other, the issue of share capital, the appointment and
powers of directors and proceedings at meetings.

Part II of Table A contained in Schedule 1 of the 1948 Act
sets out a standard form of Articles applying to private
companies, but you will usually want to make changes. A special
Article must be filed if you want to adopt it, and if you do not
you must register the restrictions that make it a private company
which are included in Part II.

The Articles of your ready-made company will usually
already have been altered to ensure that new issues of shares are
offered first to existing shareholders in proportion to their
holdings, so that you can retain control if you take in new
shareholders. There should also be a clause requiring a shareholder selling out to give existing shareholders the right of first
refusal on the purchase of his shares.

The Articles also state how your shares are to be valued. This
does not, of course, affect their nominal or par value but
reflects the market value of the shares in terms of the return on
their nominal value as an investment in the business. Nor does it
affect the liability of the shareholders, which is fixed on issue
of, and payment for, the shares.

Table A defines and restricts directors' powers in Articles 75
to 109 and you may also want to make some alterations here.
Modifications to Table A must be specific and the usual formula

is to make it apply specifically in the first Article and then to specify by number the Articles in Table A you wish to exclude in the second Article, the replacements being set out in subsequent Articles.

The Articles can be altered, provided that dissenting minority shareholders cannot successfully assert and prove that the change only benefits management or the majority shareholders at their expense or at the expense of the company. Changes are passed by a special resolution of 75 per cent of the shareholders and a copy of the amended Articles must be sent to shareholders on request and payment of a fee. The Registrar must also be notified within 15 days of the change and sent a copy of the altered Articles which is published in the *Gazette*. Again, as with any 'public' alteration (ie one which is published through the Registrar), alterations are not effective until publication. In some circumstances, you must wait for at least another 15 days after that, so rushing through a resolution does not dispose of problems immediately.

Once the Articles are registered, they bind the company and its shareholders as if all of them had signed them and constitute a contract both between and with the individual shareholders. The shareholders can therefore enforce their rights under the Articles against each other as shareholders without the company being involved, and any single shareholder can enforce his rights against the company. This can be important, as a private company is restricted in the transfer of shares. The shares can only be disposed of within a small group and a purchase can be forced on anyone with an option to purchase contained in the Articles. Rights against the company can be important when dividends have been promised but not paid.

Directors are in exactly the same position as any other shareholder. They are not entitled to a salary unless the Articles declare and fix the amount. The amount can be altered, but only with the consent of three-quarters of the shareholders. All your other rights as a director depend on your service contract, which should be contained in a separate agreement quite independent of the Articles. This must also be approved by the company in general meeting if it is for a fixed term of over five years, during which the company cannot terminate the contract by giving you notice, or can only terminate it in specified circumstances. The contract must be on show to the shareholders at the meeting and also be available for inspection at your registered office for at least 15 days before the meeting.

Your first business contracts

As soon as you start organising the business with a view to transferring it to a partnership or a limited company, you become a promoter and promoters cannot promote themselves. You can only make a profit from the sale of assets acquired to sell to the partnership or company with the consent of the partnership or company itself, after you have disclosed all the details of the transaction. This means that, if you take on associates and you have sold assets to the business at an over-valuation, your associates can object and may be able to have the transaction set aside.

Selling to the partnership

Where profits from the acquisition of future partnership assets end up depends on whether the asset is to be the partnership's or is to remain that of the individual partner.

If you sell to the partnership, the law assumes that good faith is part of your Partnership Agreement. You must therefore give your partners details of all transactions you enter into that affect the business, both before and after the partnership is formed. You can agree any arrangement your partners will accept if the asset is to remain your property, but, once it is agreed that something belongs to the partnership, any increase or decrease in its value belongs to the partnership from the date of the Agreement and the proceeds are available to creditors if the partnership becomes insolvent.

Selling to the company

If you sell any assets acquired with the intention of selling them to the company, you must disclose details of the transaction to the board of directors and to shareholders. If you are the sole director of a private company, full details of the transaction should be put on file and the sale to the company should be based on a proper valuation.

You and your fellow promoters are personally liable in any transaction you enter into on behalf of your company before incorporation,* unless you make specific provision to the contrary. To protect yourself, you should contract on the basis that you will no longer be liable once the contract is put before the board or general meeting, whether or not the company adopts the transaction. When it is adopted, the preliminary

---

* *P. Honogram* v *Lane* (1981) 125 SJ 527

contract is replaced by a draft agreement, which is executed by the company on incorporation.

STATUTORY REFERENCES

Arbitration Acts 1950, 1975 and 1979

Companies Acts 1948 to 1981

European Communities Act 1972

Income and Corporation Taxes Act 1970 (as amended)

Limited Partnership Act 1907

Partnership Act 1890

Registration of Business Names Act 1916

3
Capital and Profits

Sole trader

Business capital is what you put into the business in cash or asset value. You want to go into business and stay in business and you are on your own. You cannot invite outside or public participation and anything additional to your own resources has to be raised by way of a loan.

Your financial commitment is total but the business is not a private bank and business takings are not personal income but a source of working and growth capital for the business, free of interest. Playing fast and loose with funds which should properly and more profitably be used in the business is short-sighted and can lead to tax problems at a later stage. In addition, your borrowing capacity is dependent on your track record, which is the only criterion for investment in your expertise by your bank or any other outside lender.

Partnership

The partnership is in the same situation as the sole trader. The business depends for its capital on the partners and your Partnership Agreement should state the amount of the initial investments. The partners may, however, want or need to make short-term loans to the business or to withdraw capital from time to time and, if they want to claim interest on a credit balance, the Agreement should state that they receive a specified rate of interest per annum on the amount of capital from time to time outstanding to their credit. This should be stated to be an outgoing, to be deducted and paid as a business expense before the computation and division of profits. If this is not specified in the Agreement, the partners can only claim interest of 5 per cent on advances over and above their initial capital contribution, unless a different rate can be implied from the custom of their trade or the course of dealing between the partners.

If the partnership is dissolved, the partners can no longer claim interest on advances, although it may be months or years before winding up is completed and the capital is repaid. Advances are repayable before the partners' original capital contributions, but business debts and liabilities have the first call on the assets. If, however, you have been defrauded by your partners, you have a lien (that is, a right of retention) on all business assets, in addition to any other claims you may have on dissolution.

In most commercial transactions, one partner's signature, signing on behalf of the partnership, is acceptable to a lender. Your Agreement should specify the kind of transaction that any one partner can enter into on behalf of the business and put limits on the amount involved. (Bear in mind, however, that an outsider is not assumed to know the limits put upon the person with whom he is dealing, as the Agreement is a personal arrangement between the partners.) Loans which are secured by a charge or mortgage of business assets should be approved by all the partners.

Partners' borrowings from the business can be interest-free. If you want to charge interest, it should be provided for in your Agreement and loans of more than £5000, including the cost of the credit, must comply with the terms of the Consumer Credit Act 1974 (see Chapter 9).

A loan can be raised by taking on a limited partner, whose liability is limited to the amount advanced to the business. You will not thereby lose any control, as any involvement in the business means that he takes on the full liability of the working partners. Any other source of finance is a loan at interest on security and is dependent on your asset position and profit record.

Partnership profits

The law ignores work in progress and stock in trade, so that, unless you make provision in your Agreement, profits (less expenses) are your receipts without consideration of when the work was done or the goods sold. At the end of the year book debts can be a major item, so you should provide that they are taken into account in computing profits, subject to an allowance for bad and/or doubtful debts.

The law assumes that profits are divided equally and not in proportion to your capital contributions. The Agreement should therefore state precisely how they are to be ascertained and divided. If you take on new partners or take over an existing business, you should specify how book debts are to be dealt with.

An increase in the value of business goodwill is not taken into account in calculating profits. Goodwill is an asset that can be added to your business capital but it is best to provide that it should be disregarded or put in at book value in your annual accounts.

You will want to draw for current expenses against future profits and should provide for this in your Agreement. You should also consider whether you want to pay salaries or consultancy fees instead of a share of profits to partners who do not work full-time in the business.

Corporate capital

A limited company's capital structure is more complicated and a whole range of special terms is necessary to describe capital contributions, even if it is only the directors who put up the initial capital.

If two directors contribute £300 each to form a company with a nominal (or authorised) capital of £1000, each taking 50 shares with a part (or nominal) value of £10 each, that £600 is the company's paid-up capital for 100 shares in the company. The balance of £400 outstanding is the uncalled capital. This can be called on by the company at any time, in accordance with the terms of the Articles, unless it is later decided (by special resolution) to make all or part of it reserve capital, which is only called on if the company goes into liquidation.

Nominal capital is the total amount of share capital which the Memorandum authorises the company to issue. Since entry into the Common Market, any reference to capital on business documents or publications must be to paid-up capital. This figure need not, and generally does not, have any relationship to the actual value of the company's assets or the market value of the shares. Unlike a partnership, it only fixes the minimum value of the net assets which must be raised initially and as far as possible maintained in the business, and it is not a guarantee fund for the company's creditors. In order to see if a company is undercapitalised, you will have to look at the balance sheet. Even if the paid-up value of the shares and the value of the assets are equivalent at the outset, which is unlikely, they would in time diverge, unless you distributed all your profits as dividends; for instance, you may want to plough back some of the profits into the business or, as the company grows, issue shares at a premium.

Corporate profits

Profits mean shares of profits, unless you are considering the impact on the price of the shares and the saleability of the company. As in a partnership your contribution of capital gives you a right to your share of distributed profits but, again, it does not always set the proportion to which you are entitled.

Payment for shares can be in cash or in kind, including goodwill, know-how or an undertaking to do work or perform services for the company or a third party. Your ordinary shares, issued on incorporation, give you a claim to income on equal parts of the company's net assets. If you later issue preference shares, their preferential rights must be met before the ordinary share dividend is paid.

The rights attached to shares, including the right to dividends, depend on the terms of the company's Memorandum and Articles and even at the outset you may want to issue shares with different rights attached to them. If you attach the right to vote at general meetings to only one class of shares the company can be given a wide capital base but management will retain control.

Right attached to shares by the Memorandum or Articles can, with certain exceptions related to shareholders' pre-emptive rights (see page 44) and the reduction of the company's capital, be varied in accordance with the relevant clause permitting variation, or by written consent of three-quarters of the shareholders affected, or by their extraordinary resolution. Class rights stated to be unalterable in the Memorandum can only be varied with the consent of all the shareholders, but, if they will not agree to the change, it may be possible to effect it by way of a 'scheme of arrangement' (see page 44).

Preference shares come in all kinds of guises but they all have some preference over other classes of shares in their right to dividend and/or repayment of capital.

Preference dividends are paid at a fixed percentage rate on the price of the share before anything is paid to ordinary shareholders and you can issue several classes of preference shares, ranking one behind the other in their right to dividend.

Dividends are cumulative unless the Memorandum and Articles state that they are not, so that if they are not paid on the due date the arrears must be paid off before you pay the ordinary share dividend. If they are stated to be non-cumulative, a dividend passed is a dividend lost for ever. Participating preference (or preferred ordinary) shareholders receive their share of any surplus distributed profits after the preference and ordinary share dividends have been paid.

Preference shareholders can be in a better position than the ordinary shareholders if the company goes into liquidation after a difficult period. Accumulated arrears of preference dividends are payable after the company's creditors have been paid; it is only then that the ordinary shareholders are entitled to the return of their capital, in proportion to the nominal value of their shares, but the Memorandum and Articles can again give the preference shareholders priority. Surplus assets are usually split between the ordinary and participating preference shareholders.

Redeemable preference shares are more like debentures and are best seen in the context of loans. The clause setting out their rights must be carefully put together: an ambiguity can be extremely expensive, either because of unnecessary litigation or because you did not realise what you were selling or giving away.

Share warrants are usually issued only to holders of fully paid-up shares, although they can, for example, be attached to a debenture issue to make it more attractive, with the option to convert them into fully paid-up shares at a future date. They usually pay dividends when the coupon attached to the warrant is sent to the company. Unlike share certificates, they are negotiable, so if they are stolen or lost the original holder may have no rights against the company. Warrant-holders sometimes have voting rights but the Articles may allow them to vote only on deposit of the warrant. The company usually contacts warrant-holders only by newspaper advertisements, so they often miss meetings and may not receive their dividends promptly.

Increasing the company's base capital

You can increase the company's nominal capital by issuing more shares, provided this is permitted by the Articles. The increase must be authorised by resolution of the company in general meeting according to the terms of the relevant Article. If your Articles do not permit the increase, an appropriate Article may first be inserted by special resolution of three-quarters of the shareholders, giving the company power to increase its capital.

The new capital can be by issue of ordinary, preferred or even deferred shares, paid for on instalment terms, provided there is nothing in the Memorandum to prevent this and you may also have to alter the Memorandum to record the issue.

Notice of any increase of capital must be sent to the Registrar within 15 days of the passing of the resolution, together with a copy of the Minutes of the Meeting, the authorising resolution and the amended Memorandum and/or Articles.

Existing shareholders have pre-emptive rights to a new issue in proportion to their shareholding, unless their rights are excluded in the Articles, payment is not to be in cash, the shares carry a fixed dividend or the directors are authorised to allot shares.

The directors' authority to allot shares must be contained in the Articles or granted by the shareholders by an ordinary majority resolution in general meeting. The authority can be conditional or unconditional and lasts for a maximum of five years, renewable for a further five-year period. Directors knowingly or recklessly misleading the shareholders are liable to a fine and up to two years' imprisonment.

A new issue varying the rights of existing shareholders should be done through a scheme of arrangement, whether the rights are contained in the Memorandum or the Articles. This means an application to the court to call a meeting of shareholders. If the meeting agrees to variation of their rights by a majority in number, representing at least three-quarters of the shares, the court can approve the issue. Any shareholder can put his objections before the court as well as before the shareholders' meeting.

If you have been trading profitably and have built up reserves, the true value of your shares will have increased. If new shares are issued at more than the par (nominal) value of previously issued shares of the same class, the premium must be transferred to a share premium account, which becomes part of the company's capital. It cannot then be distributed without the consent of the court, unless you use it for a bonus or rights issue, or to provide a premium for the redemption of redeemable preference shares or debentures but it can be used to write off the expenses of another issue.

The premium becomes part of your capital structure because it is basically a revaluation of the company's assets. If bonus shares are issued to existing shareholders out of reserves or the share premium account, the premium is permanently ploughed back into the business and capitalised or converted into share capital, thus bringing the capital closer to the net book value of the assets. However, the net book value is not necessarily the same as the true net worth of the assets because of the distinction that must be drawn in your accounts between fixed assets and circulating assets under the company legislation. Broadly, the fixed assets are your plant and machinery and anything used in the business which produces income and the circulating assets are your trade creditors, stock in trade and money used in the business.

Under the 1981 Companies Act, however, new rules apply to the transfer of premiums to the share premium account if the issue is connected with a group reconstruction or merger after 4 February 1981. The transaction must be between a wholly owned subsidiary issuing shares at a premium to a holding company or to another wholly owned subsidiary in consideration for shares in another subsidiary. The new rules also apply to mergers where your company has already obtained at least 90 per cent of the equity in another company — which here means 90 per cent of the nominal value of the shares or class of shares. The agreement, scheme or arrangement by which you allot your shares must be made in consideration of the issue or transfer, or the cancellation of the remaining equity in the company taken over or for the issue, transfer or cancellation of non-equity shares. For this purpose, shares held by your holding or subsidiary company or by any other co-subsidiary are deemed to be held by your company.

Only the minimum value of the premium is then required to go to the share premium account. The minimum value is the amount (if any) by which the base value of the transferred shares exceeds the total nominal value of the shares issued in consideration of the transfer, where the base value is the lesser amount of the cost of the shares to the transferring company or their value as stated in their most recent accounts. The balance of the price can be disregarded in the value of the consideration which appears in the balance sheet.

Where your premium issue is made in consideration of the issue, transfer or cancellation of shares in a company which is, or which, by the transaction has become, your subsidiary or co-subsidiary, the premiums not yet transferred to the share premium account under the previous legislation can be disregarded in both the share premium account and the value of the consideration entered on the balance sheet.

There are also new rules for an issue, authorised by your Articles, of shares which are redeemable at the option of the shareholder or the company. At the time of the issue there must be ordinary shares in the company and at the time of redemption the redeemable shares must be fully paid up. The terms for redemption must include payment which has to be made out of distributable profits or from the proceeds of a new issue of shares made for the purpose. If a premium is paid on redemption, this must be paid out of distributable profits but if the shares were originally issued at a premium, it can be paid out of the proceeds of a fresh issue of shares made for the purposes of the redemption up to the lesser amount of the total premiums received when they were issued or the current amount then in the share premium account, including anything received from the new issue.

The shares are cancelled on redemption and the amount of the company's nominal (not authorised) capital is reduced accordingly, so that the company can still issue shares to the limit of the authorised capital, as if the shares had never been issued. The new issue is only subject to capital duty if the value exceeds the value of the redeemed shares when capital and stamp duty are payable on the difference but only if the shares are redeemed within one month of the new issue.

You cannot issue shares at less than their par (nominal) value but you can sell your services or your property to the company and be paid by a special issue of shares. This may end up as a discounted issue but this is a difficult area and careful and expert consideration should be given to such an arrangement.

An issue, such as a rights issue with an element of bonus, below the market price (but not below par) is allowed because it is not an issue at a discount as far as the company's nominal capital is concerned. Bonus (or scrip) shares may look like an issue at a discount but in fact are not. If, for example, you have sufficient in the accumulated reserves, profit and loss account, share premium account or capital redemption reserve fund to declare a dividend of £1 on your £1 shares, you can instead credit the amount towards payment in full of new shares to existing shareholders. This capitalises the amount standing to the company's credit as, instead of being distributed, it is credited towards payment for shares.

Reducing the company's capital

Under the 1981 Act, and if you have an appropriate provision in your Articles, the company can reduce its capital by buying back its shares. It can also buy back, on conditions set out on page 46 its redeemable shares, whether or not the power is contained in the Articles, provided some unredeemable shares are still held in the company. The provisions are, however, complicated and the penalties for non-compliance include imprisonment and/or a fine. You should therefore take legal and financial advice before taking action.

The payment out of capital — called the 'permissible capital payment' — must not exceed profits available for distribution plus the proceeds of any new issue made for the purpose of the transaction. If this is not sufficient to cover the nominal amount of the shares purchased or redeemed, the difference must be transferred to the capital redemption reserve. Where, however, the permissible capital payment exceeds the maximum figure, the amount standing in the capital redemption reserve account, the share premium account, the fully paid share capital and anything representing unrealised profits standing to the credit of a revaluation reserve can be reduced accordingly.

The transaction must first be authorised by special resolution of the company, passed by a majority of the shareholders entitled to vote and a copy of the purchase contract must be available for inspection at the registered office for 15 days before the meeting at which the resolution is passed and at the meeting itself.

The directors must make a statutory declaration specifying the amount paid and stating that, after a full enquiry, in their opinion, the company will be able to pay its debts immediately after the purchase and that, in the context of their management plans and financial arrangements, it will continue as a going concern for the following year, paying its debts as they fall due. The declaration must be annexed to an auditors' report stating that, also after enquiry, the capital amount has been properly calculated and that the auditors are not aware of anything to indicate that the directors' opinion is unreasonable in the circumstances. The declaration and report must be available for inspection by shareholders at the meeting which must approve the transaction by special resolution of a majority of the shareholders entitled to vote on the date of the statutory declaration, or within the following week. Payment must be made between five and seven weeks after the meeting.

The transaction receives the full glare of publicity; full details must appear in the *Gazette* and either be advertised in the national press or notified to creditors within the week following the resolution and the declaration and report be made available for inspection at the registered office by shareholders and creditors. Details of the transaction, together with the declaration, the report and a copy of the resolution must be sent to the Registrar within the same period.

Both shareholders and creditors can apply to the court for cancellation of the resolution and the court can adjourn the proceedings so that an arrangement can be agreed to purchase the interest of a dissentient shareholder or to protect creditors.

Where payment is out of distributable profits, the requirements are a little less demanding. You still need prior authorisation of the shareholders, however, and the relevant details must be sent to the Registrar within 28 days of delivery of the shares and, even if the contract is only contingent, details must be kept on file at your registered office for 10 years after completion for inspection by shareholders during business hours.

Where part or all of the payment on purchase or redemption is made by way of a new issue, the capital received for the issue replaces part or all of the capital of the shares purchased or redeemed. It can therefore increase, replace or reduce the company's capital. Accordingly, if you choose instead to use distributable profits, an amount equal to the nominal amount of the shares must be transferred to the capital redemption reserve. This is treated for most purposes as capital, so it is still tied up. It can be used, however, to pay up unissued shares in the company or to issue bonus shares. A bonus issue is therefore often called a capitalisation issue, as it releases some of the capital for distribution to the shareholders. The rate of dividend per share is the same on the increased number of shares and the shares remain part of the capital structure. The amount paid up on the bonus shares is treated as a distribution of the company's income for tax purposes, unless it is a bonus issue of fully paid preference shares. If any premium is payable on redemption of the redeemable preference shares, it must be paid out of profits or the share premium account.

Loans from the company

The provisions of the 1980 Companies Act concerning loans and lending facilities extended to directors go far beyond the bald statement of prohibition contained in earlier legislation and the results, when you have found your way through the maze, are not ungenerous.

Your company can now make a loan, extend a guarantee or provide security in connection with a loan to a director and to anyone connected with a director to a maximum of £5000. Persons 'connected with' a director are a small and exclusive group, broadly comprising the director's partner, spouse, child and step-child, a company with which the director is associated and of which he controls at least one-fifth of the votes at general meetings, a trustee of any trust under which the director, the family group or the associated company are beneficiaries, and the partner of a 'connected' person. Transactions of under £5000, including the cost of the credit, must comply with the terms of the Consumer Credit Act 1974.

There is no limit to the amount if the transaction is made in the ordinary course of the company's business and might properly have been made, on the same terms, to an outsider, or the company is in the lending business. Nor is there a limit to the amount the company can provide to enable a director properly to perform his duties, but the transaction must be approved in advance by the shareholders in general meeting or made on condition that, if it is not approved at the next annual general meeting, the company will be reimbursed within six months of the meeting.

Money-lending companies which ordinarily provide such loans to employees can lend up to £50,000 to a director to buy, or pay for improvements to, his only or main residence for tax purposes. This is, however, a maximum from which must be deducted any other cash or credit facilities already extended to the director. The money-lending company can also make loans or quasi-loans or extend guarantees to directors or their connections, provided the company would give similar credit facilities to an outsider in the ordinary course of its business. For this purpose a quasi-loan is an undertaking by the company to reimburse a creditor of the director or connected person.

Credit facilities extended in contravention of the legislation can be cancelled by the company, which is entitled to reimbursement unless restitution is impossible, the company has been indemnified for its loss and damage, or an outsider without knowledge of the contravention might suffer loss. Even if restitution is impossible, the contravenor and any director authorising the transaction are liable to reimburse or indemnify the company and, in addition, to recompense it for any consequential gain or loss (unless they can prove that they did not know the transaction was unlawful). If the transaction was made between the company and a director's connection, the connected director is not liable if he can prove that he took all reasonable steps to ensure that the company complied with the statutory requirements.

Company assets are also specifically dealt with under the 1980 Act. Non-cash assets valued at £1000, or at an amount equal to the company's called-up share capital, cannot be handed over to directors or their connections, or acquired by the company, without the prior approval of the shareholders in general meeting. Approval can be retrospective, if given within a reasonable period of the transaction. If annual accounts have been prepared in accordance with the statutory requirements, the limit is increased to £50,000 or a maximum of 10 per cent of the company's net assets as stated in the most recent accounts.

The company can cancel an unlawful transfer of assets, unless restitution is impossible or an innocent third party might suffer loss. However, in this instance, indemnifying the company for loss or damage through a third party will not save the transaction. The unwitting contravenor is excused on the same grounds as in the case of prohibited credit arrangements but the deliberate lawbreaker is liable to the company for any consequential gain or loss, whether or not restitution is possible.

Credit facilities, agreements to arrange credit and the provision of guarantees and security to directors and their connections must be disclosed in the annual accounts, unless the company's contingent net liability during the period covered by the accounts does not exceed £5000. Any other transactions or arrangements between the directors and their connections must also be included in the accounts unless the net value does not exceed £1000 or 1 per cent of the net value of the company's assets to a maximum of £5000.

There is no top limit on the amount of a loan to employees to buy shares in the company nor on an advance made by the company to set up a trust to buy shares in the company for employees, including full-time salaried directors.

Your private company can now assist you or anyone else financially to buy its shares, provided the company's assets are not thereby reduced or, to the extent of the reduction, the finance comes out of distributable profits.

The assistance can be by way of gift, loan, guarantee, security, indemnity or any other financial help which materially reduces the net assets. In this context, net assets means the difference between the aggregate amounts of assets and liabilities shown in the most recent accounts, and liabilities include amounts reasonably retained for bad and doubtful debts. The assistance must be given in good faith and in the interests of the company and be only ancillary to the company's main purpose in entering the transaction. The directors must make a statutory declaration, giving details of the transaction and stating that, in their opinion, the company will be able to pay its debts within the following 12 months as they fall due or, if the company is to be wound up, in full. This must be annexed to an auditors' report stating that, after enquiries, the auditors are not aware of anything which indicates that the directors' opinion is unreasonable in the circumstances. On the date of the statutory declaration, a special resolution approving the transaction must be passed by the shareholders, all of whom must participate in the vote, and a copy of the resolution, together with the declaration and the report must be filed with the Registrar. The holders of 10 per cent of the nominal value of the issued share capital can apply to the court to cancel the resolution and there are penalties for non-compliance with the legislation, including imprisonment and/or a fine.

The legislation enabling a company to purchase its own shares which, it was thought, would be particularly helpful to the smaller business, was followed by tax concessions to the smaller business (contained in the Finance Act 1982). This provided that transactions involving the smaller family business in this context were to be treated as straightforward sales of shares. Accordingly advance corporation tax and income tax are not payable and the sale is usually only subject to capital gains tax.

Dividends and accounting problems

Dividends must be paid from profits, not capital. Profits are defined as accumulated realised profits, not previously utilised by distribution or capitalisation, less accumulated realised losses, not previously written off. You cannot use unrealised profits from the revaluation of assets to pay debentures or amounts unpaid on issued shares. Realised profits can be distributed after account has been taken of depreciation. Under the 1981 legislation, development costs shown as an asset in the accounts are treated as realised losses and are deductible from your profits for tax purposes, except for any amount representing an unrealised profit made on revaluation of development costs. The directors can, however, elect to deal differently with the amount if they can show special circumstances justifying the decision which must be set out in an explanatory note to the accounts.

Dividend declarations are self-contained and you do not have to offset previous losses before you pay them out, nor do losses on fixed capital have to be made good before profits are ascertained, although you must make up losses of circulating capital.

What your circulating capital is for company law purposes depends on the nature of the business, not the nature of the assets. Broadly, your fixed assets enable you to produce income and what you turn over in the business, your stock in trade, sundry debtors and cash in the bank and in hand constitute the circulating assets to be taken into account before profits are calculated. Profits on circulating assets are income profits on which corporation tax is paid, but what is acceptable for company law practice is not necessarily acceptable for tax purposes nor even for accounting practice. This is, however, more an accounting than a legal problem and your best adviser initially is your accountant.

Inflation accounting
Until recently the law did not expect companies to value fixed assets on an annual basis. The value was the historical cost and assumed to remain constant, subject to an adjustment for depreciation. Stock in trade also appeared in accounts at the purchase price. However, the fourth EEC Directive, adopted in July 1978, contained new rules for the valuation of assets to prevent the distribution of unrealised profits. The rules permit the adoption of current cost accounting, a way of looking at the accounts that some of our nationalised industries quickly found appealing.

Our version, labelled SSAP 16, is a standard method of accounting to reflect the real cost of replacement of fixed assets and stock in trade. The Directive applies to both private and public companies and it is expected that most companies will have to comply with its requirements from 1982. Some of its terms have already been implemented under the 1980 Companies Act and the legislation now before Parliament. In line with the accounting provisions contained in the two Acts, the smaller and medium-sized company have been exempted from some requirements. The small company is presently defined as one which fulfils two out of three criteria, which are based on a maximum turnover of £1.4 million, a maximum balance sheet total of £700,000 and an average maximum workforce of 50, so your new business has some way to go before inflation accounting is a factor. Bearing in mind the current rate of inflation, however, you would be well-advised to take your cue from the standard being set for big business and adjust your profit figures to take into account future requirements for capital expenditure on fixed assets and escalating costs.

The required formats for accounts and the accounting principles and rules which apply to companies are set out in the Schedules to the 1981 Companies Act.

In spite of the legislation, however, the new rules have not been universally accepted and the Inland Revenue consultative paper* suggested that figures based on current purchasing power might be more realistic and criticised the new rules as giving too many options for subjective judgement.

Loans to the company

A trading company can borrow and give security without a specific provision in its Memorandum and Articles, but you should ensure that the company has the widest possible borrowing and investment powers to avoid problems with lenders and shareholders. You should, in particular, exclude the provisions of the standard Memorandum and Articles under the Companies Act 1948 which restrict the powers of the company and the directors.

A money-lending company can lodge its shares as security in a transaction entered into by the company in the ordinary course of its business and any company can mortgage partly paid-up shares for the balance remaining unpaid.

You can raise additional capital by a debenture issue. The debenture itself is a document given by the company to the debenture-holder as evidence of a mortgage or charge on its

* Sandilands Commission Report of 14 November 1981

assets for a loan with interest. The debenture-holder is a creditor of the company but often holds one of a series of debentures with similar rights attached to them, or is one of a class of debenture-holders whose security is transferable (like shares) or negotiable (like warrants).

Debentures are often described as loan capital but they are a part of the capital which is entirely different from the company's share capital. The debentures are legally enforceable debts, not just bookkeeping entries and appear as liabilities in the balance sheet. A preference share issue can also be made redeemable when it will often give the preference shareholder the right to a fixed return of dividend and capital in the same way as a debenture. The holders are shareholders but they can often vote only in specific circumstances, which may be the same as those in which a debenture-holder is entitled to vote.

If a debenture is secured by specific assets, the charge is fixed. A charge over all the company's assets is a floating charge, as the security changes from time to time. A floating charge crystallises into a fixed charge if the company is wound up or stops trading, or if it is in default under the terms of the loan and the debenture-holder proceeds to enforce the security.

Debentures, unlike shares, can be issued at a discount. They can be redeemable, with or without a premium, when the holder must be repaid on a fixed date, or irredeemable, but the interest is payable even if you are not making profits.

Most debentures are contained in a formal trust deed, giving a charge over the fixed assets, plus a floating charge over the remaining assets. They usually have a provision allowing the company to deal with present and future assets in the ordinary course of business and even to mortgage and sell them until the happening of stated events, when the trustees named in the deed can appoint a receiver.

A floating charge, allowing the company freely to deal with business assets, is not available to the sole trader or the partnership but a company can create separate floating and fixed charges. A floating charge is always enforceable after a fixed charge, in whatever order they were made, unless the floating charge prohibits a loan with prior rights on the security of the fixed assets and the lender under the fixed charge knows of the restriction. You may therefore have difficulties if you run into a basic liquidity problem and have given security on the company's current bank account as banks usually include this precaution in their lending agreements. Cheques paid into the account after a company ceases trading may be fraudulent preferences (favouring the bank), even if paid in under the 'genuine and reasonable belief' that the company's creditors will be paid within 'a short time'.* In practical terms, this may mean that the bank may insist on retaining a much larger amount in the business account than the amount of the agreed overdraft if you are having difficulties meeting bills, on the assumption that some of it constitutes a fraudulent preference and may have to be paid over to the liquidator if the business is insolvent.

If liquidity problems force the company into liquidation, a floating charge created within six months of winding up is invalid unless the company was solvent when the charge was created. Debentures or straightforward loans to the company may also be invalid as fraudulent preferences favouring individual creditors, if they were made within six months of winding up. Repayment is then postponed to the rights of preferential and secured creditors and in some circumstances the directors must repay the lender themselves and may also be liable to prosecution.

Charges must be registered with the Registrar of Companies within 21 days of creation or else they are void if the company goes into liquidation, and the creditor will not be able to enforce his security unless the court extends the time for registration. Charges on registered land must be registered under the Land Registration Act 1925 and fixed charges on unregistered land registered under the Land Charges Act 1972.

The company must also keep its own register of charges, available for public inspection at its registered office. Copies of instruments creating charges must be kept at the registered office and be available for inspection by creditors and shareholders.

If the company is a joint debtor with an individual and the loan is for less than £5000, including the cost of the credit, the terms of the loan agreement must comply with the Consumer Credit Act 1974. A joint and several obligation by the company and an individual is outside the ambit of the Act.

STATUTORY REFERENCES

Companies Acts 1948 to 1981	Land Registration Act 1925
Consumer Credit Act 1974	Limited Partnership Act 1907
Income and Corporation Taxes Act 1970 (as amended)	Misrepresentation Act 1967
	Partnership Act 1890
Land Charges Act 1972	

* *Matthews* (in liquidation) *Ltd* (1982) 2 WLR 495

4
Running the Business

Partners' responsibilities

The sole trader is restricted only by his access to capital and ability to generate profits. Sharing the load as partner or director however, your entrepreneurial talents are more restricted. Whether you are equal working partner, or effectively a sole trader with a sleeping partner who takes no part in the business, you act on behalf of the partnership and your partners and the law expect your relationship to be based on fair dealing and good faith.

You must account to the business for profits and commissions on sales and purchases of partnership assets and must not make a profit at the expense of the business. Any business income and profits not paid into the business account must be made good by all the partners, unless the transaction is one for which the partner is personally responsible (for example, as executor of a deceased partner). Outsiders dealing with the partners are entitled to assume that they act for and on behalf of the partnership, unless they know they do not or the transaction is outside the partnership's usual business, whether or not the partner has authority to complete the transaction under your Partnership Agreement.

In a trading business, you can borrow on security and draw, sign, accept and negotiate negotiable instruments; in any other business, you can only draw and endorse ordinary cheques.

All the partners take part in management, unless they have agreed to divide responsibilities. If you do not give all your time to the business, the partnership can be dissolved and you may have to compensate your more industrious colleagues. If the Partnership Agreement permits it, however, you can go into business on your own account, provided you are not in direct competition with the partnership and keep your personal and business affairs fairly and separately apart from partnership business.

The majority vote of the partners makes business decisions. If you cannot agree between yourselves, you must, if you have an arbitration clause in your Agreement, go to arbitration, or to the courts if you think it is worth taking such public and expensive action. Everyone has to agree if you take in a new partner or go into a different field of business and a dissenting partner can be forced to resign only in the circumstances specified in your Agreement.

The law assumes that you divide profits and losses equally, although you will not necessarily share equally if the partnership is dissolved.* Your share of the initial capital contribution does not give you a proportionate share of profits and you are not entitled to interest on your capital or to a salary.

You will therefore have made special provision in your Agreement for the sharing of profits, salaries and for interest on capital contributions. If the Agreement does not cover interest, you only receive 5 per cent per annum on advances made to the business. This is not added to the initial capital contribution but is payable before profits are calculated.

Whatever the partners agree is to belong to the business is a partnership asset and, if you decide that something is to belong wholly to one or more of the partners, you must specify it in the Agreement. If the partnership is to be the tenant of a partner and pays rent without any mention of a tenancy in the Agreement the partnership is his tenant and cannot be evicted unless the partnership is dissolved. The partnership's security as tenant is the property owning partner's insecurity. He stands to lose the most if the partnership splits up at short notice, as he could find himself without a tenant overnight. Partners can jointly own property but be partners with the others in its use. This should be clearly understood and spelt out in the Agreement at the outset, as any increase in the value of the property then belongs to the landlords and not to the partnership.

Anything bought after you start trading belongs to the partnership, if it is purchased in the course of business for business use or on its account. If it is bought with partnership money, it is usually presumed to be bought for the business.

Land bought by a partnership is a special case. It is categorised by the law as 'personal property' and not as real estate. This means that its value is seen in cash terms. The ongoing business

---

* *Conway* v *Petronius Clothing Ltd* (1978) 1 WLR 72

of the partnership is not affected but the land has to be sold if the partnership is dissolved. Even if you make provision in the Agreement to avoid a sale on dissolution, the land is still considered as a cash sum, with consequent complications when a partner dies and on dissolution.*

It has been said that business partners should choose each other more carefully than marriage partners because they can find themselves wholly responsible for the partnership's debts and obligations and even for its criminal offences. Division of responsibility between partners lasts only as long as each partner is willing, able and available to meet his commitments, whether liability is joint or several. If your partners are unable or unavailable, your right to a contribution from them is obviously worthless. But your responsibilities last only while you are a partner or, if your partners abandon you and the partnership is dissolved, until winding up is completed. The only exception is if a new contract is put together which extends your liabilities with an existing creditor of the partnership. You will, however, still be responsible for partnership debts if you do not let your business contacts know when you leave the partnership. Your retirement must also be advertised in the *London Gazette* and your name deleted from all business documentation. However, if a deceased partner's name stays on the letterhead, his estate does not remain responsible for partnership debts. A sleeping partner need not formally announce his retirement, except to anyone dealing with the partnership who knew of his involvement.

Directors' responsibilities

The director is a constitutional monarch, bound by the terms of his company's charter contained in the Memorandum and Articles. He is responsible to the company but not to individual shareholders, and is expected to act honestly and in the company's best interests. He must not make a profit at the company's expense and, if he has a vested interest in trans-actions in which the company is involved, it must be disclosed to shareholders. Where he owns the vast majority of the shares and is the sole director, his rule may be despotic but it must be in accordance with the law.

The names of the first directors must be filed with the Registrar of Companies on registration. Later appointments are

* *Daniels* v *Daniels* (1978) 1 WLR 78

made as provided in the Articles and details must again be sent to the Registry. There must be at least two shareholders but a director need not be one of them, although his position may then be precarious, as he will not be able to vote in general meetings unless he is given special rights. If the Memorandum states that he will take up qualification shares, they must be taken up within two months of his appointment or within any shorter time fixed by the Articles. Directors' names must be listed on trade catalogues, circulars and showcards and on all business letters in which the company's name appears.

You are not responsible for your co-directors if they are dishonest, provided you act honestly and reasonably, but you are personally liable to outsiders, to the company and to shareholders for anything you do which is not permitted under the Memorandum and Articles. You are also personally liable if you sign cheques which are not properly made out in the company's name and for misfeasance (wrong-doing), for instance making secret profits, but not for nonfeasance (doing nothing). You can be sacked for incompetence but you are not necessarily liable for the financial consequences. A director may do something badly or do nothing at all, but it is only if he is negligent or dishonest that he is responsible for consequential loss caused to the company. Active involvement in a company carrying on business for a fraudulent purpose or continuing to trade and incur debts when, to the knowledge of the directors, there is no reasonable prospect of the creditors ever being paid, can bring a personal liability without limit for all the company's debts. In addition the directors, and anyone else knowingly involved in the fraud, may also be liable to a fine and/or imprisonment.

Both you and your company have responsibilities under employment and health and safety legislation and can be convicted of crimes such as offences under the Road Traffic Acts. The directors are also personally liable for any deficit in the employer's slice of their employees' national insurance contributions.

Under the 1980 Companies Act, directors are now directed to take note of the interests of their employees as well as those of the shareholders. This is an EEC-inspired provision and something new to our law. Directors must still, however, have regard to what is in the best interests of the company and, in the absence of employee boardroom participation, which has not yet been imported from the EEC, it is questionable whether there has been a real change in our law.

More detailed provisions concerning directors' duties are promised under future EEC Directives but these will no doubt be fully discussed before they are adopted and interpretation and implementation will depend on the view taken by the government and Parliament when they come up for discussion.

Until recently companies could disclaim responsibility for commercial transactions in which directors or senior employees had involved the company without the authority or permission given by the Memorandum and Articles or the Board of Directors. The standard excuse was that the transaction was not within the power of the director, the employee or the company. Since entry into the Common Market, however, contracts made on the company's behalf cannot be repudiated if an outsider is dealing with the company's representative in good faith and the company approves the transaction. This does not mean that anyone from the managing director to the office boy can enter into any kind of transaction and an outsider can insist on completion. The contract must be one which the company's representative would normally have the authority to make in the ordinary course of business. If the company has no option but to complete an unsuitable transaction, it can turn to the director or employee for reimbursement in the hope, if not the certainty, that he will provide adequate compensation.

Directors' service contracts must be available for shareholders' inspection at your registered office or principal place of business during business hours. If there is no written contract, the company must keep a written memorandum or note of its terms and a notice must be sent to the Registrar of the address at which contracts, memoranda and copies are kept. The aggregate amounts of directors' salaries, their current or past pensions and compensation for loss of office must be shown in the accounts. If that total exceeds £40,000 per annum more detailed figures must be disclosed.

A director and his family may not buy options on the company's shares or debentures, although they can receive them as a gift, and details of shareholdings and dealings in debentures must be given to the company within five days of the transaction.

A director can be removed from office at any time by a majority vote of shareholders, after he has been given 28 days notice to prepare for the meeting. Entitlement to compensation depends on the terms of the director's service contract. A director must give the company written notice of resignation and, if the Articles allow him to nominate a successor, the appointment has to be confirmed by a special resolution of the shareholders. The Articles usually provide for some (normally one-third) of the directors to retire each year in rotation and they can, if eligible, be immediately re-elected. If, however, this would mean that the company would be only left with two directors, no one need resign.

A managing director can be appointed only if there is an appropriate provision in the Articles. Like any other director, what he does and what he earns depends on the Articles and on his service contract.

Your company must have a company secretary and his name must be sent to the Registrar on formation. There are no special qualifications for the secretary of a private company and you can be both secretary and director, provided you are not the only director, but you cannot then sign documents requiring a signature in both capacities.

The secretary is usually appointed by the board and he is an officer of the company and liable in the same way as a director and excused from responsibility on the same terms. It is often helpful if your accountant or solicitor will agree to act as company secretary for an annual salary in return for instant financial or legal advice.

Generally the secretary is involved in administration, not in management, and cannot commit the company in business transactions. He provides formal copies of contracts and company resolutions and the Articles usually state that he is one of the officers in whose presence the Company Seal is put on documents. (The seal is usually a metal disc with the name of the company on it in raised letters. It is stamped on official company documents and its use must be authorised by the directors.) The secretary is also responsible for making sure that the necessary returns are made to the Registrar of Companies and that the company's own registers are properly kept.

Auditors

The company must appoint (and re-appoint) auditors at the annual general meeting. The auditors must be members of the Institute of Chartered Accountants or of the Association of Certified and Corporate Accountants, or, in Scotland and Ireland, of the Institute of Chartered Accountants. They present a report on the company's accounts to general meetings of shareholders at regular intervals.

Auditors and accountants have become surrounded by a certain mystique in recent years as faceless manipulators of figures. They have responsibilities to management, who pay their fee; to shareholders, whose interests they must protect; and to the Inland Revenue, to whom they must account. Like everyone else, they are expected to be honest and efficient and, as they are professional advisers, the seal of the confessional is put on everything said between them and their clients. Here the client is the company and strictly their responsibility is only to make sure that the balance sheet and profit and loss account are properly prepared in accordance with the law and give a true and fair view of the state of the company and of its profits or losses. But they are watchdogs, not bloodhounds, and do not guarantee that the books and accounts show the true financial position. Their only responsibility is for any loss caused by their own negligence or fraud and that responsibility extends to anyone who might reasonably be expected to rely upon them.* Reports and conclusions must be based on proper investigation and they are entitled to access to all the necessary documents and information: it is now a crime to mislead your auditors. If your books and accounts are in any way suspect, or the auditors cannot elicit sufficient information, this must be stated in their report.

It is not the auditors' job to report to the Inland Revenue, but they do have to report to shareholders, give full and proper information and submit to questioning at general meetings. If the majority shareholders are at fault and in a position to override minority objections, the auditors' responsibility can end with the qualification they put on the accounts. That qualification and the terms in which it is expressed should be sufficient notice to shareholders and to the Revenue that something is seriously wrong. If they resign because they have reservations about the accounts, they must inform both the shareholders and the Registrar and, if necessary, call an extraordinary general meeting to make a personal report.

* *JEB Fasteners* v *Marks, Bloom & Co* (1981) 3 All ER 289

Accounts

Legally, with the exception of some professions and apart from your obligations to pay tax and to provide sufficient records for the Inland Revenue and Customs and Excise, you are not obliged to keep full accounts. Growth is, however, dependent on your track record when you look for outside financial help, including overdraft facilities from your bank. An artificial reduction in your profits to reduce your tax liability or incomplete records will bring with it a correspondingly reduced borrowing capacity and, if you decide to take in a partner, valuation will be based on your proven profit record, as evidenced by your financial records.

Proper accounting procedures are also part of the efficient administration of any business. The accounts of the sole trader and partnership are for your own and the Revenue's information only and their sole purpose is to show how business is proceeding. All that is necessary is that your books record receipts and payments from which yearly accounts can be drawn up showing assets and liabilities and, in the case of a partnership, what is due to each partner. The partners must have access to the books but they are not available to anyone else except the inspector of taxes and the VAT inspector.

Companies must be more specific. In addition to giving a 'true and fair view' of the state of the business, the books must explain company transactions. Receipts and expenses, sales and purchases, assets and liabilities must be recorded in books open to the directors' inspection and kept at the registered office or where the directors designate. As a director, you have the right to inspect the company's books at any time but knowledge brings responsibility, so make sure you understand what you are reading.

A printed copy of the balance sheet and the documents required to be attached to it must be presented to shareholders at the annual general meeting. Your company will have to attach a copy of the profit and loss account and the reports of the directors and auditors. Your accounts must be prepared for each accounting reference period of the company, usually a period of between six and 18 months ending on 31 March of each year, unless you notify the Registrar of another date. The accounts must be before the general meeting within 10 months of the end of the period and 12 months if you do business abroad. The accounts must be delivered to the Registrar within the same period, unless yours is an unlimited company.

Two directors or the sole director sign the balance sheet on behalf of the board and, if the accounts are delayed, the directors can be fined up to £1000, plus £100 for each day the delay continues, unless they are not personally at fault. In addition, the Registrar can disqualify them from acting as directors if they are persistently late in filing returns with the annual accounts.

The Companies Acts specify what the accounts must contain. Presently you must include details of directors' emoluments, with separate details of past and present directors' pensions and their compensation for loss of office. If the directors' total salaries amount to more than £40,000, you must also disclose the salary of the chairman, and if any director receives a higher salary, that of the highest paid directors must be specified. The number of directors receiving less than £5000 must be given and the number of those receiving salaries between successive multipliers of £5000. If a director waives any part of his salary, this must be stated in the accounts. Corresponding amounts for the above items for previous years must be shown.

Details must be given of loans or credit arrangements or agreements for loans or credit arrangements between the company and a director and of any transactions with the company involving a director in which he had a material interest, whether indirectly or directly. Transactions with persons connected with directors must also be disclosed.

According to the 1980 Companies Act, an interest is not material if the majority of the directors, other than the interested party, think it is not material. A connected person is the spouse or child of a director, the trustee of a trust under which they are a beneficiary, or the partner of a director or connected person. It may also be an associated company (ie one in which the director has control of one-fifth of the voting shares).

Details of credit transactions and of guarantees or securities entered into in connection with credit transactions, involving amounts of up to £5000 do not, however, have to be included.

In this context it should be pointed out that credit facilities and arrangements, loans or guarantees of over £50,000 (or, in some cases, over £5000) are prohibited unless the company is in the lending field. If the transaction is for the purposes of the business the shareholders' consent may also be required.

The salaries of employees, other than those who work mainly outside the United Kingdom, must, if they exceed £20,000, be shown in the accounts as a designated number who receive between £20,000 and £25,000. You must also give the number of employees receiving higher successive multiples of £5000 as salary. Corresponding figures from the previous accounts must also be given.

The profit and loss account must be annexed to the balance sheet, together with the directors' and auditors' reports. Copies must be sent to every shareholder and debenture-holder and to anyone entitled to receive notice of the meeting, such as the auditors, 21 days before it is to be held. Unless yours is an unlimited company, copies must also be sent to the Registrar.

Special provisions are contained in the Companies Act 1981 to exempt smaller and medium-sized companies from some of the present requirements and also the requirements for full disclosure of information which will apply to public companies and companies whose turnover exceeds £5,750,000, whose balance sheet total exceeds £2,800,000 and/or which employ over 250. Fulfilment of two out of the three criteria is sufficient to categorise the company.

The smaller company is defined as one with a turnover of less than £1,400,000, whose balance sheet total is less than £700,000 and/or which employs less than 51 people. The smaller company is now permitted to file abridged accounts, instead of accounts according to the prescribed formats for the layout of accounts contained in Schedule 1 of the Act or the copy of its accounts prepared in accordance with the more stringent requirements of the present legislation. The directors have to state on the accounts that they have relied on the 'exemption for individual accounts' because the company is entitled to benefit from these exemptions. An auditors' report must also be filed, stating that in their opinion the company qualifies for the exemption but their report must fully reproduce the text of their report on the full accounts, which have to be prepared in accordance with the present legislation.

The new rules for the preparation, presentation and publication of company accounts are contained in the EEC fourth Directive, adopted by the Council of Ministers on 25 July 1978. The Directive is part of the EEC company law harmonisation programme and applies to all UK companies, although smaller companies are being exempted from some of its provisions.

In accordance with the Directive two new concepts have now been introduced into our law by the 1981 Companies Act: prescribed formats for the layout of accounts and rules for the valuation of assets which will prevent the distribution of unrealised profits and require them to be held in an undistributable reserve. The valuation rules permit the adoption of current cost accounting and our interpretation and application under SSAP 16 is discussed on page 52.

Some further provisions of the Directive have still to be implemented and companies may be required to conform with the requirements from 1982. A consultative document has been published by the Department of Trade setting out the further changes which they consider necessary to bring our law into line with the Directive's provisions.

Keeping the shareholders informed

The Directors' Report

The Report sets out what the directors recommend should be paid as dividends and how much, if anything, should be carried to reserve and retained in the business for future investment and reserved for bad debts.

The Report must set out everything that materially affects the company's affairs and list the names of the directors, with details of their holdings in the company's share and debentures. Details of company arrangements by which they have acquired shares or debentures in the company, and in any other company, must be included.

New share and debenture issues must be listed, the company's main activity described and details given of any material changes made during the financial year. If your turnover is over £50,000 and you are carrying on business in two or more substantially different fields, you must specify the proportionate relevant profits and the extent to which your overall performance was affected by the split. If you supply goods and your turnover is over £50,000, you must state the amount of your export business, unless the Department of Trade agrees that it would not be in the national interest to disclose the figure or you act only as agent.

Changes between the market and balance sheet value of land and changes in fixed assets must be set out and political and charitable gifts listed. Unless you employ less than 100 employees, or the company is a wholly owned subsidiary, you must give the average number of employees for each week, with their total gross annual salary.

Under the 1981 Companies Act the directors are required to give a 'fair review of the development of the business . . . during the year and of the position at the end of it'. The directors are required to detail important events affecting the company during the year, indicate likely future developments and outline any activities in the research and development field. Details of directors' shareholdings and debenture-holdings can be given in the notes to the accounts instead of contained in the Report.

The 1981 Act also calls for detailed particulars of the directors' acquisition of the company's shares and for the auditors to verify the information.

Meetings

The company must hold an annual general meeting within 18 months of incorporation and once in every subsequent calendar year, 15 months being the longest permitted interval between them.

At the annual general meeting the accounts and reports are considered, dividends approved (the directors can only make recommendations in their report), directors elected, and auditors appointed or re-appointed and their fee fixed.

Any other company business is usually 'special' and requires an extraordinary general meeting, with notice to shareholders of what is to be discussed. It can be called by the directors or, subject to what is contained in the Articles, two or more holders of more than one-tenth of the voting shares (provided they are fully paid-up) can demand that the directors call a meeting within 21 days. If it is not, a meeting can be called by at least half of those shareholders within three months of their request. Holders of at least one-twentieth of the voting shares, or at least 100 shareholders with a minimum paid-up value averaging £100 for each holding, can force the company to present a resolution at the annual general meeting and to send their comments about it to all the shareholders. Notice of the resolution must be given to the company at least six weeks before the meeting, unless the date of the meeting is changed after it is sent. In exceptional circumstances a single director or shareholder can ask the court to order a meeting.

Notice of meetings and of what is to be discussed must be given to the auditors and to shareholders in accordance with the provisions of the Articles. These usually specify 21 days for the

annual general meeting, 14 and seven days for other meetings
(except one to consider a special resolution) in a limited and
unlimited company respectively, and 21 days for a special
resolution. Notice of the annual general meeting must describe it
as such and shareholders of your private company can assign
their vote to a proxy, who can speak and vote for them.

Notice is given when it has been posted and can be assumed
to be received but it is best to state in the Articles that an
accidental omission to give notice, or its non-receipt, will not
invalidate proceedings at meetings. Usually you do not have to
give notice to shareholders living abroad.

Special notice of at least 28 days must be given to shareholders of a resolution to appoint new auditors or to prevent
their re-appointment and to remove or replace directors. You
should, if possible, give notice of the meeting and the resolution
at the same time but notice of the resolution must be received
at least 21 days before the meeting.

The rules regarding notice can be waived with the consent of
95 per cent of the holders of the voting shares and they can
agree not to meet at all, but all the shareholders with voting
rights must agree before you can dispense with the annual
general meeting. The shareholders can simply sign written
resolutions, instead of putting them to the vote at a meeting but
they must also signify their agreement to waiver of notice of the
meeting.

Resolutions may be ordinary, special or extraordinary.
Ordinary and special resolutions are passed by a straight
majority of those actually present at the meeting but a special
resolution must include proxy votes. Extraordinary resolutions
need a three-quarters majority.

Most company business, including the removal of directors
and a voluntary winding up in the circumstances specified in the
Articles, requires only an ordinary resolution. Special resolutions
are necessary to change the company's Articles and its name or
objects and to reduce the capital. Extraordinary resolutions are
only needed for a voluntary winding up when the company is
insolvent and for reconstructions and mergers. Copies of special
and extraordinary resolutions must be sent to the Registrar
within 15 days of the meeting.

The chairman of the board usually runs meetings but the
shareholders can elect anyone to chair a meeting, unless there is
a special provision in the Articles to prevent it. The chairman
has to keep order and ascertain the opinion of the meeting and

he can make decisions only on very incidental points. Keeping order, however, often requires snap decisions on motions, amendments, questions and points of order and a special provision in the Articles giving the chairman of the meeting a casting vote at general and board meetings is often useful.

The real business of the company is decided at board meetings, which also deal with any formal business required by the Articles, such as approving share transfers. They can be held anywhere and at any time and usually the Articles allow the Board to delegate its powers to committees of one or several directors. The powers of the board depend on the Articles and it can usually pass any resolution that is not designated by the Articles or by the law as the province of the shareholders in general meeting. Consequently, if the powers of management are vested in the board, it effectively makes all the company's decisions but, while the board can generally manage the company in its own way, the shareholders must be kept up to date on major decisions.

If a quorum is specified in the Articles, the specified number must be present at board meetings but resolutions can be passed without calling a meeting if the board have all been notified of the resolution. If no quorum is specified, a majority of the directors must be present.

A director with a personal interest in a contract discussed at a meeting is not entitled to vote.

Directors must be given notice of meetings, unless it is impossible to reach them, if, for example, they are out of the country. Notice can be very short and informal, even unwritten, and need not state what is to be discussed, unless the Articles require it.

Minutes of all the meetings must be kept in a Minute Book, used only for that purpose, which is kept at the registered office. Decisions made at meetings are put in the form of resolutions and signed by the chairman or other officer and bind the directors if agreed in accordance with the required majority. Any procedural points which are not covered by the Memorandum and Articles can therefore be written into the minutes, provided they do not conflict with their provisions, so that the responsibilities and sphere of activities of management can be defined and minuted. You should also formally agree and minute the decision as to who is to sign company cheques if you do not adopt the form of draft resolution which is usually sent by the company's bankers when you agree their appointment.

Majority rule and minority rights

As long as management acts in good faith and in the interests of the company as a whole, minority shareholders have no power to interfere in the running of the business.

While a single shareholder can sue the company in his own name to protect his individual rights (for example, to compel the board to accept his vote at general meetings), he can seldom call on the law to act to protect what he considers to be the company's interests or to interfere with internal management. Any action has to be taken by the company itself.

This means that the will of the majority shareholders is the will of the company and the company in general meeting has the sole right to decide whether disputes should be put before the court which takes the view that if the company is defrauded, the company should take action and it is only where the board is controlled by 'fraudsters' that a minority of shareholders can take action. Even then they must first show a *prima facie* case and if damage to the company does not affect them personally, they cannot take action.*

A shareholder can, however, stop management acting illegally or beyond the powers given to them under the Memorandum and Articles and can make an application to the court if the affairs of the company are being conducted in a manner which is, or will be, prejudicial to his interests. Even then, unless there is an allegation of fraud, the Memorandum and Articles can provide for ratification of almost any action of the board by special or ordinary resolution at general meetings. If minority shareholders want to proceed against controlling shareholders, their only recourse is to the court and then only, except in exceptional circumstances, if the majority shareholders have not yet confirmed the transaction.

Where, however, the shareholder acts promptly and is able to prove that his interests have been unfairly prejudiced, the court can exercise strict control over the company by, for example, ordering that the majority shareholders buy him out, or that the company do so by reducing its capital. It can also order

---

* *Prudential Assurance Co Ltd* v *Newman Industries and Others* (No 2) (1982) 2 WLR 31

alteration of the Memorandum and Articles or bring proceedings against management on behalf of the company.

If the board is just inefficient, a shareholder may be able to do nothing. The court will support him, however, if the majority shareholders do not share a profit resulting from their 'gross negligence' and he does not have to prove fraud. Run-of-the-mill negligence, even if it leads to loss, may not attract the same support and usually the shareholder must prove that there has been some manipulation of the advantages of a majority holding to gain something to which management is otherwise not legally entitled.

The same considerations apply to a shareholders' petition to the court for a compulsory liquidation on the ground that it is 'just and equitable' to wind up the company. The court will make the order only if it considers that the shareholders have no other remedy and that they are not being unreasonable in insisting upon a winding up.

As a last resort, the company itself (by passing a special resolution), or at least 200 shareholders or at least 10 per cent of the holders of the issued shares, can call in the Department of Trade to investigate the company. Shareholders must have substantial grounds to call for an investigation and must give security for the costs of the inquiry to a maximum of £5000.

The Department will appoint an inspector if it thinks that management is, or has been, running the company with intent to defraud or mislead shareholders or creditors, or running it for a fraudulent or unlawful purpose or in a manner which is, or will be, prejudicial to the shareholders' interests, even if the company is already in voluntary liquidation. The inspector must have access to all the necessary information, books and documents and the investigation can lead to prosecution, the imposition of strict controls on management, an order to buy out minority shareholders, or liquidation. The company can itself also claim damages or the recovery of its assets from management.

STATUTORY REFERENCES

Partnerships	Companies
Law Reform (Married Women and Joint Tortfeasors) Act 1935	Companies Acts 1948 to 1981
Limited Partnership Act 1890	
Partnership Act 1890	
Registration of Business Names Act 1916	

5
Premises

Do-it-yourself conveyancing may be your choice when you buy your home and buying and selling real estate is an area of protection supervised by the Office of Fair Trading under the Estate Agency Act 1979. Investment in business premises and rent is, however, a large part of your overhead and the right location at the right price and on the right terms can be essential to your success. When you acquire business premises you should therefore seek professional advice on your legal obligations and to obtain a valuation of 'goodwill' attached to a business bought as a going concern. Rent is also an area for expert valuation, both on acquisition and on renewal of a lease.

Planning permission

You should make sure that the local authority has consented to the current use of the premises or will consent to a change of use to your chosen business activity and that there are no local by-laws which restrict the current use of, or proposed alteration to, the premises.

Expert advice is required if you need planning consents but you can make preliminary investigations yourself as to whether the use or proposed change conforms with local planning policy or reasonably relates to permitted development. You can also check whether the consents of anyone with an interest in the premises, including the freeholder and any lessee whose tenancy has at least 10 years to run, has been, or can be, obtained. A prospective buyer can apply for planning permission but you may have to pay more for the property if its value is increased by the change of use.

Certain alterations and building works do not require planning permission, including, subject to conditions, a 10 per cent addition to the building's cubic content (not to its square footage). A change within the categories of the Use Classes Order 1977 (for example, fron one shop to another) is also permitted. Consent is, however, required for a 'material' change of use, for the carrying out of demolition and most building work, and for a 'material' widening of access to the highway. (You cannot widen the access to the premises at all, if you would thereby dangerously obstruct the view of road users.) You may also require consent if you want to display outside advertisements.

If your vendor has received outline permission, based on preliminary drawings, you must ensure that the time limits on the permission have not been exceeded. Full, as opposed to outline, permission normally lasts for five years, unless another period has been specified.

If the current use is unauthorised you will have problems. Unauthorised use from before the end of 1963 can be regularised by applying for an established use certificate but, if the change is more recent, the current use is unlawful.

You must make your own inquiries as to planning permission for current, or proposed change of, use. While you can obtain your vendor's undertaking that planning permission has been obtained and insist on the insertion of a special provision in your conveyance or lease to that effect, the tenant or owner in occupation of the premises is the person responsible to the local authority if the use is illegal. Your right to sue for misrepresentation and/or breach of the covenants in your lease and to be indemnified in damages is expensive and generally of little value compared with the expense and impact on the business of an eviction without notice for non-compliance with planning regulations.

The leaseholder

If you are acquiring leasehold premises, the landlord's consent may have to be obtained to a change in the use of the premises to enable you to carry on your chosen business under the terms of the vendor's lease. The landlord cannot demand payment for his consent or increase the rent if the change involves no structural alterations even if the lease states that he can, but he can require payment for damage to the property or any diminution in its value or the value of adjoining property that he owns. The tenant must, however, pay any legal or other expenses consequent on the change and for structural alterations. These costs may be passed on to a purchaser. If the relevant clause in the lease states that the landlord cannot 'unreasonably withhold consent' to the change in use, he must give a reasonable reason for refusing consent and a demand for a sum in excess of actual compensation constitutes unreasonable refusal. The tenant can apply to the court for a declaration that consent has been unreasonably withheld but, as *in any dispute as to the terms of a lease, you should seek a legal opinion* as to what constitutes unreasonableness or adequate compensation.

A change in the use of the premises or one which simply amounts to an alteration or improvement of the property and involves no change of use can be prohibited by the terms of a lease. As is the case with any terms of the lease which solely benefit one party, the landlord can waive his rights and permit the change.

Again, if the relevant clause states that the landlord's consent cannot be unreasonably withheld, the tenant will have to pay a reasonable sum to compensate for damage to, or diminution in the value of, the landlord's premises and consequential legal or other expenses. He may also have to give an undertaking to reinstate the premises if this would be reasonable in the circumstances.

If you buy from an outgoing tenant, make sure that the terms of his lease permit him to sell or sub-let his interest in the property. If the vendor sells to you in breach of the terms of his lease, that is his problem and not yours, as, unless you knew he had no right to sell to you, the landlord will have to accept you as a tenant and seek redress from your vendor.

Even if the lease does not permit a sale or sub-let, the landlord may give permission. Where his consent is specifically required he cannot refuse permission to a sale to a suitable tenant and can only charge for his consent if his lease with your vendor provides for it. Your vendor can only pass on those costs to you if the agreement for sale specifically states that the purchaser is liable for the expenses. The 'National Conditions of Sale', which are usually incorporated into contracts of sale, require that such payments are the liability of the vendor.

In these inflationary times, there will usually be a rent review clause in your lease. It is often an increase of rent that forces a business tenant to move on, as most tenants of business premises can continue in occupation after their lease expires on the same terms as were contained in the expired lease, provided it was for a fixed period or from year to year following a lease for a stated period of months or years.

Tenants who use part of the premises for living accommodation cannot automatically continue in occupation — although they may have security of tenure under the Rent Act — and other tenancies, including the tenancy of a public house, which are exluded from this protection are listed in Part II of the Landlord and Tenant Act 1954.

Renewal is subject to negotiation but there must first be determination of the existing tenancy in accordance with the terms of the Landlord and Tenant Act 1954. Usually the landlord must give between six and 12 months' notice of termination and must state whether he will oppose your application for a new tenancy. Otherwise the existing tenancy continues on the existing terms until the tenant asks for renewal. There are strict formalities and time limits for both sides but the tenant's right to remain in occupation and directions as to the method by which he can exercise his right must be given in the landlord's notice of termination.

The landlord cannot simply ask you to leave but must base his claim on one of the statutory grounds for possession. Generally they are similar to those you might expect in a commercial lease and include persistent delay in paying the rent and failure to maintain, repair, use or manage the premises properly. In addition, however satisfactory you are as tenant, you must move if the landlord offers you suitable alternative accommodation, if he wants to let the premises as part of a larger and more profitable unit, or if he intends to redevelop or to use them himself.

If it is only a question, however, of a breakdown in the negotiations for renewal, you can apply to the county court for a new lease. This is why, in accordance with the terms of the Landlord and Tenant Act 1954, you must be sure to make application to the court for a new tenancy two to four months before service of the landlord's notice of termination or your request for renewal. However close to agreement you are at the outset, you may drift apart during negotiations and applications made out of time cannot be heard by the court and you will lose your statutory right to a new tenancy.

You can protect yourself by asking your landlord to agree in writing that he will not insist on his legal rights and, if possible, ask him to agree an extension without a time limit, but your best protection is to lodge your application in any event and at an early stage.

If the landlord cannot prove one of the statutory grounds, the court must grant you a tenancy of up to 14 years depending on what ground the landlord has based his opposition. The new lease is usually put together on much the same terms as the old one, but rent will be based on what the property would fetch on the open market. This is determined after hearing expert evidence from both sides. You will have to pay the new rent as from three months after the case is heard and, if the landlord has applied for an interim increase in rent pending determination of the case, you will have to pay this until the full increase is payable. A rent review clause can also be included in your new lease.

If the tenant has to move, the landlord must pay compensation for improvements, whoever terminated the tenancy, provided the tenant served formal notice of three months of his intention to do the work and the landlord made no objection, or did not himself carry it out in return for a reasonable increase in rent. If the landlord simply objects, the tenant can apply to the court for a certificate stating that it was reasonable to do the work in the circumstances. The claim must have been made before the end of the tenancy, within specified time limits, and, if an amount is not agreed between the landlord and tenant, it will be calculated by the court.

If the tenant or his business has occupied the premises continuously for the previous 14 years, the tenant is entitled to compensation for disturbance. This is, however, only available if the tenant has to move because the landlord wants a better return by a letting of the premises as part of a larger unit, if he intends to redevelop, or if he wants them for his own use.

Landlord and tenant law is a very technical area, with infinite possibilities for expensive error. Time limits must be strictly adhered to and leases, even the occasional ostensibly easily understood rental agreement, are best read and understood by the same kind of legal mind that initially drafted the document. Mistakes can be very expensive. Bear in mind how much your business success depends on careful investment in your premises and make an additional investment in proper professional advice on all aspects of its acquisition.

Arrears of rent

The business tenant's statutory security of tenure and compulsory compensation on moving are to some extent counterbalanced by the landlord's legal right to levy distress (or distrain) for arrears of rent, by seizing the tenant's assets as security for the amount outstanding. The assets may be sold if the landlord is not paid within five days of seizure.

Distress can only be levied in the daylight hours, excluding Sundays, and is only available against a tenant in occupation under a continuing tenancy or during the six months subsequent to the termination of the tenancy. It is not available against someone occupying the premises under a licence and the landlord's rights are subject and without prejudice to the rights of prior creditors. The landlord can distrain personally or through a bailiff and, if the goods are sold, they must be valued and any excess on realisation paid over to the tenant.

A landlord wrongfully exercising his right to distrain is liable in damages to the tenant and you should therefore take legal advice before you exercise or admit the right to legalised trespass and seizure of goods.

Conditions of work

With the law looking over your shoulder — a sleeping partner on no account to be disturbed — you must now consider the condition of your premises in the context of the Health and Safety at Work Act 1974, the Offices, Shops and Railway Premises Act 1963 and the Factories Act 1961.

The 1974 Act has defined and extended the duties of all employers, whatever the nature of their business activities. A catalogue listing more than 2000 relevant publications, intended for employers, employees and legal specialists, and which includes reports, regulations and forms, is available at £1.50 from HMSO. An annual update is also available. Commissions set up to consider conditions of work under the Act have wide powers of investigation and inspection and can close down your premises if there is potential danger to employees, so you must be aware of health and safety law and the way in which it is being interpreted.

The Health and Safety at Work Act applies to all premises where people are employed and covers about 5,000,000 people not protected by earlier legislation applying to offices, shops and factories. It also, as does some of the earlier legislation, covers independent contractors (which includes the self-employed), visitors to your premises and members of the general public who are injured by your business activities.

Legislation which specifically applies to offices, shops, factories and certain trades is dealt with later in this chapter and there is an overlap between the 1974 health and safety legislation and the earlier law. The 1974 Act is mainly concerned with the prevention of accidents and the imposition of fines and penalties for offences under the Act. The earlier law imposes responsibilities on occupiers of business premises to provide a safe system of work and a general liability in damages to anyone injured as a result of their business activities.

The old law is still the basis for claims for compensation brought by employees and third parties and employees may also claim for an industrial injury under the Social Security Act 1975, payable by the Department of Health and Social Security. Your liability cannot be excluded or restricted if an employee suffers physical or mental injury or illness in the course of employment because of defective plant, machinery, equipment or clothing used in the business.

Essentially your employees must work in reasonable safety and comfort, your premises must not be too hot, too cold, too damp or too noisy. Nor must the noise level adversely affect your neighbours. The local authority can close you down if you are polluting the environment with industrial effluent or emissions, including excessive noise and you must use the best practicable means to avoid environmental pollution.

Here, as in so many other areas of law where your actions affect the general public, you are 'strictly liable' (that is, automatically responsible) for business activities which adversely affect the health or safety of the public.*

Welfare and catering arrangements and toilet facilities must be clean and safe and you are responsible for looking after employees' clothing left on the premises. All this, however, applies with the rider 'as far as is reasonably practicable': the kitchens of the Ritz, set in the gardens of Versailles, with Vivaldi as background music are not called for. Inspectors have been appointed under the 1974 Act and there is also an Employment Medical Advisory Service (EMAS). Prior consultation and cooperation with the inspectorate and EMAS may enable you to avoid problems which may even lead to criminal proceedings.

If you manufacture, supply or import goods, your plant, machinery, systems of work and methods of handling, storage and transport must be safe, suitable and without risk to health. Any installations on the premises must be properly inspected

---

* See for instance *Ashcroft* v *Cambro Waste Products Ltd* (1981) 1 WLR 1349 where pollution permitted by a site foreman was sufficient to make the company liable under the Pollution Act, although the directors had no knowledge of the offence.

by the person who installs them. Plant and machinery should be overhauled periodically and your employees directed immediately to report defects, so that repairs can be properly effected as and when necessary. Defective machinery that has become dangerous should be withdrawn from use until repaired.

The manufacturer, supplier, installer, person responsible for maintenance and anyone else through whose hands a defective product has passed all have their own responsibilities, both to you and to anyone employed by you or injured on your premises. You are, however, in the first line of fire and directly responsible to anyone injured physically or mentally by a defect in plant, machinery or clothing used at work, even if the accident is due to someone else's careless or intentional act.

Claims must be made within three years of the injury and damages are reduced to reflect a claimant's own responsibility for the accident; after settlement you can turn to the party at fault for reimbursement. In order to ensure that you are able to meet a claim by an employee injured in the course of employment you must, subject to a penalty of £200, be insured for at least £2,000,000 in respect of claims arising out of any one incident, under the Employers Liability (Compulsory Insurance) Act 1969. A copy of the policy must be displayed on your premises for the information of employees and available on demand to an accredited inspector. This cover is, however, not required if you only employ near relatives or independent contractors.

You must ensure that the means of access to the premises is safe, and continuing instruction, information, training and supervision must be provided to protect your employees' safety and health. If your workforce is inexperienced you must take special care, and employees with a poor command of English must be clearly instructed. You can insist on the use of protective devices and special clothing and equipment if you are engaged in hazardous work and should put up warning notices and directly warn your employees of the possible results if they do not follow advice. If the dangers attendant on your business activities are not obvious or where injury might be slow to appear, employees should be duly warned of inherent risk, but the cost and inconvenience of extra precautions can be weighed against the risk and your experienced employees should not require continual reminders. Employees should be warned if they are handling dangerous substances, such as chemicals used in manufacturing processes. The manufacturer is liable for injury consequential on their use if he has not given adequate warning, but you must yourself pass on the information to your employees.

If you have more than five employees, emergency safety procedures and general rules relating to health and safety at work must be listed in a written statement setting out the responsibilities of all levels of management and employees. It must be kept up to date and the employees informed of its contents. If your employees are members of a trade union they can appoint a safety representative, who must be consulted when you establish your health and safety precautions, and they can also ask for a supervisory safety committee to be appointed.

If you design, manufacture, import or supply goods you are responsible for your merchandise, unless the purchaser undertakes to carry out his own safety checks. Even then you must give proper instructions for their use and carry out research to minimise existing and potential health and safety hazards, unless you could reasonably have relied on someone else's expert research. The purchaser has recourse to his supplier but an employer is still responsible to an injured employee.

Your responsibility for the safety of the premises continues even if you employ someone else to supervise safety measures. You should therefore be very careful how you delegate this potentially expensive liability, as your only defence is that you reasonably relied on expert advice or information or on the established practice of your trade.

In addition, you remain responsible for your employees when you send them elsewhere to work for you but only to take 'reasonable' care that they are operating within a safe system of work. What is 'reasonable' depends in each case on the individual circumstances of the premises, the work and the employee. The full weight of the responsibility, however, will usually fall on the person who owns the premises to which you send your employees.*

Both you and your business can be prosecuted under the legislation and can be held responsible for an employee's breach of the regulations. Fines are unlimited for a serious offence and you can face up to two years' imprisonment. Some continuing offences carry a continuing daily fine and the premises can be

* *R v Swan Hunter Shipbuilders* (1981) Crim.LR 883

closed down if health or safety is at risk.

Obviously you cannot guarantee safety on the job and you are not 'nurse' to an 'imbecile child'.* Your employees are expected to follow orders and safety regulations and to take reasonable care of themselves and anyone else affected by their work. Fortunately, the law assumes they work carefully, competently and reasonably skilfully and take proper care of your property, but if there is an accident you can be liable for employing unsuitable people – a known practical joker involves you in any accident he causes, although an unavoidable action by a responsible employee may not. Even when you have specifically forbidden an employee to do something, you are usually responsible for any damage he causes while he is working for you. If he deliberately and voluntarily chooses to put himself and others at risk, the claim against you may be proportionately reduced.

You and your business can also be convicted for certain offences committed by an employee which are regarded as your offences, if, for example, a lorry is on the road carrying an insecure load in contravention of road traffic legislation. However, each offence must be seen in the context of the harm it is designed to avoid and there are defences available to the employer in some circumstances (as, for example, in the case of *Portsea Island Mutual Co-Operative Society* v *Leyland* (1978) ICR 1195, where the employer was not convicted of an offence, although an under-age employee was taken on, as he was engaged without the employer's knowledge and against his instructions).

Self-employed people and independent contractors have their own responsibilities but, although they must not expose anyone working with them to risk, you are still personally responsible for the safety of your premises.

Responsibility for and to temporary workers depends on whether they have a contract of employment or have worked for you sufficiently long for you to be considered their employer. If they are engaged through an employment agency, you are responsible only if they have a personal obligation to do the work. Some agencies act as the employer, deducting tax, insurance and so on from the employee's salary, but if they act as a placement bureau you are responsible for anyone they send

* *Smith* v *Austin Lifts* (1959) 1 All ER 81

to you. If you lend an employee or borrow someone else's the employer's responsibilities may be acquired with the employee, particularly if there is a question of liability to outsiders.

The end result, however, of all the hair-splitting definitions which have been considered over the years is that as employer or owner of the premises you are usually responsible to anyone affected by your business activities. Accidents resulting in personal injury or death are your responsibility, however many warning notices are posted on the premises and liability for loss or damage can only be avoided if it is reasonable in the circumstances to place the responsibility on other shoulders.

Factories

Your premises may fall within the legal definition of a factory and you will then have additional and specific legal responsibilities.

If your employees are engaged in 'manual labour by way of trade, or for the purpose of gain' you are running a factory, even if you only have a high street shoe repairers. Not surprisingly, the definition has been the source of much expensive legal discussion and if you are faced with a claim under the Factories Act you should seek legal advice.

The occupier of the premises has the responsibility under the Act but only if he is in 'control' of the premises. If you have a self-service car wash or a do-it-yourself workshop, you may have sufficient 'control' over the premises to be responsible for the safety of the premises and the entrance and exit, for the machinery and substances used and for preventing the emission of noxious or offensive substances. Your 'labour-only sub-contractors' can also turn to you for compensation. However, the 'responsible employee' can also be charged with offences and any claim against the occupier will be reduced accordingly.

The provisions of the Factories Act are generally framed to protect employees and independent contractors working in an industrial environment against risks incurred every working day by their proximity to machinery and other hazards. For example, potentially dangerous machinery must be safely fenced to protect anyone working on the premises but an occasional visitor will not necessarily be protected under the legislation. You are not, however, responsible for injuries sustained by an employee as a result of using unfenced dangerous machinery for his private work or out of working hours for a purpose unconnected with the work for which he was engaged. There are some exceptions to the requirement for fencing, including when it is in the course of being overhauled, but you must still meet the requirement of providing a safe system of work.

Both the premises and access must be made and kept safe for anyone using the factory, so far as this is reasonably practicable and you are also responsible for ensuring that access maintained or provided by an independent contractor working at the factory is safe for your employees, provided that it was intended they use it. Here, however, you can turn to the independent contractor for compensation in case of accident and you should insert an express clause to that effect in your contract with him. If you do not do so or have no written agreement, you can claim compensation under the Law Reform (Married Women and Joint Tortfeasors) Act 1935 but the amount of his contribution to your damages will be a matter for the discretion of the court.

Floors, steps, stairs, passages and gangways must be soundly constructed and maintained and you are responsible for accidents resulting from faulty fittings. In addition, they must be as far as is reasonably practicable free from obstruction or substances likely to cause anyone to slip.

The health and welfare provisions applying to factories are much the same as those which apply to offices and shops and are summarised under a separate heading but, in factories, there will usually be a factory inspector who ensures that the provisions are observed.

Employees must be protected by the provision and easy availability of suitable goggles or effective screens to protect their eyes and the 1974 Act requires suitable protective clothing and equipment to be supplied when necessary.

The occupier must provide the Health and Safety Executive with details of the nature of the work, his name and the name of the business, the factory address and whether any mechanical power will be used. Written notice of any accident causing death or disablement lasting more than three days and precluding normal work and of an industrial disease specified by the regulations under the 1974 Act or by lead, phosphorous, arsenical or mercurial poisoning must be given to the Executive.

Offices and shops

The Offices, Shops and Railway Premises Act applies to offices and shops. An office, for the purposes of the Act, includes any building or part of a building solely or principally used as an office or for office purposes and to further such activities (including rooms used as a staff canteen and storage rooms).

A shop is also defined by the Act and covers any premises used to carry out retail trade, while a shop assistant is anyone wholly or mainly engaged there to serve customers, take orders or dispatch goods but trade goes further than simply buying and selling. It includes retail sales at auctions, lending books for profit, hairdressing and barber shops and the sale of refreshments and intoxicating drinks. Also included are buildings where a wholesaler keeps or disposes of stock, buildings to which the public have access to effect their own repairs, either themself or by using the advice of an expert, premises used to store and sell fuel and the staff canteen.

Like the Factories Act, the 1963 Act is framed so as to protect employees and independent contractors against risks which are part of their everyday working environment and occasional visitors and customers will have to seek compensation under the general law.

The occupier of an office or shop must give the local authority two copies of a written notice stating his intention to occupy or use the premises at least one month prior to occupation or use. Written notice of accidents causing death or disablement lasting more than three days, which precludes normal work, must also be sent to the local authority.

Health and welfare provisions

Factories, shops and offices must comply with specific provisions under the 1961 and 1963 Acts to safeguard the general health and welfare of their employees.

The premises must be kept clean and sanitary, and dirt and refuse must be removed daily from the floors. Detailed provisions for washing walls and ceilings and redecorating are contained in the Acts. Proper drainage must be provided where necessary to a manufacturing process.

A factory must not be overcrowded so that there is risk of injury to health. Each employee must have a minimum of 400 cubic feet of space, discounting 14 feet above floor level and there are similar provisions which apply to shops and offices but they do not apply to a room which is open to the public or part of a shop used for the sale of goods to customers.

Proper and suitable lighting, heating and ventilation must be provided and sufficient and suitable sanitary conveniences maintained and kept clean and properly lit. Drinking water must be accessible and there must be first-aid supplies on the premises, with a responsible person in charge. A qualified nurse or person qualified in first-aid must be in charge if you employ more than 50 people.

The Secretary of State for Employment can require medical supervision where there is a risk of injury to health because of the type of work carried out, the introduction of new processes or substances, the employment of young people or a change in the conditions of work.

Employer protection

With the weight of all the legislation on the employer, you should prepare a safety at work scheme, after consultation with your employees or their trade union representatives, and it should be reviewed annually. You should provide protective equipment and clothing, with instructions on its proper use and regularly remind employees of the risks involved in a failure to use it. Notices of emergency and safety procedures and directions for the use of protective clothing and equipment should be prominently displayed on the premises. If the use of safety equipment is made part of the contract of employment or a provision of the works' rules, you can — after due warnings — fairly dismiss an employee if he does not observe the procedure.

Your back-up protection, however, is the compulsory and voluntary insurance of risks which, however careful you are in your choice of employees and method of work, cannot be avoided.

Special legislation for certain trades

Restaurants and snackbars must be approved by a food inspector and comply with public health and fire regulations and a hotel sleeping more than six people must have a fire certificate from the local fire authority. A going concern should already have a fire certificate but, even if the fire authority has recently inspected the building, you should make sure that no further alterations or improvements are required.

If you intend to serve drinks, you will have to negotiate for the transfer of an existing licence, or make application for the grant of a new licence from the local magistrates' court, where you should be represented by a solicitor.

Cafes, restaurants, pubs and any establishment serving food

or drink on the premises must display their prices. If you provide service at tables, the prices must be displayed at or near the entrance to the cafe or restaurant, so that they can be read by the customer before he enters. In pubs and self-service restaurants the price must be shown at the point where the customer makes his choice and sometimes also at the entrance to the service canteen.

Prices do not have to be displayed for *bona fide* clubs, works' canteens, school canteens and boarding and guest houses where food is only offered to residents.

The Food and Drugs Act 1955 and the Food Hygiene (Market Stall and Delivery Vehicles) Regulations 1966 apply to mobile food shops and you should make inquiries at the Environmental Health Department, which may require you to obtain a licence.

Street traders require licences in areas such as town centres and sea fronts. Some local authorities will allow you to trade without a licence but others will not allow street trading at all except for news vendors. Licences may be issued by the Borough Secretary, the Licensing Division, the Engineering and Surveyors' Department, the Chief Trading Standards Officer or the local police. If you are selling food you must notify the Environmental Health Department.

If your shop employs staff you must register under the Offices, Shops and Railways Premises Act (as amended) and change of ownership must be given to the local authority for rating purposes.

Employment agencies are required to obtain a licence from the Secretary of State for Employment before starting in business. Under the Employment Agencies Act 1973 (as amended) licences are required for employment agencies and business involved in entertainment and modelling but not those dealing with nurses and midwives. Information on this can be obtained at regional offices of the Department of Employment. Agencies for qualified nurses and midwives are licensed under the Nurses Agencies Act 1957 and licences are obtainable from your local authority.

Licences are required from the Environmental Health Department for pet shops and boarding and breeding kennels to which the Pet Animals Act 1951, the Animal Boarding Establishments Act 1963 and the Breeding of Dogs Act 1973 apply.

If you are hiring cars by the hour, you will not usually require a licence but you may require a licence for a mini-cab business. Taxis generally need a licence and the Local Government (Miscellaneous Provisions) Act 1976 applies to the registration of private hire cars, although not all local authorities have adopted its provisions.

Licences from your local licensing justices are usually required for betting agencies and offices, snooker halls and bookmakers.

The following are just some of the trades which require licences and you should check with your local authority on the local requirements, as each trade is licensed under specific legislation: fireworks; pharmacy and poisons; premises used for offensive trades under the Public Health Act 1936; scrap metal dealers; auction sale rooms; milk dealers and dairies; ice cream manufacturers and dealers; manufacturers of sausages and preserved meat; hairdressers and barbers; cinemas and theatres; and rag, cloth and other material dealers.

Opening hours

There may be restrictions on opening hours, which you would like to be varied. Shops in some areas are open until all hours in flagrant disregard of the law and you should inquire whether special dispensation has been obtained from the local authority to allow you to stay open without fear of the law, which applies to any place, other than a mobile shop or the old-established street markets, where retail trade is carried on.

Sunday trading is also restricted and shopkeepers all over the country traffic in illegal goods on Sundays, opening for trade in contravention of legislation which, if properly enforced, would adversely affect profits.

Legally, unless special permission has been obtained from the local authority, you can offer for sale only a selected variety of merchandise to meet the shopper's most urgent Sunday needs: kosher meat if you observe the Jewish sabbath by closing on Saturday; otherwise strictly vegetarian foods, sweets, tobacco, flowers, newspapers and magazines. You can also sell car, motor-cycle and aircraft accessories and a choice of drinks from licensed premises, during licensing hours and, if you are a chemist, medical supplies.

During the 18-week holiday season, you can, in addition, sell bathing suits, fishing tackle, photographic supplies, toys, books, stationery and souvenirs.

STATUTORY REFERENCES

Control of pollution Act 1974

Employers' Liability (Compulsory Insurance) Act 1969

Employers' Liability (Defective Equipment) Act 1969

Estate Agency Act 1979

Factories Act 1961

Fatal Accidents Act 1976

Health and Safety at Work Act 1974

Landlord and Tenant Act 1927

Landlord and Tenant Act 1954 (Part II)

Law Reform (Contributory Negligence) Act 1945

Law Reform (Married Women and Joint Tortfeasors) Act 1935

Law Reform (Miscellaneous Provisions) Act 1934

Offices, Shops and Railway Premises Act 1963

Social Security Act 1975

Town and Country Planning Act 1971

and specific legislation applying to certain trades referred to in the text.

6
Taxation

A book about business would be incomplete without some discussion of taxation but your first and best adviser on tax matters is your accountant. His general knowledge of the relevant law and practical experience of its application should be sufficient for your requirements and as a general practitioner, with a specialised knowledge of accountancy and tax, he will refer difficult questions of law to a specialist.

This chapter is therefore an explanatory guide to the relevant tax provisions and their principal implications, rather than a discussion of the complexities of revenue law, which is very much the province of the expert.

The tax bill for the business is based on business profits but how it is calculated and when you pay depend on whether you are personally assessed to tax as a self-employed person as a sole trader or partner, or whether the business is separately taxed as a limited company.

The main taxes affecting business are income tax, payable by the sole trader and partner, corporation tax, payable by limited companies and national insurance contributions. You will also be liable to VAT if your business turnover exceeds £17,000 in your accounting year, or £6000 in any quarter.

You may have other taxable income or be liable for capital transfer tax or capital gains tax on the disposal of capital assets. If you employ people full time, you will be responsible for the administration and payment to the Revenue of their PAYE payments under Schedule E of the 1970 Act, covering wages and salaries from employment. As a shareholder in your company you will pay corporation tax on your dividends.

The sole trader and the partnership

The sole trader is taxed as if business income were his own earnings. Partnership profits are a tax on the partnership itself and the business, not the individual partners, pays the bill.

The partners, however, are personally and jointly, not severally, liable to the Revenue but, provided the partners are alive and solvent, they share the tax liability in the same ratio as that in which profits are shared. The proportion is the one actually existing at the time the business is assessed to tax. As tax under Schedule D, which covers income from trades, professions and vocations, is paid on a preceding year basis, this may not necessarily be the same as the ratio in which profits were shared during the year in which they were earned.

A partner's salary is part of his share of the profits and interest on his advances to the partnership are also added to business income and taxed as business profits, although the interest will not be part of his share of the profits.

In order to ascertain your profits, you must prepare a set of accounts, comprising a profit and loss account and balance sheet, drawn from the books which record daily business transactions and, unless you have specialised knowledge of both accountancy and tax, the accounts should be prepared by a professional accountant.

Accounting periods and commencement provisions

The first accounting period of a new business can be any period that you and your accountant choose. The second period will generally be 12 months ending on a date which then becomes your usual 'year end' or 'accounting date'.

The new business is taxed from commencement of trading to the following 5 April on its actual profits. The second year's tax is based on the profits of the first 12 months' trading. By the third year you will be on the normal basis of taxation of profits for the accounting year ending in the previous fiscal (tax) year, which is assessed to tax on the 5 April following your accounting date. You can opt for both the second and the third years also to be assessed on an actual basis, which will reduce your tax bill if the second year's profits are lower than the first.

There are advantages in your choice of the first accounting period. For instance, a profit for income tax for the year ended 30 April 1982 of £5000 will be the assessment for the tax year 1983-84. Any other income earned by you or your spouse (above the personal allowance) will be added to this. If your only income is from the business the £5000 is treated as if it were your salary and your assessment, showing a deduction of the married person's allowance and, say, £1000 for building society interest, will be as follows:

	£	£
Profit for income tax		5000
less mortgage interest paid	1000	
married person's allowance	2445	3445
		1555

Income tax payable: 1555 @ 30% £466.50

The £466.50 is payable in two equal instalments on 1 January 1984 and 1 July 1984, 20 months and 26 months after the end of the year in which you earned the profits.

Once you have been in business for three years or more, your profit is assessed in the tax year on 5 April following the end of your accounting year, so that profits accruing to 30 April 1982 are assessed to tax in the fiscal year 1983-84 and you obtain the maximum period of credit for payment of tax. If you had chosen a year end of 31 March, you would have obtained an average of only 12 months' credit.

During the opening years your assessment to tax is tied to the commencement provisions. If, for instance, you start business on 1 July 1982 and choose an accounting year and date of 31 December, your assessment to tax will be calculated as follows:

On profits of:

£1200 from 1 July 1982 to 31 December 1982: 1st period
£3600 from 1 January 1983 to 31 December 1983: 2nd period
£6000 from 1 January 1984 to 31 December 1984: 3rd period

your tax bill will be:

£2100 in the tax year 1982-83: actual year basis
£3600 in the tax year 1983-84: first 12 months' trading
£3600 in the tax year 1984-85: preceding year basis.

Out of the first 18 months' profit, nine months have come in for assessment twice and three months of it have been assessed three times. It is therefore advantageous to keep profits low during the first three years. However, if you make a loss in the first two years, before you are on the normal preceding year basis, you will only be allowed loss relief once.

Closing years

The advantages of the commencement provisions are to some extent outweighed by the closing year provisions, as the year in which you stop trading is also taxed on an actual basis. The basis period extends back from the date of discontinuance to the preceding 6 April. Assessments for the penultimate and pre-penultimate years of assessment will already have been made on a preceding year basis and they will be recalculated on an actual basis. If the aggregate of taxable profits in those two years, made on an actual basis, exceeds the aggregate of the two assessments already made, additional tax can be charged on the excess. If necessary, the profits disclosed on the accounts will be time apportioned.

A partnership is deemed to stop trading and restart when there is a change of partners, other than a change in corporate partners. You can elect to 'continue' trading when there is a change and must confirm your election by written notice sent to your tax inspector within two years of change, signed by all the partners involved in the partnership both before and after the change. The discontinuance rules do not apply if a sole trader dies and the husband or wife continues to carry on the business.

Tax relief for pre-trading expenditure

Some business expenditure, such as wages and rent and rates, now qualifies for tax relief if it was incurred by a business not more than three years before the start of trading.

Losses

The income of the sole trader or partner, like that of his employees, is subject to an ascending rate of tax, starting at 30 per cent on the first £12,800 and rising to a maximum of 60 per cent on incomes over £31,500. This is subject to your personal tax reliefs and a deduction for part of the premium on life assurance policies before assessment to tax.

You can, however, unlike your employees, deduct from profits any 'revenue' or day-to-day business expenses, wholly and exclusively incurred in carrying on the business.

If your accounts for the year show a loss, you can have this set against any other income for the tax year in which the loss was incurred and against income for the following year. Losses must be set off first against earned income and then against unearned income, which is subject to an additional tax of 15 per cent if it exceeds £6250 per annum. Any balance remaining can be carried forward and set off against future profits or carried back to be set off against earlier profits.

The sole trader and partner can, in addition, carry back any losses incurred in the first four years' trading and set them against earlier income from any other source, including their salary, in the three years before they started the new business.

Allowable business expenses

The following are the most important day-to-day expenses which can be deducted as revenue expenses from your profits before they are assessed to tax:

1. Runnings costs, including heating, lighting, rent, rates, telephone, postage, advertising, cleaning and repairs — but not improvements, which are a capital expense — insurance and the use of special clothing. If you use your home as business premises, you can claim up to two-thirds of the running costs as a business expense but you may thereby disable yourself from claiming a proportionate part of the capital gains tax exemption for your private residence and have to pay the tax on some of the capital gain arising on sale.

2. Development costs. If these are shown as an asset in a company's accounts they can now be treated as a realised loss except for any amount which represents an unrealised profit on revaluation of the costs.

3. The cost of goods bought for resale and materials for manufacturing. You cannot deduct capital expenditure on plant, cars or machinery but some smaller items, such as typewriters, may be allowable.

4. Carriage, packing and delivery costs.

5. Wages and salaries, other than your own or your partners'. Your spouse can receive a salary, provided there is a reasonable amount of work done for the business and, if income from other sources is less than the personal allowance, the amount will be free of tax.

6. Interest on loans and overdrafts incurred wholly in connection with the business, but not interest on partners' advances.

7. Hire, hire purchase and leasing charges. Only the amount related to rental can be deducted, not the actual cost or cash price of the article, which is a capital expense.

8. Insurance. You can deduct any related business insurance, including that taken out to cover your employees but excluding your own national insurance contribution and premiums paid on your own life insurance (which is subject to personal tax relief).

9. Subscriptions to professional and trade organisations.

10. Travel and hotel expenses on business trips which relate to eliciting business but not travel between home and office if you have a fixed place of work. You can also claim the running expense of your car, including petrol in the proportion in which you use it for business purposes.

11. Entertaining of overseas customers but you will have to show evidence of a connection between your export business and the amounts claimed; you can also claim for entertaining your own staff.

12. Some legal and other professional fees, such as audit fees or the cost of legal advice and court actions related to the business but not for penalties for breaking the law, for instance parking fines.

13. Bad debts actually incurred. This can be claimed if specific customers are named and you can show that they are unlikely to meet their obligations, for instance where the account is overdue and they ignore reminders. A general provision for a percentage of unspecified bad debts is not allowable against your tax.

    Trade debts outstanding count as income, even if not paid by the end of the accounting period. Debts owed by you are costs, even if they will not be paid until the next accounting period.

14. Business gifts costing up to £2 per recipient per annum, excluding food, drink and tobacco. All gifts to employees are allowable but they may have to be disclosed on the employee's tax return and tax paid on the amount.

15. The VAT element in business expenses is allowable, for example VAT on petrol for your car, unless you are a taxable trader for VAT purposes. The VAT on the purchase of your car is allowable in any event, however, as it cannot be reclaimed in your VAT return.

Capital allowances

From time to time you will incur capital expenses as you acquire or replace permanent fixtures, fittings, machinery and vehicles used in the business. For both income tax and corporation tax purposes, the depreciation which you deduct in your accounts is replaced by capital allowances which are deducted from your tax bill.

You can deduct a 'writing down allowance' of 25 per cent a year to a maximum of £2000 on the cost of private cars.

Other capital assets qualify for a first-year writing off allowance of the total cost in the tax year of acquisition. If you do not have sufficient profits against which the full amount can be set off, you may want to claim the allowance at the rate of 25 per cent a year, which is calculated on the proportion which has not yet been written off. An asset written down from a cost price of £3000 at 25 per cent per annum will therefore yield allowances of £750 in the first year (25/100 x £3000) and £562.50 in the second year (25/100 x £2250) and so on.

Second-hand plant and machinery qualify for the full first year allowance and the 25 per cent writing off allowance in the same way as new equipment.

The value of your premises can be written down at varying rates depending on their use as follows:

1. New industrial buildings at 75 per cent of the construction cost in the first year, excluding the cost of the land, plus 4 per cent for each year of use. The 1982 Finance Act has made the allowance available in addition to buildings used for the maintenance and repair business (small industrial workshops) and for a retailer's warehouse. The same Act also extended the relief to a licensee or lessee. There is no first-year allowance if the building is not new but the cost can be written off over the remaining life of the building, except for any amount exceeding the amount paid by the original user.
2. New 'small' industrial workshops, to a maximum of 2500 square feet, at 100 per cent, excluding the cost of the land (until March 1985). The relief is available to landlords as well as to owner/users.
3. Agricultural buildings at 30 per cent in the first year, the balance over seven years.

4. Hotels at 20 per cent in the first year, the balance over
   20 years.

A development grant on plant and factory buildings available
when you set up in a development area cannot be deducted from
the cost for the purpose of calculating the capital allowance.

Hire purchase is treated for tax purposes in the same way as
any other form of purchase. The cash price is the cost price on
which is based the capital allowance and the interest is allowed
as a trading (revenue) expense, as and when it is paid.

Leasing is not purchase, whether of real estate or any other
item of capital expenditure. The leasing company claims its own
capital allowance while the lessee can claim the rentals against
tax as trading expenses.

Business know-how and goodwill bought for a capital sum
can be written off over six years.

Taxation of intellectual property, comprising patents,
registered trade marks and designs, copyright and know-how is
an area for expert advice. What may look to be a capital sum
may be taxed as income and even a lump sum for the absolute
assignment of a licence to produce, market or otherwise exploit
a product may be taxed as a trading receipt in some circumstances. Proper tax planning, however, can ensure that income
and capital payments and receipts are treated in the most tax-
efficient manner.

If you are registered for VAT, you will already have reclaimed
the VAT element on the purchase in your quarterly or monthly
VAT returns, so that your capital allowances must then be
calculated on the net amount, excluding VAT, except in the
case of cars.

As a sole trader or partner paying income tax, capital
allowances are kept separate from your profits and cannot be
carried forward against tax for future years when they are not
used in the current year. In a new business, capital allowances,
like losses, are given only once and are not applied in each of
the tax years forming the basis of the assessment.

Companies paying corporation tax can, however, treat capital
allowances as trading expenses, which often converts a profit
into a loss for tax purposes. The loss can be carried forward
indefinitely and set against future profits.

Stock relief

If you hold stock — whether as material for manufacturing, work in progress, or finished goods ready for sale — it must be valued at each accounting date.

The difference between the value of your opening and closing stock represents the cost of your sales but in times of inflation its value appreciates and, if this is taken into account, you would show a paper profit which would rapidly disappear as you replaced existing stock at higher prices. The Inland Revenue therefore allowed tax relief on amounts by which your stock increased in value as shown in your accounts between one year and the next. It did not distinguish between volume and price and was concerned only with the purchase price of the stock. As this gave rather more relief than was compensated for by inflation, 10 per cent of the net profit for a sole trader or partnership and 15 per cent for a company was deducted from the increased price to calculate the amount of relief.

A new system of stock relief was introduced by the 1981 Finance Act for accounting periods ending on, or bridging, 14 November 1980 with certain transitional arrangements. Relief is calculated by applying the increase in the value of stock volume in a single index over the period of account to the value of stock and work in progress at the beginning of that period; special provisions apply for the first period of trading.

The index is to be compiled monthly: provisional figures are available within one month after the month to which they relate, and final figures are available two months later. The first £2000 of stock and work in progress will not qualify for relief.

There is no restriction by reference to business profits and you will still be able to make a partial claim or apply for succession relief. There is not clawback of relief unless business ceases or there is a major drop in your business activities as compared with a previous period of account during the preceding six years. Relief is free of clawback after six years and any unused relief cannot be carried forward after that period.

Transitional provisions apply for periods of account ending on, or bridging, 14 November 1980 and you can still claim relief under the old scheme for the lesser of an amount exceeding £10,000 or 25 per cent of the relief available under the new scheme, without taking into account any increase in the value of stock after 14 November 1980. If you claim deferment of clawback under the old scheme in the transitional period of account, however, you can claim stock relief under the old scheme for that period up to the full amount of the deferred charge.

Business start-up scheme

The 1981 Finance Act introduced a new tax relief in the form of a 'business start-up scheme', which enables a private investor not otherwise connected with the business to make a minority investment of between £500 and £10,000 in the 1981-82 tax year and £20,000 for subsequent tax years in a new business and to obtain income tax relief on his stake. You can carry forward the part of the relief not utilised in 1981-82 to the following year, provided you do not exceed the £20,000 limit.

The relief is available during the first three years of a company's business life, or by a self-employed person starting in business or incorporating business activities during the first three years' trading. Usually you must hold the investment for at least five years but there is now no restriction on the amount you can deduct in calculating a chargeable gain when you sell the shares.

The details of the scheme are complicated, running to 17 pages in the 1981 Act, and the relief is hedged with restrictions. Wholesalers, retailers and anyone in the property business or offering financial services do not qualify and the relief is not available to an investor who receives payment from the business. If you are a company, you cannot have or acquire a subsidiary within five years of taking on the investor(s), the company must have only one class of share capital and the investment is confined to 30 per cent of the equity.

If any of these or any other conditions are infringed tax relief is revoked retrospectively and the investor has to pay interest on the tax relief, which the Revenue tax as a loan from the Treasury. You and your investor should therefore seek advice from your accountants before becoming involved in outside finance.

Tax relief available to traders on start-up costs and on the incidental costs of raising loan finance incurred before the commencement of trading is more straightforward and is extended to traders generally.

Computing taxable profit

Your tax bill is based on the profits shown in your annual accounts, but it may not coincide with the tax year which ends 5 April, and your taxable profits will not coincide with the profits shown on your accounts.

Certain costs which are genuine business expenses are not allowable for tax purposes, for example, entertaining customers other than foreign buyers or their agents. Nor can you deduct depreciation against your profits, although you can claim writing down allowances which have a similar effect. These and other expenses which are not allowable against tax must therefore be added back to the profits.

Certain profits must be deducted from your Schedule D assessment, because they are taxed on a different basis and under another heading. These include gains from the disposal of capital assets, bank interest paid on money in a deposit account and income from sub-letting part of your premises.

The accounts will be adjusted by the various tax reliefs and allowances and the final taxable profit is then agreed, possibly after negotiation and correspondence with the tax inspector.

Corporation tax

The limited company pays corporation tax and must prepare more detailed accounts to the prescribed standard set by the Companies Acts, audited by a qualified accountant.

Profits are similarly adjusted by various allowances and deductions to calculate the taxable profit for corporation tax, which is agreed between your accountant and the tax inspector. Corporation tax is, however, related to fiscal (tax) years, so that, if your year end is 31 December, you are only assessed on profits made in that year and there is no special concession for the opening years of business.

Companies pay advance corporation tax (ACT) on their share dividends. The dividend is paid net of tax to the shareholder and three-sevenths of the gross amount is paid directly to the Revenue by the company within three months of distribution of the dividend, which is set off against the company's total corporation tax liability at the year's end. In addition, corporation tax is normally payable nine months from the end of each accounting period.

Since 1973 the rate of corporation tax has been 52 per cent. Companies making smaller profits pay a reduced rate of 40 per cent up to £90,000. Profits between £90,000 and £225,000 are subject to marginal relief, giving a gradually increased rate to the full 52 per cent rate at £225,000.

Allowable expenses against profits are about the same as those for the sole trader and partnership except that you can deduct employees' salaries, including those of the directors, although they will themselves be liable to income tax on the amount. Your national insurance contributions will be at the employed rate and you will pay PAYE on your salary, which is paid over to the Revenue monthly. In practice the profits of small companies are usually taken out as directors' remuneration and you can often decide the amount after the accounts for the year are completed, when you know your actual profit.

Interest relief for investment in a close company

You can obtain relief on interest paid on a loan used to purchase shares or lend money to a close company after 9 March 1982, provided you have been involved for the greater part of your time in the conduct and management of the business.

Comparisons

As sole trader or partner your business losses can be set against any other taxable income you or your spouse earns. If you have already paid tax on it you can claim a refund. Trading losses of a company are locked into the company and can only be carried forward to be set against future profits or carried back to set against a profit of the previous year.

If you are starting a new business after having paid substantial tax on your salary, you can set losses accruing in the first four years of trading against your salary and any other income of the three years before you started business, so that you can claim repayment of some or all of the tax deducted while you were on salary. A company director cannot claim this concession.

On the other hand, if you make losses as a sole trader or partnership and then convert the business into a limited company, any unrelieved losses can be converted to losses carried forward against your new company's profits.

Taxation on private use of motor vehicles may be more favourable with a company. The sole trader or partner has to agree a proportion for private use with the tax inspector. There is a fixed scale for private use of a company car, based on the age and size of the car, which usually results in a lower taxable amount to an individually negotiated figure.

The main tax considerations affecting your choice are set out in the table overleaf. The advantages and disadvantages depend partly on the size of the business, the number of people you employ and whether you have a substantial shareholding.

If you paid substantial tax on high earnings before going it alone, you may decide against forming a limited company, at least initially, so that you can make use of the retrospective loss allowance. If the personal service of the proprietor is really the essence of the business, it makes sense to trade as a sole trader or in partnership. If the personal touch is removed from your customer relations and you want to project an established image, a limited company may be the preferred vehicle. The nature of your business may well be the decisive factor but there are no absolute criteria and much depends on your decision concerning the other advantages and disadvantages of limited liability.

Capital transfer tax

The introduction of the tax replacing estate duty was potentially disastrous for the small business and it is now treated as a special case and the value of your interest in the business or your controlling shareholding is reduced by 50 per cent for assessment to the tax. There is in addition a 30 per cent reduction in the value of land, buildings, machinery and plant used by a controlled company or partnership and the value of a minority shareholding is reduced by 20 per cent. No tax is payable on transfers under £55,000. The percentage paid thereafter increases from 30 per cent on amounts between £55,001 to £70,000 to 75 per cent on cumulative lifetime transfers of over £2,500,000. From April 1983 the tax bands to which the varying percentages apply will be index-linked to changes in the retail prices index.

	Sole trader/partnership	Company
Tax basis	Income tax on profit after allowances	40 per cent of profit after allowances
Timing of payment	12/23 months later depending on accounting year	Directors' salaries immediately under PAYE
Retrospective loss allowance for new business	Allowance for four years against previous three years' income	Not available
Capital allowances	Only available in first year of business	Deducted from profits in account year asset acquired
Losses	Can be set off against other income	Locked in to company and can only be set against company profits
Losses conversion	Can be used if a conversion to partnership or company	Can only use in company reconstruction
National insurance	Lower contribution as self-employed	Higher contribution as employee, but some extra benefits
Pension	Self-employed retirement annuity	Can form company pension scheme with more tax relief
Car	Private use taxed as negotiated with tax inspector	Can use company car with established criteria for private use*

*Summary of tax advantages/disadvantages
of types of business organisation*

---

* Directors and higher paid employees are taxed on company cars which are also
available for private use on a sliding scale which varies in accordance with the value
of the car and its cylinder capacity. (Petrol provided free when an employee uses a
company car is now taxed under PAYE the amount varying with the car's engine
size, and reduced by 50 per cent if the car is used mainly for business purposes
(ie a minimum of 18,000 business miles during the tax year). If the employee pays
for petrol used in the company car for private use — which includes travel back and
forth to work — the charge is cancelled. The provisions do not apply to petrol
provided for business use in the employee's private or hired car but the employer
must notify the Revenue (on form P11D) of the cost of petrol supplied.

Capital gains tax

Both individuals and companies pay capital gains tax if they sell or give away assets at an effective rate of 30 per cent of the gain less any necessary connected expenditure. Disposals by an individual are exempt where the real or notional gain in any tax year is less than £5000. From 1983-84 the limit may be index-linked to reflect increases in the retail price index for the year ending 31 December before the beginning of the tax year. Gains on the disposal of some goods and chattels including those used in a business are also exempt if the disposal proceeds (not the gains) do not exceed £3000 and there may be a reduction in the tax if the top limit is exceeded by a small amount.

From 1983-84 gains may be reduced by increasing the allowable expenditure in accordance with the increase in the retail prices index.

Disposal of the business is liable to tax but, if you sell and buy another business within three years, you can defer payment until you finally dispose of the new business and stop trading. If you have owned the business for more than 10 years and sell when you are 65 you can claim relief at the rate of £10,000 a year to a maximum of £50,000. The relief is particularly advantageous if you have been using your private residence as business premises and claiming tax relief for running expenses on a proportionate basis. The first £5,000 capital gain is now exempt from tax and further relief can be claimed to the £50,000 limit. Restricted relief applies to taxpayers between 60 and 65 years of age.

Value added tax

If the taxable outputs of the business (ie your charges to customers for goods and services) exceed or are likely to exceed £17,000 a year or £6000 in any quarter you must register with Customs and Excise for VAT.

Not all goods and services carry VAT. Some, such as basic foodstuffs, coach operators, books and newspapers, are zero-rated. It is sometimes advantageous to apply for voluntary registration. As a zero-rated trader, for instance, buying supplies and equipment from VAT-registered traders, you can claim repayment of the 'input' tax charged to you by your suppliers. If both your customers and your suppliers are registered for VAT, your registration will not affect them and you can claim repayment of input tax. You can also apply for voluntary registration if your taxable outputs are less than £15,000, although the Customs and Excise have a discretion to refuse your registration.

You can obtain full details of the system from Customs and Excise, who will supply you with booklets and notices about VAT which are relevant to your trade or profession. Registration involves considerable administration and records must be kept for three years and be available for inspection. As your own tax inspector, you must be accurate and efficient and once registered you must charge VAT at 15 per cent on all your sales and services which are not zero-rated. Sales invoices must show your VAT-registered number and full details of the sale, including the VAT rate charged and the amount. There are simplified requirements for invoices under £50.

You must have some kind of record — a day book or sheet — listing all invoices received by you on which VAT has been charged, including those zero-rated and these must be totalled to show total purchases excluding VAT and the VAT amount. Invoices must be filed and available for inspection.

At the end of each VAT accounting period, quarterly or monthly, you must complete a VAT return of all your outputs charged on sales, showing their total value and the amount of VAT charged. Against this can be set off the total of your inputs (VAT on your purchases) and the amount of VAT you have paid. If your outputs exceed your inputs, you must pay the balance to Customs and Excise. If you have paid out more tax that you have received, you can claim the difference from Customs and Excise. Zero-rated traders usually account for the tax monthly but you can choose VAT quarter end dates to coincide with your own accounting year if you account for VAT quarterly, although there may be restrictions if you choose 31 March or 31 December and if your annual sales exceed £50,000.

There are special schemes for retailers, businesses dealing in second-hand goods, motor car dealers, and suppliers of vending and gaming machines. There are special requirements for discounts, free gifts, samples, coupon schemes, returnable containers, hire purchase and 'self-supply' (where you take goods away for your own use from your business premises), and building work can be rated at zero or 15 per cent. Relief is available on the VAT element of bad debts.

The Customs and Excise Department is usually very helpful but you will also need to consult with your accountant, as he will use your records in the preparation of your accounts. In addition to continuing information from Customs and Excise, you may also be able to obtain advice and information from your trade association.

PAYE

If you employ staff you are responsible for deducting PAYE from their wages. It must also be deducted from your own salary as a company director. The sums deducted must be paid monthly to the Inland Revenue.

The tax office will send you a tax deduction card for each employee for the year ending 5 April. Weekly or monthly, you will have to enter details of tax, pay for each period and for the year to date. Deductions are based on the employee's tax code number, allotted by the tax office, and you will also receive a set of tax tables from which you will be able to abstract the correct amount of tax due.

At the end of the tax year you must make out a Form P60 for each employee with details of pay and tax deducted for the year. Form P35 must be sent to the Revenue, summarising the tax and graduated national insurance contributions of all your employees during the year.

When an employee leaves he is entitled to a P45, which you must complete and give to the employee to hand to his new employer in order that the tax record is continued. Part of the P45 is sent to the tax office, showing the employee's code number and the amount of pay and tax deducted.

National insurance contributions

The sole trader or partner is self-employed and pays contributions in Class 2, usually a weekly amount, *and* in Class 4, based on profit and collected annually. The company director pays contributions as an employee and the company makes a contribution as the employer.

Rates of contribution vary from year to year and for the tax year 1982-83 are as follows:

1. *Sole trader/partner:*
   Class 2: flat rate of £3.75 per week. You can apply for the small earnings exception if you expect your earnings to be less than £1600 in the 1982-83 tax year.
   Class 4: earnings-related 6 per cent of profits or gains between £3450 and £11,000 per annum.

2. *Company director/employee:*

Class 1	Employee (%)	Employer (%)
If within the State Pension Scheme	8.75	12.2
Contracted out rates:		
On first £29.50 per week	8.75	12.2
On earnings between £29.50 and		
£220 per week	6.25	7.7

Neither employee nor employer pays a contribution on earnings under £29.50 per week and the sole trader or partner earning less than £1600 is also exempt from contributions. No further contributions are payable by a director/employee earning over £220 a week or £11,439.96 a year. The sole trader or partner makes no further contribution once earnings reach £11,000 per annum but, once the Class 4 contribution becomes payable on earnings between £3,450 and £11,000 per annum, his contribution is substantially higher, particularly when compared with the rates payable if the company contracts out of the State Scheme.

In addition, the sole trader and partner are not entitled to unemployed or industrial injury benefit, which is available to the company director/employee and there is also a difference in the entitlement to pensions.

Pensions

The sole trader or partner is entitled to the self-employed person's State flat-rate pension at retirement age, which is not related to previous income. You can, however, take out a self-employed pensions policy with an insurance company and the premium is totally allowed against income tax if it amounts to no more than 17½ per cent of your net earnings. The percentage increases to 20 per cent for taxpayers born between 1913 and 1916 for 1982-83 and subsequent years and increases again in two-year bands to 21, 24, 26.5, 29.5 and 32.5 per cent for taxpayers born in 1907.

Your company can 'contract out' of the State Pension Scheme. If you do nothing, you will have 'contracted in', which means that the 7.75 per cent rate on earnings and 13.7 per cent employer's contribution is payable and your employees will receive the State earnings-related pension on retirement. If your company contracts out you will pay the lower rates on higher incomes and must make your own pension arrangements although you can have a tax-free retirement annuity policy which will top up your pension even if the company contracts into the State Scheme.

STATUTORY REFERENCES

The aforementioned obligations to the Inland Revenue and HM Customs and Excise are exhausting but by no means exhaustive. Accordingly the statutory references are kept to a minimum, as further details are available from the Inland Revenue, HM Customs and Excise and the Department of Health and Social Security.

Capital Allowances Act 1968

Companies Act 1981

Finance Acts 1965, 1972, 1975, 1976, 1980, 1982

Income and Corporation Taxes Act 1970 (as amended)

7
Insurance

Insurance is an overhead and a guarantee against loss; how much you carry is a commercial decision, based on calculating the odds and deciding whether the cost of the premium is a reasonable investment in the context of the possibility of loss. You must, however, know what you are buying and your arrangements should be made through a broker or agent specialising in the appropriate field. Insurance is a competitive business and it is therefore worth 'shopping around' and comparing quotations.

Law of the contract

Unless you include a clause stating that your insurance contract is to be governed by English law, cover for losses under agreements with foreign suppliers and customers may be governed by foreign law. If nothing is stated, it will turn on the circumstances in which you concluded the contract or what was ostensibly agreed at the time. Entitlement to the proceeds, however, depends on the law of the place where the money is payable.

The distinction is between whether the insurer owes the money at all, which is governed by the law of your contract, and to whom the proceeds belong, which is governed by where it is to be paid out. Insurance monies are generally payable, subject to anything in the policy, where the insurance company carries on business but the destination of the proceeds when an insured person dies depends on the law of the country where he was domiciled at the date of his death.

The insurance agreement

The first step in effecting insurance is to submit a proposal or application to a broker or insurance company giving details of the risks you want covered. The insurance contract is not complete until a final offer is unconditionally accepted. The insurers can, however, accept your proposal, subject to payment of the premium. A non-marine policy can be agreed verbally and you must settle the principal terms, specifically the items and sum to be insured and the risks to be covered. The point at which the contract is concluded is based on the same principles as any other contract and once you agree the principal terms, you can often be immediately protected pending formal acceptance by the insurers, although they can withdraw after making inquiries.

Cover can be arranged informally on the issue of a cover note, which is your temporary contract. It is distinct from the later formal policy, unless the insurers combine the two by sending the cover note on receipt of the premium, when the cover note is a 'deposit receipt'.

A temporary cover note to renew an existing policy does not extend your cover automatically as it may only be an offer to insure, requiring acceptance but the note becomes a deposit receipt when you pay the premium. Some policies are expressly self-extending but, if there is no provision for renewal, you must come to a new arrangement with your insurers, unless they renew on the 'usual' or 'previous' terms.

Insurance offered by your broker through underwriting members of Lloyds, or through marine underwriters of insurance companies, is usually submitted on a 'slip' (literally a slip of paper) containing brief details of the risk to be covered. Accepting underwriters mark the amount they are willing to cover and your insurers have to issue the policy on those terms.

Terms and conditions

Insurance law is a special branch of general contract law, dealing with what are rather coyly styled 'contracts of the utmost good faith', with special ground rules relating to disclosure and misrepresentation.

Unlike any other business transaction, the parties to an insurance contract must make full and accurate disclosure of anything which might affect the risk insured and you must keep your insurers informed of any change in the risk. Some policies specifically forbid any changes and if, for example, you introduce certain stipulated dangers on to your premises, even temporarily, your policy will be cancelled. If you do not make full disclosure and mislead your insurers, even unintentionally, they can refuse to meet your claim and cancel the policy.

Generally you must tell them if you have had any previous claims and state whether the items are covered by other insurance.

Valuations

If you overvalue your merchandise, the insurers can cancel the policy. You do not have to claim for the actual loss, as you can agree the value of items insured when you take out the policy under a 'valued policy' and the claim is based on that value. Usually, however, your cover is limited to a specific amount, which is the maximum you can claim.

If you do not have a valued policy, you can usually claim the market value of anything lost or the cost of restoration or repair to the limit of the sum insured, subject to any average clause.

Average clauses

Most insurances now include an averaging restriction, which can be expensive in these inflationary times, particularly under long-term policies. The average clause restricts your claim to the current market value of the goods, taking account of depreciation.

You will therefore almost inevitably find that you are insured for less than replacement value, unless you are claiming for stock which is quickly turned over in the business. Insurance for replacement value is available but the premiums will of course be correspondingly higher.

Consequential loss

Consequential loss arising from, for example, the destruction of your stock in trade can be claimed only if it is specifically included. If you are simply covered for loss of goods, you can only recover their value and cannot make a claim for loss of profits. This also applies to damage caused to your premises. Loss of rent or loss of custom is not recoverable unless specifically insured.

'New for old' allowances

A discount on your claim is usually included on the basis that you are acquiring new articles to replace those which have depreciated in value because of use.

Marine insurance

Marine insurance developed on slightly different lines to other insurance, but the main difference is that the value you can claim is that of the goods at the time they were insured and not the value at the time of the loss. In addition a claim is automatically subject to averaging unless it is specifically excluded in the policy.

Legal rights and obligations

Most policies state the terms and conditions upon which they are granted and some define their legal effects and enlarge or restrict your legal rights and obligations. These should be carefully and expertly considered, as you may sometimes be entitled to damages if the insurers refuse a claim because they allege you are in breach of contract.

Cover

You must know the extent of your cover and the excluded risks. Insurance claims are based on abnormal circumstances. Normal wear and tear and inherent vice are usually excluded, even if the policy covers 'all risks'.

'Inherent vice' is, rather disappointingly, defined as natural behaviour of the item insured, so that insurance of animals or an accident policy excludes death by natural causes.

Other generally excepted risks are riot, act of God, civil commotion and war but you can cover almost any risk at a price; the only real difference between insurance and placing a bet is that insurance contracts are enforceable under English law.

Accident policies cover accidents caused by anyone's carelessness, including the insured person's, but deliberate damage is only covered if someone else is responsible.

'All risks' means compensation for all loss or damage caused in the circumstances set out in your policy.

Period of cover

The period for which you are covered depends on the items and risks insured and the wording of the policy.

Transit risks are usually covered from the time the journey begins until it ends and the goods are insured as soon as they are given to a carrier. You should, however, check the wording of the policy to ensure that you are covered during loading and unloading and while goods are warehoused or left loaded overnight or unattended. Your policy should cover all methods of transport, by land, sea and air, so that you have a claim if there is an unforeseen change in transit arrangements.

Time of loss

The time of the loss is the time of the accident, whenever it is discovered, except in marine insurance, or if it is attributable to something that happened outside the period of insurance. The cause of loss can therefore be crucial.

Your claim must be based on one direct and operative cause — the 'proximate' cause — which is not necessarily the latest in time and you may discover it is an excepted risk.

If, for example, theft by an employee is excepted and goods are stolen from your premises, you cannot claim if an employee is one of the thieves and his connivance is considered to be the proximate cause of the loss.

Fire insurance is also restricted in some circumstances. If a fire on your premises causes an explosion, you are covered for your own damage but not necessarily for that caused to other buildings, although you are covered if neighbouring buildings are damaged by the fire itself.

Notice of loss

Generally notice of loss must be given within a specified time and it is best to give it as quickly as possible. Oral notification may be sufficient and you must give sufficient details to enable the insurers to ascertain the nature of the claim. Written notification is better, however, as you then have records to which to refer and if the policy calls for specific requirements and sets a time limit, and you do not give notice in appropriate terms, the insurers can reject the claim.*

Proof of loss

Sometimes proof of loss or damage must be given in accordance with the terms of the policy and you usually have to report loss

---

* See for instance *Grundy (Teddington) Ltd* v *Fulton*, Law Society's Gazette 26 August 1981, where the cover on goods in transit was only for their normal route, so that thefts outside the route were not covered.

or theft to the police or appropriate authorities. If goods are damaged in transit, there should be no problem of proof if they were intact at the start of the journey and damaged or lost at its end.

In some circumstances you may also have to prove the amount of the loss and policies covering loss of profits usually require assessment by auditors.

Settlement

You will need advice to establish a claim under a cover note, before the full policy is issued or received, as your entitlement depends on the circumstances of the claim and the type of insurance. The same applies to a claim made after the renewal date of an existing policy, if you have not renewed it.

Settlement is usually negotiated with the insurers and their assessors. If it is substantial or complicated and there are disputes as to value or the circumstances or extent of the loss, you should negotiate through your own assessor or valuer. Some policies include a clause referring disputes to arbitration but most insurers do not enforce it if you prefer to have liability, but not the amount of the claim, decided in court. This does not, however, apply to marine or aircraft insurance or to a specially negotiated arbitration clause.

Acceptance on both sides must be unconditional and payment by the insurers is irrecoverable unless they can prove fraud or that payment was made because of a genuine mistake as to the facts.

Usually you settle for cash and a claim for lost goods stands, even if the goods are found. The insurers are then entitled to claim them as salvage and they are also entitled to damaged goods, if you have claimed for replacement on the ground that they are beyond repair.

Insurance of your business premises

It may be your option as to whether you accept repair or replacement of goods, or rebuilding or reinstatement of your premises. Where, however, the insurers wish to rebuild or reinstate your premises, either under their option or under an obligation under the Fire Prevention (Metropolis) Act 1774, you must accept.

The Act, in spite of its name, applies to most of the United Kingdom and, if the insurers choose to reinstate, they cannot limit the expense unless the policy sets a limit and the work must be completed within a reasonable time. Either the landlord or tenant can insist that the insurance company — but not if it is a Lloyds' underwriter — rebuild or reinstate if the premises are burnt down or damaged by fire, unless the insurers suspect someone in occupation of the premises is responsible for the damage. They do not have to replace trade fixtures or any fixtures not attached to the freehold and can restrict what they spend to the sum insured. You can settle with them and/or do the work yourself. It is possible, however, to insure fixtures and fittings separately.

Leasehold premises can be insured by the landlord or the tenant or both of them. As tenant, the insurable interest is only as tenant in possession, so that you can only recover your own loss, unless you are liable to the landlord for the value of the entire premises, either under the covenant to repair or under the general law. Usually your liability is commensurate with your liability to pay rent, which continues to be payable even if the covenant does not require you to repair in the event of fire, or if the premises are totally destroyed. It remains payable whether or not your landlord has insured the premises himself or covenanted to do the repairs.

Consequently a tenant usually covenants to insure the premises if he has covenanted to repair, which effectively makes him the insurer of the full value of the whole premises, even if the covenant is for a fixed sum. If he does not insure for that amount, or the loss is due to an excepted risk, the tenant has to pay the balance or the whole of the loss himself. Normally the tenant insures at the commencement of the lease and, if he does not pay the premium on renewal, he is in breach of the insurance covenant. The landlord can then claim damages or, if he has reserved a right of re-entry for breach of the terms of the lease, forfeit the lease.

If the tenant is not bound to insure, the landlord must do so but the tenant is liable for increases in the premium due to changes on his own premises. He cannot recover under the landlord's insurance, even if the landlord is not bound to repair and he continues to be liable for the rent, even if the premises are destroyed. He may, however, be entitled to claim reinstatement under the 1774 Act. If the landlord's covenant is stated to be for the benefit of both himself and the tenant, the landlord must use the proceeds of his claim to reinstate, even if he has not covenanted to do so.

The normal cover for fire can, at an increased premium, be extended to include 'special perils', including explosions, earthquakes, damage caused by aircraft, subterranean fire, riots and civil commotions, bursting or overflowing of water tanks, apparatus or pipes, impact and malicious damage. This can be negotiated on a replacement or reinstatement basis and the policy can be extended to include the cost of any fees payable to architects and/or surveyors incurred as a result of rebuilding. You will also want to cover the contents of the building for loss or damage to stock, plant, machinery, fixtures and fittings and for the removal of the debris resulting from building damage.

Burglary insurance

Cover for loss or damage caused by theft involving entry or exit by forceful or violent means but not shoplifting is also available. Your insurance company will usually require the premises to be properly protected and you will save time and money if you make inquiries in advance as to what they require.

Engineering insurance

The Factories Acts require some plant to be inspected by a 'competent' engineer and specialist insurers will provide a proper inspection service. If part of your plant is vulnerable to damage or breakdown and potentially dangerous you should obtain appropriate cover.

Money insurance

You can insure against loss of money by an employee. The cover extends to loss by any cause except theft by an employee, which can be insured under a fidelity bond or policy and is discussed later in this chapter.

Money insurance however is usually arranged on a selective basis, according to the needs of the insured and can cover losses during and outside business hours from a safe or outside a safe. You can also cover loss of national insurance cards, trading stamps and cash in the custody of collectors or at your private residence and money in transit between your premises and the bank or Post Office. The policy can be extended to include a benefit for personal assault, usually on the basis of a capital sum or weekly benefit if employees are assaulted while carrying money in the course of their employment. The premium is normally based on the total amount of cash, bank notes and open cheques handled in a year.

Insurance of goods

Deterioration of stock can be covered and other claims for insurance on goods depend on whether the goods are at the claimant's risk at the time of the loss (see page 146). Rights may have to be ceded to the insurance company, which reimburses the claimant itself.

You can insure before you buy goods by taking out a 'floating policy' to cover, for example, 'all the goods in the warehouse or otherwise ascertainable at the time of the loss' to a fixed amount, or take out a 'declaration policy' for goods to be declared from time to time. Another blanket method is to take out an 'open policy', insuring against all risks by sea and land, which normally requires you to notify the insurers as soon as you know that goods of the class insured are at your risk and that they are in transit.

Once risk passes to you, the goods are insurable, even if they are still on the seller's premises.

The buyer also has an insurable interest if ownership alone has passed to him (if, for example, the seller agrees to delivery specifically at the buyer's own risk). If the goods are destroyed the buyer can recover from the insurers what he must pay to the seller. If the buyer becomes insolvent after risk has passed to him and the seller still has the goods, the seller has a lien on them for the price and can retain the goods. If the seller has already parted with them he can reclaim them if they are still in transit. Either way he has an insurable interest.

The seller's lien does not affect the buyer's insurance once the risk passes to him and the right to stop the goods in transit does not mean that the seller can claim under the buyer's insurance.

There are several commercial variants: for example, a seller can insure under an insurance inclusive CIF (cost, insurance, freight) contract for the buyer's benefit; if the contract is agreed on an FOB (free on board) basis, the buyer carries the cost of the insurance. There are other computations and you should check your insurance and sales documents to ensure that there is adequate cover and to find out who is entitled to claim against the insurers.

Liability insurance

Liability insurance of goods or property covers your liability to employees or to the general public as employer, owner or occupier of a building and usually covers the actions of your employees, unless fraud or criminal acts are involved.

Public liability insurance usually covers claims relating to injury, disease or damage to property of a third party, but excludes injury to your own employees, damage to your own property if you are in occupation and some kinds of liability under commercial contracts. It can be extended to cover liability arising out of goods sold or supplied and, if the business involves work away from your premises, it should be extended accordingly.

If an employee is injured at work you are usually held responsible whether or not you were personally at fault and you are legally required to take out appropriate insurance with authorised insurers under the Employer's Liability (Compulsory Insurance) Act 1969. There are some exceptions to the requirement, for example, where you only employ your family. The Certificate of Insurance must be prominently displayed on the premises and, provided you employ trustworthy and trained personnel, your insurers cannot refuse a claim.

You are required to record details of injuries at work in a special 'Accident Book', which is useful evidence in support of any claims by, or against, you.

Personal accident and/or sickness insurance

You may wish to provide an employee scheme for accident or sickness cover as a 'fringe benefit'. You might also consider health insurance for yourself if the business is dependent on your services.

Motor insurance

It is an offence to use a motor vehicle on the highway unless you have insurance cover under the Road Traffic Acts, but the legal requirement, usually called 'road traffic cover', only indemnifies you for your legal liability for death of or injury to third parties. Usually you will want at least third party cover, which also indemnifies you for damage to third party property and you can extend the cover to include loss of or damage to your own vehicle by fire and theft. Comprehensive cover also includes accidental damage to the insured vehicle. When insuring vehicles used in the business you must specify the use in your proposal to the insurers.

Even under road traffic cover you will usually be insured

personally as driver of any vehicle. Your policy is therefore automatically transferred if you change your car, even if this is because your own car has been stolen or destroyed and you have made a claim on your insurers.

Fidelity bonds and policies

Insurance against theft by your employees is obtainable under fidelity bonds and policies and you can also take out insurance in the form of a guarantee for due completion of contracts and payment of debts. The insurers or underwriters stand surety for the risk, or else you can be insured against losses arising from specified dishonesty and for non-completion of a particular contract or non-payment of a specific debt.

Guarantee insurance is different from guarantee by a surety, as the surety will reimburse you if you are unpaid but he is under no obligation until there is a default and the principal (actual) debt remains unaffected.

As with other insurance you must make full disclosure of all material facts, including the financial position of the debtor and a guarantee must be contained in a written document.

Fidelity policies cover you against an employee's breach of confidence or a loss resulting from his dishonesty but they only cover you for his negligence if it is specifically included and some policies only cover theft. The cover is usually restricted to a particular employment in a stated capacity for a fixed period, as the risk depends on the opportunity. Default within the period of the guarantee is usually covered, even if the loss is discovered afterwards. The conditions imposed by the policy are usually the same as those contained in other insurance contracts. Notice of loss may be necessary but usually not notice of suspicion.

Credit insurance

Credit insurance to cover your business abroad is dealt with more fully at the end of Chapter 9 but debts are usually insured on the basis of an indemnity. If they are not paid when due, you can make a claim and the insurers pay you and have your rights against the debtor. Cover is sometimes confined to non-payment in specific circumstances, but, if it is for non-payment on a fixed date, the cause is irrelevant. You do not usually have to sue the debtor or enforce any security unless you are claiming a deficiency.

The cover continues even if you enter into a 'scheme of arrangement' with the creditor, as the debt, or part of it, remains unpaid and the arrangement does not change the risk. You usually have to carry a small part of the loss yourself with credit insurance, depending on what causes the loss.

Insurance against claims under employment legislation

Some specialist insurers as well as general insurers will cover you for claims by employees under the employment legislation. They often provide an advisory service on personnel relations in the hope that the employer will avoid problems and they can minimise claims. Cover is also available for the costs of general litigation.

Insurance of key personnel

You can insure against loss caused to the business by the death of members of senior management. Cover can be for direct loss caused to the business, to provide cash on the death of a partner to enable the firm to buy his share or to engage someone to take over management of the business.

STATUTORY REFERENCES

Defective Premises Act 1972

Employers' Liability (Compulsory Insurance) Act 1969

Employers' Liability (Defective Equipment) Act 1969

Factories Act 1961

Fire Prevention (Metropolis) Act 1774

Marine Insurance Act 1906

Occupiers' Liability Act 1957

Road Traffic Act 1972

Sale of Goods Act 1979

8
Employment Law

Employer's obligations

As soon as you take on one employee the law takes an active part in your day-to-day activities. The network of legislation through which you must pick your way is studded with fines and penalties and you may also have to comply with industrial practice and collective bargaining agreements. As with the system of work legislation, contravention can prove to be far more expensive than taking preventive measures, so you should have a good knowledge of what is required of you. If an employee alleges that he has been unfairly or wrongly dismissed, your first and best defence is that you have followed the procedure required by the employment legislation.

The safe and happy working environment you have created in accordance with your legal obligations must now be filled with competent employees.

If you have even one employee, apart from members of the family, you must conform to the provisions of the Employment Protection (Consolidation) Act 1978 and associated legislation. With the exception of non-executive directors and the self-employed, the legislation applies to everyone from the apprentice on the shop floor to top management. Directors are covered by the Act if they have a contract of service or one can be implied from the circumstances of their employment.* Partners taking a share of the profits are self-employed but they are employers under the Act and if there is a major split in the partnership the employees may be in a redundancy situation as dissolution may terminate their contracts of employment.† (Self-employed workers are also treated differently from employees for the purpose of PAYE deductions for income tax and for insurance contributions under the Social Security Act 1973.)

* *Parsons* v *Albert Parsons* (1979) ICR 271
† *Tunstall* v *Condon* (1980) ICR 786

Temporary employees are covered by the Act if they work for you under a contract of employment for more than 16 hours a week or have been continuously employed for between eight and 16 hours a week for five years. They are not, however, protected under the unfair dismissal provisions if the contract is only for temporary work and they are brought in to replace someone on maternity leave or temporarily suspended on medical grounds and were notified in writing when taken on that the employment would be terminated at the end of the relevant period.

Outworkers and homeworkers have different rights. To protect yourself you should check with the Advisory, Conciliation and Arbitration Service (ACAS) to ensure that their wages and the terms and conditions of their employment comply with any orders issued by a wages council or joint industrial council in your trade or industry.

Written statement of employment

Each employee must be given a written statement of the terms of his employment within 13 weeks of starting work, unless he works for less than 16 hours a week, is married to the employer, or normally works abroad. He is entitled to certain minimum periods of notice on dismissal and is protected against unfair dismissal. He can also claim redundancy or guarantee payments if you cannot provide work or sufficient work to constitute full-time employment according to the original terms upon which he was engaged.

The statement under the 1978 Act must give the names of the employer and employee, the position of the employee and the date he started work and state whether any other employment is to count as part of his continuous period of employment (for the purposes of protection under the legislation), when you must specify the earlier date. The hours of work, how much and when he is to be paid, pension rights and entitlement to holiday and sick pay must also be specified. It must also state whether a contracting out certificate under the Social Security Pension Act 1975 is in force for the employment. (The Act relates State pensions to earnings and attempts to maintain their value in the face of inflation. Partial contracting out of the State scheme is allowed if your occupational pension scheme meets certain requirements.) Disciplinary rules must be set out in the statement and the person to whom the employee can make complaints about conditions of work should be specified.

Much legal energy and argument has gone into distinguishing between employees and the self-employed. The difference is important under the employment legislation, and it also affects some of your other obligations as an employer. For example, your responsibility for the safety of your workforce when they are not working on your premises, your liability for the actions of your employees and your obligation to deduct income tax and national insurance contributions are all determined by their status.

The courts have tried to resolve the question in a number of ways. The traditional approach was to regard an individual as an employee if the person for whom he worked controlled not only what work was done but how and when it was done. More recently the courts have taken the view that an individual is regarded as an employee not only if the person for whom he works controls how and when the work is done, but also if the terms of the contract of employment, either expressly or impliedly, indicate that he is working for you rather than for himself. Much depends on whether he is described as being self-employed or as being an independent contractor. Here again, however, the court may not necessarily agree that he is self-employed simply because he or the person for whom he works says that he is. They will look at his conditions of work, and for key criteria such as how he is paid, who is responsible for tax and national insurance deductions, whether the 'employer' provides equipment and whether the employee takes a profit or a loss on the work.

When you have a collective agreement the statement can usually simply refer to it, as it contains most of the information required by the 1978 Act. Draft forms of the statement, works' rules and disciplinary and grievance procedures can be obtained from the Department of Employment and ACAS gives general advice on employment legislation.

If you do not provide your employees with a statement and do not have a proper disciplinary procedure, your involvement with a conciliation officer, who deals with disputes before they reach the industrial tribunal, and with the tribunal may be short, unsatisfactory and expensive.

Notice

The length of notice of termination of employment must also be specified in the statement. There are mandatory minimum periods of notice which cannot be overriden by an agreement for shorter periods but the employee's right to receive the specified period of notice can be waived and you may offer payment in lieu of the required notice. Currently an employee continuously employed for four weeks is entitled to not less than one week's notice and employees in continous employment for between two and 12 years must receive a week's notice for each year of continuous service. Employees employed continuously for over 12 years are entitled to not less than 12 weeks' notice. The employer, on the other hand, is only entitled to a week's notice from an employee who has been employed for four or more weeks.

Contract of employment

The statement is not a contract of employment but is evidence of some of the terms and conditions that may be implied in an individual contract of employment. The full contract can be oral or written, and may be the result of prolonged negotiation or of casual conversation. However, it is safest formally to agree all of its terms, at least in the case of senior employees, so that you both know where you stand.

The contract should cover wages (including bonuses and commission), overtime payments, sick pay, travel allowances, pensions and so on, and should also state what behaviour will result in dismissal. Works' rules can be included as terms of the contract, or you can impose them outside it. Works' rules should be put together after consultation with employees or their trade union or staff representatives and should include a requirement to follow your safety at work scheme. As a term of the contract they have to be negotiated, otherwise you can change them at any time. If you specify the method of performing the work and set out safety and disciplinary procedures outside the contact, a breach of the works' rules automatically results in (fair) dismissal, provided the rules and procedures are clear and reasonable.

Since terms of the contract of employment can only be varied by agreement, if you demote an employee without sufficient reason, his consequent resignation may amount to dismissal (termed constructive dismissal) and may be unfair under the Act. If he does not object, he is taken to have accepted the change in his thereafter modified contract. A contract can, however, expressly permit substantial variation and it can also be implied from conduct or from the terms of your collective agreement.

Trade union agreements apply to non-union members only by agreement but a local employers' association in your trade or industry or a section of an independent recognised trade union, of which one of your employees is a member, can lodge a complaint with ACAS that your employees are worse off than comparative workers in comparable employment, whose terms and conditions of employment have been settled by an agreement or award between the relevant employers' association and a trade union representing a substantial proportion of such employees. If ACAS cannot deal with the complaint, it must be referred to the Central Arbitration Committee, whose secretary is appointed by the Secretary of State for Employment.

Wages

In the absence of expressly agreed terms governing payment of wages or a rate determined in accordance with the terms of a collective agreement, an employee can claim reasonable remuneration in relation to the work carried out, based on the mutual understanding that the services provided were to be paid for.

Women are entitled to be paid the same wages as the men working in the same or basically similar work and there are several legislative provisions covering a wide variety of statutory enactments, with the basic purpose of providing particular groups of workers with a minimum wage, to be paid in cash.

'Workmen' must be paid in cash and not in kind, in accordance with the provisions of the Truck Acts, which cover anyone involved in the supply of goods and services or engaged under a contract of service where physical exertion forms a substantial part of the job. Cash includes cheques, money and postal orders and bank or Giro transfer.

Only certain deductions are permitted from 'workmen's' wages and they must not exceed the real value of the benefit supplied. The deductions are confined to the supply of medicine or medical attention, the supply of fuel, the supply of food prepared and eaten on the employer's premises, for rent payable for a house let by the employer for the employee's personal occupation, and for the reasonable and actual use of materials, tools, machines, standing room and light which enable the employee to complete the work. You can also deduct fines for breaches of discipline, which are dealt with later in this chapter. Deductions, however, can only be made if you have a written agreement with the employee and signed by him, or a notice is continuously and conspicuously displayed on the premises where the employee can read and copy it. The amounts deducted must be fair and reasonable in the circumstances and a written notification of the sums payable and the reason for the deduction must be handed to the employee.

Wages may be payable in the form of commission for work done on your behalf and you must allow the employee to carry out the job and earn his commission in accordance with the terms of his contract. You must also give him sufficient work to enable him to earn the amount of commission contemplated as being reasonable in the circumstances.

You are not under a general duty to provide work but you must pay for work done. If, however, you are providing some kinds of employment, for example, as an entertainer or journalist, the opportunity to work and the related publicity that may bring other work is an essential ingredient of the agreement with the employee. Accordingly, your failure to provide work will constitute a repudiation of the contract of employment, even if the agreed wages are paid during periods of inactivity. If you engage an employee for a fixed period to discharge specific duties, for example, as a director, and the position is lost through amalgamation, thereby abolishing the position. You will have to pay damages for the premature termination and consequent failure to provide work in accordance with the contract of employment to reflect his loss of salary for the remainder of his contract.

Some sections of the workforce not represented by large and influential unions are within the scope of the supervision of wages councils representing particular trades. The councils include employers and employees in the trade with the addition of three independent persons, one of whom acts as chairman and can make orders specifying minimum wages, the duration of holidays, the amount of holiday pay and any other terms and conditions of employment. They publish details of their proposals and notify relevant employers, who must display the proposals where their employees can read them. Both employers and employees have at least 14 days to decide whether to make certain representations regarding amendments. The proposals are thereafter incorporated as implied terms in the contract of employment of every employee within the scope of the order, even if the individual's contract expressly provides otherwise.

Inspectors employed by the Department of Employment are responsible for the enforcement of wages orders and can enter an employer's premises, question personnel and examine your records of payment of wages. An employer failing to observe the terms of a wages order is liable to a fine of £100 and may be ordered to pay the difference to the employee between the wage paid and the minimum to a maximum of two years' back pay. Records should be kept for three years, as failure to keep records will result in another fine of up to £100. In addition, the employee has a contractual right to sue in the civil court for up to six years' arrears of pay.

In recent years some wages councils have been abolished and replaced by statutory joint industrial councils, on the assumption that, because the industry concerned has an organisation of employers and is sufficiently covered by trade union representation, employment issues can be negotiated through collective bargaining procedures.

Fair Wages Resolution 1946

A 'fair wages' clause is incorporated into any agreement concluded with a contractor for the completion of work done on behalf of the government, for instance, a contract to erect a new hospital for the National Health Service. The clause attempts to ensure that all the employees, not only those involved in the government work, are paid the currently accepted rate for the type of work and that the hours and conditions of work are no less favourable than those commonly accepted locally. A copy of the Resolution must be displayed in the workplace and you must ensure that your sub-contractors engaged in the work also observe its requirements. Disputes concerning implementation are referred to the Secretary of State for Employment, with, if necessary, further reference to the Central Arbitration Committee. The employee cannot, however, sue his employer and claim the accepted fair wage if it is more than that which was agreed in his contract of employment.

Similar provisions are contained in certain legislation applying to other trades, including the Road Traffic Act 1960, the Films Act 1960 and the Sugar Act 1956.

Sick pay

You can make whatever provision you wish on payment to employees who are absent through illness or accident. Usually an express term providing or withholding payment during illness is included. You may wish to provide for a decreasing scale of payment during prolonged absences, but the employee is entitled to full pay if absent through illness during the minimum period of notice required by law, whatever is in the contract of employment. If there is no mention of payment during illness, the employee is entitled to his full wage, including bonus and commission, unless there is an implied term in the contract or a trade custom negativing his right to payment.

The employee can claim sickness benefit under the Social Security Scheme, whether or not he is paid by the employer. You may wish to include an express term providing that the amount of sickness benefit should, therefore, be deducted, whether or not the benefit is claimed. The amount provided under the Scheme has recently been reduced, in line with other social security benefits, and increases are limited to up to 5 per cent less than the annual rate of inflation.

From 6 April 1983 the employer is required to make statutory payments of sick pay and reclaim payment from the Department of Health and Social Security.

The theory behind the legislation is to cut down the paperwork involved in dealing with claims but it may do just the reverse as reimbursement is only available for payments properly made in accordance with the legislation.

Payment must be made only during periods of 'incapacity' which last for at least four days beginning on the first day that the employee is off sick and ending on the day he returns to work, or when he leaves the employment, or is excluded from claiming the payment or at the end of the tax year. Payment cannot be made for the first three days unless two separate periods of at least four days' absence are separated by not more than two weeks, in which case the periods are linked and the waiting time for payment applies only to the first period. Even when you decide the employee is entitled to the payment, he can only receive payment for qualifying days, ie those days upon which it is agreed that he normally works; problems can therefore arise with part-time workers unless you are specific as to their hours of work. The provisions apply to all employees except those over the State Pension age, those earning less than the National Insurance lower earnings limit (presently £29.50

per week) and pregnant employees during the eleven weeks prior to the expected confinement and eight weeks thereafter. Married women paying the reduced rate of National Insurance contribution who previously had no claim to sickness benefit, are however, covered by the new legislation.

You will usually have to complete a form for an employee who is excluded from claiming the statutory benefit, so that he can make his own claim to the DHSS. Once that claim is admitted he cannot claim benefit from you for 57 days beginning with the last day of the period of incapacity. His only option if he wishes to make a further claim is to go again to the Department, thus triggering off another 57-day exclusion period.

The complexities of the legislation may tempt an employer to dismiss for sickness but the Department of Health and Social Security may order that the payments continue for the full eight weeks, in spite of the (probably unfair and possibly wrongful) dismissal.

The system of 'self-certification' by which an employee can take a week's sick leave without seeing his doctor is already in force and while the employer can reclaim the full amount of sick benefit paid under the existing legislation, he cannot claim repayment of his (employer's) National Insurance contribution. Again, however, you may want to include an express term in the contract of employment providing that the benefit be deducted, whether or not the employee claims payment from you or from the DHSS.

Itemised pay statements

You must provide an itemised pay statement giving details of gross wages and of any variable or fixed deductions and the net amount payable before, or at the time of, payment of wages. Only the aggregate amount of fixed deductions needs to be included if the employee has received a standing statement of fixed deductions. The standing statement can be amended in writing and must be reissued annually, as amended.

Employers and trade unions

Your employees can belong to any union they wish and take part in union activities as agreed with you, or as provided in their union membership agreement. You may find that industrial relations are simplified by the fact that you will be negotiating with a representative or representatives of your workforce, rather than with individual employees, and the ACAS codes of practice contain useful and practical guidance concerning disciplinary practices and procedures and what is considered to be reasonable disclosure of information to the union in collective bargaining. You will not, however, have to deal with a closed shop unless a secret ballot has been held in which 80 per cent of those entitled to vote have voted in favour of the application of a union membership agreement which is confined to a single recognised independent trade union. Dissenting employees cannot be forced to join the union if they object on the ground of conscience or other deeply held personal conviction. The union cannot insist on dismissal of an employee who was not, at the time of the agreement or since, a member of the union specified in the agreement, nor unreasonably exclude or expel an employee from membership.

Government codes of practice are available under the 1980 Act setting out the factors which should be taken into account by both employers and unions when negotiating a closed shop agreement and the subjects which should be covered by the agreement. They suggest that no action should be taken by the union or the employer where an employee has been excluded or expelled from the union before an appeal or complaint has been determined, that no employee should be dismissed if expelled from the union for refusing to take part in industrial action, and that the agreement should be subject to periodic review.

If you contract to perform work under a 'union only' agreement and have to dismiss a non-union member, you can now turn to the union or other person who forced the dismissal for a contribution or indemnity towards any claim for compensation made against you for unfair dismissal.

A union is generally not deemed responsible for the unofficial activities of its members but the union is liable in damages for interference leading to breach of your commercial contracts unless the action taken is in contemplation or furtherance of a trade dispute.

A contract to perform work under a 'union only' agreement is now invalid and a dismissal for non-union membership is automatically unfair unless there is an established union membership agreement approved by a five-yearly ballot of 80 per cent of the employees entitled to vote. When the dismissal is unfair, the complainant and the employer can ask for anyone, including the union, to be joined to tribunal proceedings and to provide an indemnity or contribution to damages claimed by the employee.

A union is generally not responsible for the unofficial activities of its members but it is liable in damages for interference leading to breach of your commercial contracts, unless the action relates wholly or mainly to, or is taken in contemplation or furtherance of, a trade dispute.

The trade dispute must now be a personal matter between you and your workforce and it is unlawful for your employees to bring in outsiders. Peaceful picketing in contemplation or furtherance of a trade dispute is permitted by your own employees in order that they may peacefully obtain or communicate information or peacefully persuade other employees to work or stop working. Picketing must be at or near the employees' own place of work, although trade union officials representing their picketing members can visit them to give moral support. The government code of practice suggests that it will be rare for the number of lawful pickets to exceed six and often a smaller number will be all that is required. Interference with your commercial contracts by secondary action is now illegal but you should take expert advice before entangling yourself in trade union law or alienating your workforce and its representatives.

Anti-discrimination legislation

You must not without good reason discriminate against employees because of their colour, race, ethnic or national origin or, if you have more than five employees, because of their sex or marital status and jobs must be advertised and offered accordingly. The Sex Discrimination Act cuts both ways and men, as well as women, can complain of less favourable treatment.

Women receive different death, marriage and maternity benefits. Pension rights and retirement benefits also differ except, since 6 April 1978, in the terms relating to access to occupational pensions.* The European Court has stated that employers should ensure that any differential between hourly rates of pay and payment for part-time work does not amount

---

* *Worringham* v *Lloyds Bank* (1982) WLB 950

to indirect discrimination where a lower part-time rate is paid to a group composed exclusively or predominantly of women,* although economic facts affecting the business may justify different wages for men and women who are not contemporaneously employed but do the same work.†

In spite of EEC provisions, however, women's hours of work and the type of work they may do are restricted on the same lines as those of employees under 18, unless they do managerial, seasonal or cleaning work.

Maternity benefits

Maternity pay can be claimed after two years' continuous employment, even if the employee is fairly dismissed because of the pregnancy. Dismissal is usually only fair if the employee cannot continue to work efficiently and has refused suitable alternative work. Under the Act, suitable alternative employment is work suitable in relation to the employee and the appropriateness of the new work in the circumstances, and the employee must suffer no substantial detriment. Repayment of the benefit can be claimed out of the Maternity Pay Fund administered by the Secretary of State for Employment.

In order to claim maternity pay, the employee must, at least 21 days before her absence or, if this is not reasonably practicable, as soon as possible inform the employer, in writing if so requested, that she will be (or is) absent from work wholly or partly because of pregnancy or confinement. If she wants to return to work she must inform the employer in writing within the same time limits that she intends to do so and give him the expected week of confinement or, if confinement has occurred, the date. The employee may also be sent a written request, at least 49 days before the beginning of the expected week of confinement, asking for written confirmation of her intention to return to work. She will then only be entitled to do so if she replies within 14 days or, if this is not reasonably practicable, as soon as possible and the request must be accompanied by a written statement informing her that she will not be able to return to work if she does not reply within the statutory period.

The employee has no right to return to work if, immediately

---

* *Jenkins* v *Kingsgate (Clothing Productions) Ltd* (1981)
† *Albion Shipping Agency* v *Arnold* (1982) ICR 22

she takes maternity leave, the employer and any associated employer employed less than six people or it is not reasonably practicable for the employer or his successor to take her back or offer suitable employment.

If more than five people are employed there is no right to return to work if it is not reasonably practicable for the employer or his successor, for a reason other than redundancy, to take her back and she has unreasonably refused suitable alternative employment.

A pregnant employee attending a clinic for ante-natal care on the advice of a general practitioner, registered or certified midwife or health visitor can take time off with pay during working hours to attend the clinic. She must, on each occasion except the first appointment, produce an appropriate certificate confirming the pregnancy and an appointment card or appropriate documentation showing that the appointment has been made. A complaint of unreasonable refusal of time off, or of failure to pay for time off, may be made to the industrial tribunal for a declaration and a compensatory award against the employer.

Employing the disabled

If you have more than 20 employees, 3 per cent of your workforce must be registered disabled persons, unless you are engaged in a particularly dangerous trade.

Employees with criminal records

Under the Rehabilitation of Offenders Act 1974 a criminal conviction carrying with it a penalty not exceeding two and a half years' imprisonment becomes 'spent' after a period of time which varies, according to the severity of the penalty and whether further convictions have been recorded in the interim, up to 10 years. When the conviction is spent, the offender is legally rehabilitated and the offence ceases to exist for most legal purposes. A potential employee is entitled not to disclose spent convictions and neither the fact of the conviction nor the failure to disclose them is a legitimate reason for dismissal. Lying about a past conviction which is not yet spent, however, is a ground for fair dismissal and a large number of professions are excluded by the Act itself and under the Rehabilitation of Offenders Act 1974 (Exceptions) Order 1975.

Exposure of employees to health risks

Employees who have been in continuous employment for four weeks and exposed to certain health risks under specific legislation òr suspended because of illness are entitled to up to 26 weeks' pay, unless they are unable to work or unreasonably refuse alternative work.

Guarantee and redundancy payments

Anyone employed continuously for at least four weeks who is not provided with work for more than 12 weeks can claim guarantee payments for every full day he is not working, unless he is a seasonal worker, was only taken on for 12 weeks, the failure to provide work is due to a trade dispute, or the employee unreasonably refuses alternative work or does not comply with the employer's reasonable requirement to make his services available. A casual worker, even if apparently qualified as having worked the necessary number of hours and weeks, may not be able to claim the payment.

The maximum claim is £9.15 daily for five days in any three-month period, unless the employee is covered by, for example, a collective agreement.

If lay-off or short-time working lasts for more than four consecutive weeks or more than six in any 13 the employee can claim redundancy payments. You can agree to them or serve a counter-notice in response to the employee's notice, stating that you reasonably expect to be able to provide at least 13 weeks' continuous employment. If the work does not materialise or you withdraw the counter-notice the employee is entitled to the payments.

If an employee is made redundant after two years' continuous employment, he can claim redundancy payments even if he immediately finds alternative employment elsewhere or has volunteered to be made redundant, unless he could not adapt to new methods or unreasonably refused alternative work. The amount of the payment depends on his age and the length of his employment. An employee under 18 has no claim; employees between the ages of 18 and 22 can claim half their weekly wage for each continuous year of employment; employees over 22 can claim one week's pay, and those over 41 one and a half week's pay per year. Entitlement is for a maximum of 20 years' employment to a maximum of £135 per week. The top limit for redundancy entitlement is 60 for women and 65 for men and payments are reduced by a tapering process for women aged 59 and men aged 64. A 41 per cent rebate can be claimed from the Redundancy Fund, which is made up of contributions from employers and employees and administered by the Secretary of State.

When you are making redundant an employee who is a member of an independent trade union, you must consult with representatives of his trade union at the earliest possible opportunity. If you are contemplating major cutbacks in your workforce of between 10 and 99 employees within the same establishment the earliest possible opportunity is at least 30 days before the first dismissal takes effect. Dismissal of 100 or more employees in the same establishment requires a minimum of 60 days' prior consultation, and in both cases the Department of Employment must also be notified of your proposals in writing at least 30 and 60 days respectively before the first dismissal takes place.

Your reasons for the proposed redundancies must be given and details supplied of how many and which employees you propose to dismiss and on what basis they are selected. 'Last in first out' (LIFO) is generally the safest and fairest method. The employees' representatives do not necessarily actually have to agree that their members' best interests coincide with the interests of management, but you must give reasons for disagreeing with any counter-proposals.

If there are special circumstances which make it not reasonably practicable for the employer to go through the necessary consultation procedures. You must take all reasonable and practicable steps to comply with the requirements. Insolvency alone is not necessarily a special circumstance in which it is impracticable for an employer to consult with employees' representatives before dismissing staff, as, according to the Court of Appeal, insolvency is not 'uncommon'.*

Under the 1980 Companies Act, companies can now make financial provision for employees if the company is being taken over or wound up, even if there is no appropriate provision in the company's Memorandum or Articles, provided the payment is duly authorised by a resolution of the directors or an ordinary resolution of the shareholders.

* *Mailways (Southern) Ltd* v *Willsher* (1978) ICR 511 and *USDAW* v *Lean Bacon* (1981) 1 RLR 295

Employees' obligations

Although you and your employees have felt constrained to spell out all the details of your working relationship, the law assures you that you enjoy each other's trust and confidence and that your employees will serve you faithfully. Employees must follow all lawful and reasonable orders and take proper care of your property. Their only reward for their work must be what they receive from you and they must not disclose confidential information about your business, unless obliged to do so by the law itself.

Patents, discoveries and inventions

Patents, discoveries and inventions usually belong to the employer if made during working hours, although, depending on the employee's contract, position and salary, their benefits may have to be divided between you.

Your employees should sign an appropriate agreement to protect you against the disclosure of confidential information but the courts will not enforce one which effectively stops them making a living. You can, however, ensure, by the insertion of an appropriate provision in the contract of employment, that they do not pass on information about your secret processes or lists of customers and stop them from directly competing with you, although you cannot stop them using their technical skill or their knowledge of the trade. If for any reason, including wrongful or unfair dismissal, you repudiate the agreement containing the provision, you may not be able to enforce the restrictions put on the employee.

References

References can be difficult and you do not have to supply them.* An employee can sue you for a bad reference, unless it is true or made without malice. If it is untrue or too favourable, you may have to face an action by a subsequent employer, unless you disclaim all liability for its contents, which rather defeats the object of the reference.

* *Gallear* v *J F Watson & Son Ltd* (1979) I RLR 306

Inducing breach of the contract of employment

Persuading someone to leave his employment to join you is actionable by the ex-employer as an inducement to breach of contract.

Disciplinary powers of management

These are set out in the codes of practice issued under the employment legislation and available from ACAS and you also have some rights under earlier legislation.

Under the Truck Acts 'workmen' supplying goods and services for a wage, persons engaged under a contract of service where physical exertion forms a substantial part of the job and shop assistants can be fined or have deductions made from their pay for a breach of discipline which is likely to cause loss to the employer. The wrongs for which a fine is levied should be set out in a rule book, a copy of which should be given to the employee, and he should acknowledge his agreement to the procedure by his signature. Fines can also be levied under the Acts for bad or negligent work and damage to your property, provided the fine does not amount to more than your actual loss.

Fines must be fair and reasonable in the circumstances and the offences. Your power to impose the fine and the amount should be set out in the individual contract of employment or in a notice continuously and conspicuously displayed where your employees may read and copy it. Details should also be included in the collective agreement unless the rules are based on trade practice.

Government codes of practice

The first code of practice available from ACAS and issued under the Employment Protection Act 1975 states that disciplinary procedures should be fair and worked out with the employees and union concerned and it is best to include all disciplinary powers in an agreed disciplinary procedure. The code sets out what is fair and efficient and a copy is a worthwhile investment.

The procedure should specify who can take action and in what circumstances, for example, a breach of the works' rules. The employee must have an opportunity to put his side of the case and have the right to appeal to a senior level of management or to independent arbitration. The code also sets out the respective responsibilities of management and employees and is a useful guide to procedures concerning disputes and grievances.

The second code of practice deals with the disclosure of information to trade unions for collective bargaining purposes. The third covers time off for trade union duties and activities and the fourth code, which is approved by the Health and Safety Commission, deals with safety representatives appointed under the Health and Safety at Work Act 1974 and also contains guidance notes.

There are also two government codes of practice issued under the 1980 Employment Act on picketing and the closed shop.

The codes do not have the force of law but are taken into consideration in the context of the relevant legislation as a supplement and guide to the legislation and give some indication of acceptable standards.

Dismissal

The unfair dismissal provisions contained in the 1978 Act apply to anyone who has worked for you full time for a continuous period of two years and anyone continuously employed for between eight and 16 hours a week for five years. If, however, you and an associated employer employ more than 20 people, the provisions apply to anyone who has worked for you full time for a continuous period of one year, instead of the two-year qualifying period which applies to a smaller organisation.

The following are not protected under the unfair dismissal provisions:

1. Employees who have reached normal retiring age (60 for women and 65 for men).
2. Employees with a fixed term contract of at least one year, if they have agreed in writing that they will not make a claim under the unfair dismissal legislation.
3. Employees who work less than 16 hours a week.
4. Employees covered by a dismissal procedure agreement designated and approved by the Secretary of State for Employment.
5. Employees who work or are resident abroad.

There is no qualifying period if an employee is dismissed for trade union activities, for membership of his union or because of pregnancy, or sex or race discrimination, and dismissal is then automatically unfair under the legislation. A dismissal for non-union membership is, however, only unfair if you have a union membership agreement which has been approved by a five-yearly ballot of the relevant employees (see page 129). Under the 1982 Employment Act you can fairly dismiss an employee while on strike, provided you have given him written notice that he will be dismissed if he does not return to work within a specified time and he is dismissed while still on strike.

An employee with job security under the employment legislation should be dismissed in strict conformity with the relevant code and with the terms of the individual contract and fair dismissal can only be based on one of the following:

1. The capabilities or qualifications of the employee, provided that his contract states he must hold the qualifications.
2. The employee's conduct.
3. Redundancy.
4. The fact that the employee cannot continue in his job without breaking the law.
5. Some other substantial reason.

Even if you can fairly dismiss an employee, you should follow the procedure set out in the code. Written or, if this is not possible, oral warnings should be given by someone in authority, making it clear what is complained of and that the consequence of a failure to heed the warning will be dismissal. Usually you will have to give a second warning and if this is disregarded you can consider suspension or dismissal. The second warning and the relevant facts on which you have based your decision should also be put in writing.

You must be able to show that in all the circumstances, including the size of the business and your administrative resources, you acted fairly and reasonably in treating the relevant facts as sufficient reason for dismissal, having regard to the substantial merits of the case and that the proper procedure was followed. You must give the employee at least two chances to explain himself, or dismissal is almost automatically 'unfair'.

Summary dismissal is hardly ever justified. Even if an employee seems incapable of working properly he should not be dismissed without a warning but should be given an opportunity to explain himself* and to mend his ways. Gross misconduct, such as persistent drunkenness on the job, wilful

---

* *Clarks of Hove Ltd* v *Bakers' Union* (1979) 1 All ER 152

refusal to obey lawful and reasonable orders, dishonesty, gross neglect or breach of the works' rules may exceptionally justify summary dismissal, but there is usually time and justification for a warning before you have to take action.

When you have to dismiss because of redundancy, you should follow the consultation procedure if required. You will usually have to show how, by whom and on what basis selection was made and generally 'last in first out' is reasonable in the circumstances.

An employee whose job is to drive for you can reasonably be dismissed if he loses his licence if you are unable to offer him suitable alternative work.

Dismissal for 'other substantial reason' could include a business starting up in competition with you run by an employee's family, which takes advantage of your trade secrets or connections.

Placing an employee in an untenable position, which compels him to resign ('constructive dismissal'), may amount to unfair dismissal. It will usually be a breach of the contract of employment as well and may therefore constitute wrongful dismissal.

If you do have the right to dismiss you must give the notice specified in the individual contract of employment or wages in lieu. If there is no specified period of notice it must be reasonable in the circumstances, bearing in mind that the minimum periods under the employment legislation range from one week after four weeks' continuous employment to 12 weeks after 12 or more years' continuous employment. Written reasons for your action must be sent to the employee within 14 days of dismissal.

A company director with a service contract is protected under the legislation. Even if he is the sole director and majority shareholder, he can claim redundancy payments if the company goes into liquidation but only salaried partners can claim redundancy payments against the partnership.

Remedies for unfair dismissal

If the dismissal is unfair the employee is entitled to reinstatement in the same job or re-engagement in a similar job. He can also apply to an industrial tribunal for compensation, and either of you can appeal against its decision to the Employment Appeals Tribunal and thereafter to the ordinary courts.

Compensation awarded by the tribunal depends on what the employee actually loses in money terms, in addition to the amount of any benefit he might reasonably have expected to receive. The current maximum award is £7000, though there is an additional punitive award of up to £135 per week for 52 weeks if you ignore an order for reinstatement or re-engagement.

The basic award of a half to one and a half week's pay for each year of employment, depending on the employee's age, is reduced if the employee unreasonably refuses re-instatement, he has immediately found alternative work, his conduct was a contributory factor in the dismissal or conduct of which you were unaware merited dismissal.

If the employee loses his case, he does not have to pay your costs unless the tribunal decides that he made serious and unfounded allegations. If he has been dismissed because of trade union pressure, the union or third party, such as a company for which you have had to sign a 'union only contract', may be ordered to contribute to, or indemnify you for, your costs.

Remedies for wrongful dismissal

When the dismissal is wrongful because you have broken one of the terms of the individual contract of employment, the employee can claim damages under the general law. This may amount to far more than compensation under the employment legislation.

Directors' service contracts are subject both to the company's Articles and to their individual contract, but they can be dismissed at any time for a price. Senior employees often have a contract for a fixed number of years and they are entitled to compensation for loss of office, unless they are themselves in breach of contract.

Damages are generally based on what the employee loses and expects to lose by instant unemployment. He must seek comparable alternative employment to minimise his loss but the claim can be substantial if he is unable to find comparable work.

Whatever the legal or financial consequences, however, you cannot be forced to take an employee back. If he was unfairly dismissed, the tribunal may, if it is practicable, decide he should be reinstated or re-engaged but you always have the choice of paying compensation instead.

STATUTORY REFERENCES

Companies Acts 1948 and 1980

Contracts of Employment Act 1972

Disabled Persons Employment Act 1958

Employment Acts 1980 and 1982

Employment Protection Act 1975

Employment Protection (Consolidation) Act 1978

Equal Pay Act 1970

Factories Act 1961

Films Act 1960

Race Relations Act 1976

Rehabilitation of Offenders Act 1974

Road Traffic Acts 1960, 1972 and 1974

Sex Discrimination Act 1975

Social Security Act 1979

Social Security (No 2) Act 1980

Social Security Pensions Act 1975

Sugar Act 1956

Trade Union and Labour Relations Act 1974

Truck Acts 1831 and 1896

Wages Councils Act 1979

9
Trading

This chapter covers some areas of law that directly affect your day-to-day search for profits, the law of sale of goods and consumer credit, including hire purchase.

These areas of law, like insurance law and the law of landlord and tenant, are based on contract law, which is concerned with agreements between willing parties, who exchange promises — a promise to deliver goods or services in return for a promise to pay, a promise to cover an insured risk in return for payment of the price, and so on. Where third parties are involved, with whom you have no agreed obligations, for example, where you are liable in negligence to a person injured on your premises, different rules apply. Most of your business arrangements, however, are made by agreement between the parties.

The words contract and agreement are therefore used interchangeably in this chapter, as a contract is simply the sum total of the promises made between the parties, plus any extra terms which the law may imply into the agreement, and contract law dictates the remedies available to both sides in the event of non-performance.

In theory, although with some important exceptions, oral agreements are enforceable in exactly the same way as written agreements but you will require evidence of the agreement through conversations or correspondence before you are able to show non-performance and there is no substitute for a written contract setting out all the agreed terms. You can generally agree terms between yourselves, although the law is an occasional third party. Complicated legalese is not necessary: all that is required is a clear statement of the terms and a clear understanding of the penalties consequent on non-performance.

Law of the contract

If you do business abroad you should try to agree the inclusion of a clause stating that the contract will be governed by English law, so that disputes can be settled in accordance with English law, for convenience, (relative) speed and a considerable saving in costs. In the absence of a specific clause, the law of your contract will be what was ostensibly agreed at the time or what can be inferred from the circumstances in which you conducted the contract.

You may, however, still find yourself dealing with foreign courts, as the judgement of an English court is not automatically or easily enforceable in other jurisdictions, although there are procedures by which you can ensure that any assets in this country are held here pending reference to the courts, so that if you win your case you can enforce judgement in England.

Settling disputes by arbitration

You may also want to insert a clause referring disputes to arbitration by a person to be agreed between the parties or, failing agreement within a specified period, the president of your trade or professional association or the president of the Institute of Arbitrators.

There are several arbitral courts in London, including the London Court of Arbitration, which deals with anything from a small claim to an international dispute or a shipping claim, and the Institute of Travel Agents, which deals with small claims. Other old-fashioned arbitral tribunals cover the commodity markets. These include the Sugar Association, the Coffee and Cocoa Associations, the London Metal Exchange and the Baltic Exchange, which deals with maritime claims. Your trade or professional association will give you information and advice on procedure, which is often left to experts in the field rather than to lawyers. International disputes can also be referred to the International Chamber of Commerce, the headquarters of which is in Paris but which has several national committees, including one in London, or to other international tribunals. The tribunal in the United States, for example, is frequently used because of its speed in dealing with problems compared to the US courts.

For the purposes of arbitration, the proper law of the contract, in the absence of an express clause, is that which has the closest and most real connection to the contract. The proper law decides on the validity and effect of the arbitration agreement, but the conduct of the arbitration procedure is governed by the law of the country where the arbitration takes place.

New rules governing arbitration have been introduced by the 1979 Arbitration Act and will, it is hoped, induce the English commercial community to follow international practice and to refer commercial matters to the commercial arbitration tribunals.

With the exception of contracts concerned with shipping and insurance, disputes arising out of commodity contracts or those involving a foreign national or non-resident, you can make an exclusion agreement agreeing to refer disputes to arbitration and excluding 'any right of appeal or other resort to the English courts in respect of any arbitration which might arise under the contract'. The arbitrator's decision is then final and binding, although there is a very restricted right of appeal to the courts and you can always turn to the courts if there is an allegation of 'misconduct'. Misconduct in this context means any infringement of the rules of 'natural justice', a legal term which means that you are entitled to a fair hearing and an opportunity of stating your case. A foreign national or non-resident is an individual who is a foreign national and habitually resident outside the UK, or a body incorporated outside the UK or whose central management and control is exercised abroad.

Shipping, insurance and commodity contracts can also exclude a right of referral to the court, provided the parties made the agreement after the commencement of the arbitration of the award, it does not concern a contract governed by foreign law or is not one to which a foreign national or non-resident is a party at the time of the arbitration agreement.

If you have not excluded your right to appeal to the courts, you can appeal on a question of law arising out of the award but only with the consent of the parties to the arbitration or if the commercial court thinks that the matter substantially affects the parties' rights. A further appeal to the Court of Appeal requires the consent of the commercial court or the Court of Appeal and there must be a question of public importance to be decided or some special reason why the matter should be reconsidered.

Appeal is, however, only possible if the appeal court has access to all the necessary information, so you should ensure that the arbitrator makes a 'reasoned award' setting out the basis of his decision.

Reference can also be made to the courts on a preliminary point of law arising in the course of a pending arbitration, with the consent of the parties and of the arbitrator. In addition, the court must be satisfied that determining the question will substantially save costs and is one in which leave to appeal on a point of law would be likely to be given.

Even if you have no basis for an appeal you may still be able to obtain a court hearing after the commencement of the arbitration, as the court has a discretion to stay the arbitration and must do so if it is a non-domestic agreement to which a foreign national or non-resident is a party or if it is expressly or impliedly governed by foreign law.

Buying and selling for cash

When money changes hands in exchange for goods, casually or by formal written agreement, the law is a third party in the transaction.

As manufacturer, middleman or retailer, your third party is the Sale of Goods Act 1979 and associated legislation. Hire purchase and consumer credit legislation apply to some sales on credit and your transaction, for cash or on credit, may also be affected by the customs of your trade.

Buyer protection

Although most of the sale of goods legislation only applies if you have not agreed the terms of payment and delivery, buyer protection is much wider than is generally believed.

A commercial buyer is legally entitled to assume that the seller owns his goods. The private buyer has additional, more basic protection: goods offered to the consumer must be suitable for the purpose for which they are purchased and must correspond with samples, descriptions and display items.

Obviously, there are some qualifications: if the price is low, you take your chances. You cannot claim for defects pointed out at the time of sale, nor is the seller responsible if the buyer is given an opportunity to examine the goods.

The statutory buyer protection now also covers contracts for services and some agreements to hire goods which are outside the hire purchase legislation. Services include repair and maintenance arrangements where you can legally expect work to be carried out in a reasonable time, with reasonable care and skill and, if you have not expressly or impliedly agreed the price, at a reasonable price.

In commercial situations — that is, not involving the 'consumer' you can exclude the statutory quality guarantee altogether but neither buyer nor seller can be entirely unreasonable and, if the seller has a monopoly, he will probably not be able to exclude it. But price and quality go together — you still only get what you pay for.

Exclusion and exemption clauses

You can restrict or exclude your liability for the quality and quantity of your goods under an appropriately drafted clause in your contract. It is not illegal to attempt to exclude or avoid liability for negligence or non-performance of your commercial obligations but under the Unfair Contract Terms Act 1977 the exemption clause or notice posted on your premises has no legal effect.

Widely framed indemnity clauses are also illegal. However large the notice displayed on your premises or the print in your contracts, any accident which results in personal injury or death is a commercial risk you take on as part of your commercial obligations.

Parliament, however, concedes that we are not perfect and there is a statutory defence under the Act. You can restrict your liability for loss and damage, but not for personal injury or death, provided the clause in your contract or notice to third parties is reasonable in the circumstances. In commercial transactions the relative bargaining strength of the parties and the price charged are relevant factors. But the law has again come to the aid of the consumer. The manufacturer's guarantee is just that: a guarantee that the goods are fit to use and safe to use and the retailer is the only link in the chain of responsibilities that can put a limit on liability to the customer.

There are exceptions to this optimistic re-evaluation of civic responsibility. It is legally taken for granted that you are in safe hands when you or your merchandise travel on the high seas or by scheduled airline and insurance companies are presumed not to be careless at all, possibly because their business is to pay for the carelessness of others. Contracts dealing with copyrights and patents are also excluded from the legislation, as are international contracts where the parties are resident outside the jurisdiction of the English courts.

Defective product liability

Under present UK law financial responsibility for defective products varies. A purchaser generally has an automatic right to compensation from the seller, but, where there is no commercial/contractual link, compensation is usually only available from someone who is clearly at fault.

The EEC draft Directive on liability for defective products, which has been under consideration for a considerable period, goes much further. If a product causes death, injury or damage, liability is 'strict' (legally automatic) and compensation must be paid. By whom it must be paid allows the victim a far wider choice than under UK law and includes persons who may not only be entirely blameless but may also be unable to pass on their financial liability to the person at fault. In addition, insurance of the increased liability may be extremely expensive and, in some instances, unavailable.

The Directive puts the responsibility on the 'producer'. This is defined to extend to everyone in the chain of supply, from the manufacturer of component parts and finished articles, through the middleman, who contributes to the making of the product, to the person who packages, carries or installs it. Suppliers of 'in-house' merchandise and, failing any other identifiable link in the chain, any other supplier are also liable, as is an importer, who may because of legal boundaries not be able to export his claim against a foreign supplier.

Anyone proving damage can claim compensation, whether or not the fault can be proved or a defect was discoverable in the light of the technological and other knowledge available when the article was first put on the market. Compensation is payable not only for damage causing injury and death but also for property damage, which can in some circumstances be excluded in UK law and, when payable, is limited if the claim is for purely financial loss.

Another extension under the Directive is the time limit during which claims can be made. Six and three years are the UK limits for contractual and negligence claims respectively. Under the Directive, claims must still be brought within three years of the victim becoming aware of the damage and the defect. But the producer's liability under the Directive lasts for 10 years, a period which makes nonsense of the fact that he cannot put in a defence of lack of technical knowledge at the time the article was put into circulation.

Civic responsibility, however, has its limits. Damage arising from nuclear accidents and from primary agricultural produce and craft and artistic products not subject to industrial use are excluded. And the Directive only applies to goods put into circulation in the course of business. The emphasis here, however, is on 'circulation' and unfortunately anyone injured by anything at any time can usually point to something which at some time was produced for commercial use.

Thus the circulated article affects a vast horde of prospective claimants and the financial top limits are not reassuring: approximately £17,000,000 for the totality of claims based on damage caused by identical objects with identical defects and about £34,000 for individual claims. The latter figure, however, is not a top limit as claims can in addition be made under the established heads of damages under present UK law. The Directive has been much criticised but there is no doubt that an extended degree of public protection will be introduced into our law in line with EEC requirements within the next few years.

Manufacturers who believe this places them in a very vulnerable position should not draw too gloomy a conclusion from claims made in the US. Insurance cover for defective products has been with us for many years and the 1969 legislation, making employers liable for damage caused by defective equipment used at work and directing that the liability be insured, is an instance of one area of strict liability which has already been absorbed into our system. Professional negligence cover has also been mandatory in the UK for many years but the cost of the cover is still far lower than it is in the United States. Access to a free National Health Service and the State-run Industrial Injury Schemes are also factors to be considered.

Another factor is that our legal system encourages out of court settlement, not least perhaps because awards have no relationship to legal contingency fees and compensation is assessed on well-established guidelines by the judiciary, not by a jury, and claims by a careless user will still be reduced or rejected.

Payment of compensation and insurance of the payment may produce major problems for manufacturers and suppliers, but insurance is a commercial transaction and it is to be hoped that market forces will ensure that cover is obtainable at a marketable price.

Illegal contract terms

In a commercial transaction buyer and seller can come to any agreement they please but there are some legal limits to their freedom of action.

Unfair or anti-competitive trade practices, such as price-fixing and exclusive dealing between manufacturer and retailer, which require the retailer only to stock certain goods or force a buyer to pay a higher price than he would normally pay as a condition of supplying him with goods he cannot obtain elsewhere, may lead to an investigation by the Office of Fair Trading and the Monopolies Commission. It is an offence to infringe safety regulations that apply to some manufactured goods under the Consumer Safety Act 1978. A wholesaler may only be able to claim damages from the supplier in the event of infringement but the customer can claim direct from the manufacturer under the Act.

Agreement for sale

The first move in a transaction is an offer and once a firm offer is accepted, the contract is complete. An offer to supply a specific quantity of designated goods, to be delivered over a fixed period at a fixed price, means that on acceptance the whole consignment is accepted, even if delivery is by instalments, as and when ordered. If the agreement is to deliver 'up to a specified maximum quantity as and when demanded', the buyer can revoke what is essentially a standing offer at any time, as each order is placed under a separate contract, but he must accept goods already ordered.

Acceptance by post is received when the letter is posted, even if it never reaches the seller. You can, however, cancel your offer to sell at any time before acceptance but you should confirm the refusal before you sell the goods elsewhere. Oral or telexed acceptance is, literally, received when it is heard or seen.* If the seller does not ask for formal or written acceptance, the goods are accepted when the buyer acts as if they were his, by, for example, selling them or incorporating the articles into his own products.

Payment and delivery

The law makes assumptions which can favour buyer or seller but it will not put the whole contract together; if you have not agreed the price you may have no agreement at all, unless it is a minor detail in an otherwise binding commitment. The buyer

---

* *Brinksobon Ltd* v *Stahag Stahl & Stahlwarenhandelsgesellschaft mbH* (1982) 1 WLR 264

then has to pay a 'reasonable' price, which may or may not coincide with what you had in mind.

A deposit is usually forfeited if the sale falls through because of the buyer, but a part payment on account of the price must be returned.

You can take delivery as soon as you pay the price, unless you have agreed other arrangements. The owner of the goods takes the risk and can be at risk even before delivery, because he may be the legal owner of the goods before they reach your premises. Accidental damage or loss is then your problem and the seller can sue for payment, unless he is at fault.

A clause (called a *'Romalpa'* clause after a successful litigant) which provides that goods remain the seller's until full payment has been received, has become increasingly popular as a result of the increase in bankruptcies and liquidations. The protection is useful if you are dealing with a distributor or ultimate user of goods but not if you are selling raw materials or the goods are to be mixed or processed with other goods or the proceeds of sale, when registration of a charge under the Companies Acts has been suggested as being more effective.*

If you have not agreed between you at what point the goods become the buyer's, ownership depends on whether the merchandise consists of 'unascertained' or 'specific' goods. Specific goods are those which are identified and agreed upon at the time you make your contract. Any other goods are unascertained, whether you buy from bulk stocks or designate a particular type (for example, 'twelve clocks from stock' or 'twelve clocks'). Goods that have to be manufactured or acquired by the seller after the contract is made ('future' goods) are categorised in the same way.

When specific articles are sold, ownership passes from seller to buyer when they intend it to do so, but the intention can be inferred from the contract or from what was said or done at the time.

If the question is still open, the law makes the following rules:

1. Specific finished articles in a deliverable state are the buyer's as soon as his offer is accepted, whatever the time of payment or delivery.

* *Aluminium Industrie Vaasen B V* v *Romalpa Aluminium Ltd* (1976) 1 WLR 676; *Borden (UK) Ltd* v *Scottish Timber Products Ltd* (1979) 3 WLR 672; in re *Bond Worth Ltd* (1979) 3 WLR 629

2. If the seller has to put the specified articles into a
   deliverable state, by, for example, weighing them to
   ascertain the price, they are the buyer's when he is
   notified that they are ready to deliver.
3. Specific goods in the process of construction or
   manufacture do not belong to the buyer until all the
   necessary materials have been set aside and identified.
4. Sale or return specific goods held by the buyer without
   any indication that they are accepted are the buyer's
   within a reasonable time or at the end of the period
   agreed between buyer and seller.
5. Future or unascertained goods in a deliverable state,
   sold by their description, become the buyer's when they
   are handed over to him or to a carrier or are put into
   storage.

Delayed payments and short deliveries are commercial risks that
should be covered in your contract. If you do not specify the
terms, the law spells out in detail how payment and delivery are
made:
1. You can refuse delivery of more or less than you
   ordered, unless the amount is negligible. Once accepted,
   the whole consignment must be paid for, *pro rata*, at the
   contract price.
2. When merchandise is mixed with goods which you did
   not order, you can return those not ordered or accept
   them all.
3. If the first consignment of a delivery in instalments is
   unsatisfactory, you can reject all the goods. Here again,
   once they are accepted, you cannot refuse later
   deliveries, although you must have a reasonable
   opportunity to examine the merchandise before you can
   be taken to have accepted it.
4. If instalments are paid for on delivery you may be able
   to refuse later deliveries, unless the problem is not
   sufficient to justify repudiation of what is essentially
   one continuing contract.

It is therefore best to indicate on what terms you accept goods,
or you may have to pay the full price for faulty merchandise.
   You need not pay until the goods are delivered, unless you
have agreed on payment in advance. If they are lost or destroyed
while at your risk (see page 150) you have to pay the seller, even
if they are still on his premises. If the seller asks you to take

delivery, you may be responsible for loss or deterioration and for storage charges if you do not take them within a reasonable time.

If you want to reject the goods, you must inform the seller but you do not have to return them. The seller can ask you to hand them over, even if you have already paid and can sue you if the rejection is unjustified. But leave the merchandise intact if you want to reject it as faulty. If you use or repair it you cannot return it, although you may be able to acquire it at a reduced price.

The buyer must always give a reasonable time to pay, unless other arrangements have been agreed and, once you pay, the seller must deliver or pay damages. It is only when very special merchandise is involved however that the courts will order delivery whatever the cost to the seller, so, if he cannot deliver the specified articles ordered, the buyer may be forced to accept damages.

If the buyer does not pay or offer the full price or meet the agreed credit terms, the seller has a right of retention on his goods for the price and he can stop them if they are in transit or sell them elsewhere. Even after the goods are delivered to a carrier, he can stop them in transit but holding up delivery pending payment is only possible when the seller has reserved the right, unless the carrier is an independent middleman. Delivery of an instalment contract cannot be held up to extract payment for earlier deliveries.

Misrepresentation

If the seller deliberately misleads you in order to close the deal, you may be able to claim damages as well as reimbursement. Avoidance of the contract on this ground depends on proof that the seller's misrepresentation persuaded you to enter the transaction. It is possible for the seller to restrict or exclude his liability for misrepresentation but it must be done in specific terms. If, however, the seller is careless or genuinely mistaken, you can usually cancel the contract, provided you have not agreed to accept the goods and can return them intact and no one else is involved. Bear in mind, however, that a seller does not have to point out defects in the goods, although he must answer your reasonable inquiries and you may have a claim against him if they are entirely unfit for your purposes.

Criminal law

Under the Trade Descriptions Acts 1968 to 1972 it is an offence to apply a false trade description to goods or to supply, or offer to supply, goods to which a false trade description has been applied. A false trade description is exhaustively defined under the Acts to cover statements as to quantity, size, methods or the place of manufacture, production, processing or reconditioning, composition, fitness for the purpose, strength, performance, behaviour, accuracy and other physical character- istics, testing and results of testing, approval by any person — including the person by whom the goods are manufactured, produced, processed or reconditioned — previous ownership and any other history.

The Acts apply to almost any statement, including oral statement or an advertisement, but the statement must be false, which includes situations where the customer is misled into buying the goods.

The Acts also apply to descriptions of services and accommo- dation, to unfair pricing, and to misleading indications of British origin on imported goods. The local weights and measures authorities can take proceedings under the Acts, make test purchases, and enter premises and seize goods to ascertain whether an offence has been committed, but generally action is only taken on simple cases where there is a public need for protection after an inspector has received several complaints.

As a trader you are better off bringing civil proceedings than relying on the criminal law, as there is usually also a civil wrong. Procedurally, civil action is easier to bring and the civil court can grant an injunction to restrain further wrongful acts, usually very quickly. The award of costs is much higher than in the magistrates' court, which cannot award damages or an account of profits, where the most you will achieve is the imposition of a small fine.

Misleading bargain offers

Uninformative or misleading bargain offers are prohibited under the Trade Descriptions Act. Manufacturers, retailers and advertisers must not offer mythical bargains which use false comparisons. Genuine or informative claims are still permitted. These may include comparisons with future or past prices, the prices of other named retailers and comparisons with recommended retail prices, except where this is specifically prohibited.

Buying and selling on credit

The consumer credit legislation is the third party in credit transactions and the 1974 Consumer Credit Act and associated legislation applies to credit arrangements for up to £5000 (including any insurance or optional charges but excluding interest). There is no £5000 limit if a private borrower is overcharged for credit. The Act extends most of the earlier law relating to hire purchase to a wide range of credit agreements, including cash loans and financial accommodation to partnerships and individuals (other than bearer bonds). Anyone advertising credit terms or involved in credit brokerage or the supply of credit references is also covered by the Act. It is aimed at stopping unfair practices in the provision of credit and credit brokerage. Prosecutions can be brought under the Act and, unlike the sale of goods legislation, you cannot opt out by agreement.

Most of the 1974 Act is now in force but some credit arrangements are still covered by the Moneylenders Acts and associated legislation and by the Banking Act 1979. The 1974 Act applies to all loans and credit arrangements except those made by banks, exempted lenders and companies with a capital of over £250,000,000 that provide a 'highly specialised banking service'. Except for the central banks of the member States of the EEC and exempt lenders, banks must be licensed under the 1979 Act and must comply with the strict requirements of the banking legislation.

The general principles of contract law, as set out in the first part of this chapter, apply if the debtor is a company, the credit is over the £5000 limit or is governed by the banking legislation.

Anyone giving advice on credit terms must have a licence from the Director of Fair Trading. Advisers include the retailer, the lender, the credit broker, credit reference agency, debt counsellor or collector and your professional advisers.

Licences are valid for a 10-year period at a cost of £80 for the sole trader and £150 for other applicants, plus £10 for each additional category of business activity. Existing licences have been extended for a further seven years to 3 August 1985. Licence holders must notify the Office of Fair Trading of changes that might affect their licence, such as a change in their main place of business or of the company's officers or a change of partners. Unlicensed advisers will be prosecuted and will not be able to enforce their agreements, although their customer/borrower can do so.

Borrowers are entitled to know if there are any problems with their credit references and it is illegal to send out unsolicited credit cards or circulars about credit to anyone under 18. Unsolicited cash loans can only be offered at the lender's place of business.

Ownership, acceptance and delivery under credit agreements

When you buy on hire purchase, you hire the goods with an option to purchase them and they remain the seller's property until you exercise the option.

Conditional sale and credit sale agreements are contracts for the sale of goods even though the price is paid in instalments. In a conditional sale, the customer does not own the goods until all the instalments are paid but in a credit sale he owns them as soon as the contract is made.

Hire purchase and conditional sale agreements are covered by the 1974 Act but the sale of goods legislation applies to credit sale agreements. The Act does not deal with acceptance and delivery, so that the situation is the same as it is for contracts for the sale of goods for cash.

Credit agreement

Most sales on credit are three-cornered situations: the dealer sells for cash to a finance company and the finance company sells or hires to the customer.

The customer's form, completed and signed, is his offer to the finance company to buy the goods on credit. When the dealer completes the form, it is also his offer to sell the goods to the finance company. The finance company can accept or reject both offers, which are — more than incidentally — made on its own forms and incorporate the terms it wants to include. The finance company is therefore responsible for the quality of the goods, because it sells directly to the customer.

'Regulated' agreements under the Act (that is, between the borrower and the lender) should be carefully drafted. Until draft forms of agreement are obtainable from the Office of Fair Trading, your initial agreements should be professionally drawn up.

Details of the transaction and the cost of the credit must be contained in a written agreement, including a term giving the borrower a right to pay off the debt before the agreed date, his right (if any) to cancel and to whom notice of cancellation can be given. The agreement must be signed by, or on behalf of, both the lender and the borrower.

The right to cancel is designed to give the borrower a cooling off period to consider whether he wants to go through with the transaction. If he does have a right to cancel, he must give notice within five to 14 days of signing, depending upon the type of agreement. He must be given copies of the agreement and, if it is inaccurate, the agreement and any security on which it depends is enforceable only by court order. In some circumstances the lender may not be able to enforce it at all.

There are special formalities for mortgages. The borrower must be given a period of up to 14 days to consider the transaction before he signs the agreement and the mortgage is only enforceable by court order.

Generally, if the agreement states that the lender can cancel in specified circumstances and they have arisen, notice of cancellation must be served on the borrower. The notice must give sufficient details of the borrower's breach of the agreement, such as a failure to keep the article insured, to enable him to put it right and state that, if he cannot do so, he can pay a specified sum in compensation instead. It must also inform him of the consequences of a failure to comply with the notice, and there is a minimum of seven days before the lender can pursue any action allowed by the agreement.

The lender does not have to give notice before suing for arrears of instalments. A borrower's right to draw on a credit can also be restricted or deferred without notice if he is in arrears or if, for example, a credit card holder exceeds his credit limit.

Once the borrower has paid over one-third of the total price the lender can sometimes only enforce a regulated agreement by court order, but the borrower can always apply to court for a time order for extra time to pay arrears in an action brought by the lender. Once the borrower is served with notice he can apply direct to the court for the time order, without waiting to be sued by the lender.

Security agreement

If any security is taken it should be included in the regulated agreement or in a document referred to in the agreement. If the security is given by the borrower, a separate security agreement must be in a prescribed form. It must be in writing, signed by, or on behalf of, the guarantor or indemnifier, otherwise it is unenforceable without a court order. However, if the security is given by a third party, under, for example, a recourse agreement between a finance company and a dealer, or because the borrower is considered a poor credit risk, it does not have to comply with the Act.

Special formalities apply to some kinds of security, for example, mortgage of goods and assignment of life assurance policies and the security is usually only enforceable if the regulated agreement is enforceable, unless it is an indemnity for a borrower under the age of 18.

The security agreement and any linked agreement with the lender are automatically cancelled with the regulated agreement, as is any other linked transaction, such as a policy taken out to insure repayment, or service and maintenance arrangements.

The borrower can return the goods and claim repayment of instalments, plus any fees or commissions over £1. He need not hand over the goods until he is repaid, either by the lender or by the supplier of the goods. Any goods traded in part exchange, or an equivalent sum, are returnable within 10 days of notice of cancellation.

Credit buyer's protection

Buyer protection is the same whether you buy for cash or credit. The customer is still entitled to assume the dealer owns the goods, but the quality guarantee is extended by the lender, not by the dealer. Both the dealer and the manufacturer can be held responsible if the goods are not checked before delivery.

Consumer hire agreements

Consumer hire agreements are covered by the Act if the credit is for more than three months and the total repayments are less than £5000.

The lender can repossess the goods without a court order if payments total more than £300 per annum or the agreement covers specialised goods for the borrower's business or goods that the borrower had leased to someone else. However, since the lender cannot enter the borrower's premises without his permission, he will usually need a court order anyway.

Hiring industrial plant and machinery

The £5000 limit means that most agreements for the hire of industrial plant and machinery will be outside the 1974 Act. Some manufacturers of plant and heavy machinery, including lorries and rolling stock, offer their own financing, usually through dealers. Their credit arrangements are flexible and you can often lease the machinery, which remains the property of the manufacturer or the dealer, depending on their agreements. The cost of hiring is then a deductible business expense for tax purposes.

If you buy under a credit sale agreement, you own the goods as soon as you have concluded the contract and can take advantage of the capital allowances allowed by the Inland Revenue. The interest charges are still deductible as a business expense and you can take the full capital allowances as soon as you start to use the machinery and the capital component of the price can be written down in your books. Cars for your own use can be purchased on the same terms but the capital allowances are lower.

Mortgages

A mortgage from a building society or local authority is outside the Act and some other loan arrangements are specifically exempted.

If the borrower is a private individual a second mortgage on land, whether for purchase, a bridging loan or the borrower's general use, is covered by the Act, whatever the amount of the loan.

Mail order

Mail order transactions are outside the Act, but they often contain a cancellation clause and the buyer is protected in the same way as in any other sale of goods contract. Unless you are holding on to the goods to compel repayment you must hand them over on written request, but you do not have to arrange for their return to the mail order company and you are not obliged to pay for unsolicited goods.

Indemnities and guarantees

The sale of goods legislation, applying to sales for cash, applies also to the agreement between the finance company and the dealer, unless they agree otherwise. Because the finance company runs the risk, it often requires the dealer or a third party to give an indemnity or guarantee against loss. It may also insist on the customer obtaining insurance cover for instalments that might not be forthcoming because of sickness or unemployment and for the repayment of the balance outstanding on death.

Remedies for non-performance

If the goods are unsatisfactory an over-the-counter purchaser from a retailer under a conditional sales agreement can reject the goods, even if he has accepted delivery, provided he has not confirmed the transaction or accepted the goods. If a transaction is protected by the 1974 Act the customer can cancel it. In addition, if the supplier goes into liquidation and the cash price is between £30 and £10,000, the finance company is jointly liable with the supplier to the customer. Under the Act a deposit must be repaid to the customer by either the dealer or the finance company, even if the finance company never received it. On a retail sale for cash the customer can refuse a credit note and is entitled to his money back if the goods are unsatisfactory.

Although the law assures that you can assume a seller owns his goods, this is not necessarily the case in practice. You can claim damages and/or the price if the goods are not his, but if he is not available you may have to hand them over to the rightful owner, unless he was involved in the sale. You can keep your purchase if you buy through an agent such as a car dealer, and a private buyer from a car dealer can keep the car even if a finance company is still owed money on it under a previous sale.

It is worth taking advice as it may be possible to retain the goods when the seller had no right to them at all, if, for example, the owner has made no attempt to claim them at the time of the sale. Buying from a market trader is not always a bad risk: if you think he is honest, you can legally become the owner of a real bargain, provided the goods are not so cheap that you are 'on inquiry' and should have known they might have been stolen and that you buy between sunrise and sunset at an old-established street market.

When the seller does not deliver the goods life and the law become difficult. If they have disappeared or perished at the time you agreed to buy, you pay nothing. But 'perish' has a special meaning in this context. Damage may not be sufficient to constitute perishing and you will only be entitled to damages for the deterioration, unless you have previously agreed otherwise.

If the transaction becomes impossible or illegal, possibly because of a change in the law, the contract is 'frustrated' and need not be carried through. If nothing has been delivered you may be entitled to reimbursement but, in some circumstances, you may be responsible for the seller's necessary expenses. If the risk has passed to the buyer, because, for example, the contract is for specific goods, you have to pay for the whole consignment and claim separately for damages. However, this is another complicated area of law and you should seek advice before you take action. The customer can also sue the dealer under the ordinary rules of contract for any untrue statement made about them.

Although it is virtually impossible to cover every contingency, many problems can be avoided by prior agreement between buyer and seller.

When an agreement for cash or credit is not completed, you can only be compensated if you can show that there has been a consequential loss, although you can agree in advance a reasonable penalty for non-performance.

If the goods are simply not satisfactory, you can usually claim damages. It is only if there is a 'substantial failure' to perform the contract or you are able to claim the statutory buyer protection that you can withdraw from the transaction altogether and reject the goods or claim return of the price. Substantial failure means, in effect, receiving something entirely different from what you bargained for.

Sometimes you can claim damages as well but they are compensation for purely incidental problems between buyer and seller, however large the claim. They are normally confined to any obvious consequential losses incurred in the usual course of your business and you must take reasonable steps to minimise your loss.

STATUTORY REFERENCES

Arbitration Acts 1950, 1975 and 1979
Banking Act 1979
Bills of Exchange Act 1882
Companies Act 1948
Competition Act 1979

Consumer Credit Act 1974
Consumer Safety Act 1978
Fair Trading Act 1973
Finance Acts 1971, 1972 and 1976
Hire Purchase Act 1964
Law of Property Act 1925

Law Reform (Frustrated Contracts) Act 1943

Misrepresentation Act 1967

Moneylenders Acts 1900 and 1927

Policies of Assurance Act 1867

Protection of Depositors Act 1963

Restrictive Trade Practices Act 1965

Sale of Goods Act 1979

Sale of Goods (Implied Terms) Act 1973

Supply of Goods and Services Act 1982

Trade Descriptions Act 1968

Unfair Contract Terms Act 1977

Unsolicited Goods and Services Act 1971

10
Cash and Credit at Home and Abroad

Bank accounts

The sole trader and the partnership
When you open the business bank account, you will have to give references. For a partnership account the bank will want the names and a description of the partners, details of their authority and involvement in the business and a copy of the Partnership Agreement.

All the partners usually sign the mandate (agreement), which gives instructions as to the conduct of the account, for example, who is to sign cheques and request advances, and includes details of the partnership's assets and liabilities. The partners will have to confirm that any securities to be held by the bank are to apply to existing and future liabilities and undertake to give notice of any change in the partners or the Partnership Agreement.

The mandate stands until the account is closed or the business wound up. In the case of a partnership it continues even if there is a change in the partnership name or the partners, but an incoming partner should give formal assent to its terms. An outgoing partner remains liable to the bank, although the bank often prefers to break up the account when he leaves, as it is then easier for them to retain his liability.

If the firm is dissolved because of the death or bankruptcy of a partner, the business can still operate the account but cheques drawn by the deceased or bankrupt partner must be approved by the partnership, unless the mandate specifies other arrangements. The bank can stop the cheques to retain their rights if the account is overdrawn.

Companies
The opening and running of a company account are more complicated because of the protection afforded by limited liability.

The bank will require the Certificate of Incorporation, the Memorandum and Articles of Association (which set out the authority of the directors) and a certified copy of the board resolution appointing them the company's bankers. The resolution must give detailed instructions about the operation of the account as it is the mandate between the company and the bank. Usually your bank will give you a printed form of draft resolution, which is filled out and formally passed at the first board meeting after you have conditionally agreed the arrangements, and signed by the chairman of the meeting and the secretary. Specimen signatures of those authorised to sign for the company and a description of the capacity in which they sign are usually given on the form. The mandate can be terminated by board resolution and ends if a receiver is appointed, the company goes into liquidation or the account is closed.

Overdraft arrangements are usually made by one or two members of the board, who give undertakings on behalf of the company, and the bank may want you to pass a formal resolution requesting the facility. If the business gets into difficulties, the bank often requires the company to open a separate account, to which all cheques for salaries and wages are debited and records are kept which show the amount of preferential wages and salaries due. Transfers are made from the ordinary account to cancel advances which lose their preferential character; interest and charges on the account are debited to the ordinary account.

Guarantees

The bank will usually want a guarantee from you to cover overdrafts on the business account. The sole trader's or partners' guarantee is a regulated agreement under the Consumer Credit Act 1974 if borrowings are within the £5000 limit, but the directors' guarantee is not.

Both partners' and directors' bank guarantees are usually joint *and* several (although the partners' commercial guarantee is normally joint) and they can be open guarantees or limited to a fixed amount.

Joint or several, you have to pay the full amount of the claim; you can turn to your co-partner or co-director for a contribution or indemnity (that is, for repayment of part or all of the amount paid) but the difference may be crucial to a creditor. If he sues one party under a joint liability, his claim stops there and he cannot turn to the other party if he fails to obtain payment. Under a several liability, however, he can sue each party in turn.

As guarantor you normally have rights against the creditors, the principal debtor — here the business — and your co-guarantors, but the standard bank guarantee limits your rights. As far as the principal debtor (ie the one who actually directly owes the debt) is concerned, your rights depend on its being able but unwilling to pay its debts, apart from any claim you may have if the business is wound up. Usually, if you pay the debt (and, under a bank guarantee, you must usually pay immediately on demand), you can turn to the principal debtor and set off anything the creditor has already paid, but this will not arise where the principal debtor is the business.

You can set off payments already made when you pay off any other creditor and then you are entitled to any security given for the debt by the principal debtor or anyone else. You can also call on the creditor to sue the debtor or sue him yourself or 'prove' (ie establish your claim) in the bankruptcy or liquidation for the amount.

Even under a bank guarantee you are entitled to call on your co-guarantors. If you pay more than your share, whether your liability is joint or several, you must make allowance for any security taken over from the creditor and payment made to you by the defaulting principal debtor. Again this will not arise under a bank guarantee. If the liability is joint only you can be sued for the whole sum and, once the creditor obtains judgement, he cannot sue your co-guarantors, even if he does not receive the full amount of the debt; several liability means that he can, if necessary, sue each of the co-guarantors in turn.

A bank guarantee is continuous but a deceased guarantor's estate may not be liable under a joint liability, so you should make sure that your co-guarantors sign on behalf of 'their heirs, their executors and administrators'.

You only remain liable as guarantor after the debt is paid by the business if the payment is a fraudulent preference or problems arise on fraudulent trading. In some circumstances directors are also liable if floating charges are invalidated when the company goes into liquidation.

In the context of bank overdrafts and loans generally, you should bear in mind that minimising profits for tax purposes can be an ultimately expensive pastime. Lenders lend on profit performance and by keeping profits and therefore tax low you may discover at a later stage that your profit record will not support adequate financing for the business.

Payments

The larger and more successful your business the more compli-cated its financial dealings. Most transactions will be for cash or credit but you will seldom receive payment in cash, unless you are in the retail trade.

The more esoteric financial arrangements involving bills of exchange and commercial credits are usually the province of large or old-established businesses, although bills are in fairly common use in some manufacturing trades and in heavy industry. If you do business abroad, it is mainly carried on under letters of credit.

Whatever the method of payment, your books will be debited and credited with money amounts in return for goods and services. Instead of cash in your hand, however, you receive pieces of paper carrying rights varying with their content, quite apart from any intrinsic value they have because of the credit-worthiness of the signatories.

The main feature of all the paper, including the cash, is that it is negotiable. This means that it, and the rights and obligations that go with it, is transferable with or without an endorsing signature, depending upon whether it is payable to 'order' or 'bearer'.

If you hold a negotiable instrument you can sue on it. If you give value for it in good faith (when you become a 'holder' in due course), it is valid even if it was invalid before it reached you, provided it is current and unconditional and appears to be properly completed, unless an essential signature is forged.

The main types of negotiable instruments you will come across are bills of exchange (and a cheque is a bill), promissory notes (which include bank notes) and bankers' drafts (which can be treated as bills or promissory notes). A bill of lading — the detailed receipt given by the master of a ship when goods are sent by sea — is semi-negotiable and, once invalid, it remains invalid. Postal and money orders are marked to be not negotiable and a money order is void 12 months after issue.

Enforcing payment

Cheques, banker's drafts, promissory notes and bills are promises to pay on a specified date and you can enforce payment through the High Court at minimal cost. The law takes the view that a promise to pay is sacred and once you have delivered formal notice of dishonour on presentment of the cheque, bill or note, the signatory has no defence to the action. If he disputes your right to the money, he must pay up and sue in a separate legal action, giving evidence of his entitlement to the return of the money.*

You cannot, however, obtain a better title to payment than a payee. For instance, a cheque written in discharge of an (illegal) gambling debt, to the knowledge of the payee and therefore invalid remains invalid and unenforceable by anyone subsequently receiving the cheque.†

Cheques

A cheque is an unconditional order from one person (the drawer) to another (his bank, the drawee) to pay a sum of money on demand. Payment can be to a specified person or 'to bearer'. If it is payable 'to cash or order', it is *not* a cheque, as there is no payee, although it is still a valid order for payment.

If the amount expressed in words and figures is not the same, the bank usually returns the cheque to the drawer but you are entitled to claim the written amount if the difference is very small, or the smaller amount in figures.

A post-dated cheque is valid but the bank usually refuses to honour it before the due date. Strictly a cheque does not have to be dated but the holder (unless he is a holder in due course) may not be able to cash it.

A cheque is not a continuing security but you can be called upon to pay the amount at any time up to six years from the date of issue, whether or not your account was in funds at the time it was presented for payment. If the cheque has been in circulation for a long time, however, the bank usually treats it as overdue and will generally treat a cheque as stale after six months and return it for reissue.

---

* *Montebianco Industrie Tessili SpA* v *Carlyle Mills (London)* (1981) 1 Lloyds' Rep 509 and *Power-Curber International* v *National Bank of Kuwait SAK* (1981) 1 WLR 1233, for the same rule concerning bills of exchange and letters of credit respectively.
† *Ladup* v *Shaikh* 3 WLR 172

If you lose a cheque, you can ask for another. If, however, someone else has presented it for payment and the amount has been paid out, you may have to reimburse the payer, even if it is stopped, as it is negotiable by a holder in due course. If it is lost in the post it is only payment to you if you asked for payment by post, and if it is not crossed anyone can cash it. Once crossed, it must be cleared through a bank account and even a holder in due course has no claim against the drawer, as the endorsing signature will have had to be forged.

The payer is not covered in one important area. If you sign a cheque payable to a non-existent person and it is endorsed in the same name, a holder in due course can claim payment from your bank, unless there is something obviously wrong with the cheque. This can happen quite easily when you are signing cheques to suppliers or employees which are prepared for your signature. Even if the cheque is marked 'not negotiable' it is still transferable. If it is marked 'not transferable' it is only payable to the original payee. If you add 'account payee only' between the parallel lines of the crossing, which is the direction to the receiving bank, the bank is responsible if the money goes into the wrong account.

A cheque only comes to life when it is handed over or when you inform the payee that you hold it on his behalf, unless it is not to be presented until a later date.

The holder is the person to whom it is first made payable (the payee) or the endorsee named in the endorsement or anyone holding a cheque payable 'to bearer'. The holder can alter the crossing but other alterations without the drawer's permission usually invalidate the cheque. However, a holder in due course can sometimes enforce payment if the alteration is not readily apparent. If it is endorsed after alteration it is valid for the altered amount against the endorser.

The holder of a cheque takes the cheque on exactly the same terms as the payee and, for example, if the cheque is stopped, will not be able to enforce payment. A holder who has, before it is overdue, given value in good faith for a cheque, which is regular on its face, without notice of previous dishonour or cause to believe that the previous holder did not have good title to the cheque, becomes a holder in due course and is in a stronger position. He can freely negotiate the cheque and claim payment through your non-existent payee and may be able to enforce payment of an undated or stopped cheque or of a cheque which you have been fraudulently induced to issue, provided he has no notice of the fraud.

If you are fraudulently persuaded to write a cheque, it is valid until it is stopped. In exceptional circumstances you can claim that it is void even against a holder in due course. You have to prove that you were not careless or that you thought you were signing an entirely different kind of document. This is, however, part of the wider field of contract law and you will need expert advice before you can consider repudiating a cheque.

A bearer cheque is negotiated by handing it over; if it is payable to order, it must also be endorsed. Endorsement includes both adding your signature to the cheque (thus assuming liability for the amount) and delivering it to another holder. If the endorser does not name an endorsee, the holder can write his own or someone else's name above the signature. This does not make him an endorser, although he may still be liable on the cheque when he delivers it.

If you sign or endorse a cheque on behalf of anyone else, you should limit or negative your personal liability. Your signature alone on a negotiable instrument, without any mention being made of the business, will usually mean, in the event of non-payment by the business, that you alone are liable.* Cheques sometimes have 'without recourse to me' or 'sans recours' written on them. This is adequate, but describing yourself as agent or representative is not. If it is a business cheque you should sign 'for and on behalf of' followed by the name of your principal or the name of the business *and* words describing the capacity in which you sign.

A company's name must be on all cheques, bills of exchange, promissory notes, endorsements and orders for money. Cheques signed 'for and behalf of . . .' or 'per pro' by your partners, co-directors, employees or agents are only enforceable against you, the partnership or the company if the signatory was authorised to make the disbursement or the payee could reasonably have expected him to have had such authority.

One partner's signature is, however, normally sufficient on cheques paid by, or to, the business as the payee or endorsee of a partnership cheque can reasonably expect partners to have authority to sign partnership cheques, whatever is in your

---

* *Maxform SpA* v *Mariani & Goodville* (1981) 2 Lloyds' Rep 54

Partnership Agreement, unless he has been informed or is aware that this is not the case.

A cheque made out to more than one payee must be endorsed by all of them, unless one is authorised to sign for the others, so that one partner's signature is therefore sufficient on partnership cheques. You can direct that endorsees be paid jointly on the cheque itself but you cannot split the face value to direct that specific amounts be paid to different endorsees.

If you lend money on an accommodation cheque — by post-dating it and making it payable to someone who makes an advance on it to a third party — you are liable to the holder for value, in whatever capacity you sign the cheque.

As soon as the cheque is dishonoured, the bank must give notice of dishonour to anyone who has endorsed it.

It is no longer entirely safe to assume that cheques will be cleared and paid into your account within three days and you can ask your bank to obtain 'special (expedited) clearance' for a fee, if you wish to receive prompt payment.

Banker's drafts

If you are not prepared to accept payment by cheque, you can ask for payment by banker's draft. The draft is an order for payment made directly by the payer's bank but his bank is the drawer and pays out to you direct.

The draft states the amount and place of the payment and the name of the beneficiary (payee). When it is crossed, it works like a cheque and is crossed in the same way. Make sure your name appears as beneficiary and the bank signs both as drawer and drawee. A draft, like any other negotiable instrument, is only as good as its signatories.

Promissory notes

Promissory notes are conditional or unconditional promises to pay on demand or on a fixed or determinable future date, a fixed sum to, or to the order of, a specified person or to bearer. They can be made payable with interest or stated instalments.

Often the promise to pay is stated to be at a monthly rate, plus interest on the amount outstanding, with a provision that if an instalment is not paid the whole amount becomes due. 'We promise to pay' means that the signatories are liable jointly but you can give a specifically joint and several promise.

The payee need only present a note for payment if a place is specified and an endorser is only liable if it has been presented. If it is payable on demand it must be presented within a reasonable time of the endorsement.

Notes, like bills, are negotiable and bearer notes are negotiated by being handed over; if payable to order, they must also be endorsed.

A note payable on demand is not overdue simply because a reasonable time for presentment has elapsed since it was issued or endorsed but you can have problems with an overdue bill. This is because a note, although ostensibly intended to be presented and paid on the due date, is often given as security on a debt. What is considered to be a reasonable time for presentment is therefore longer than it is in the case of a bill but all your other legal rights and remedies are the same as those of a holder of a bill of exchange.*

Documentary finance

If you do a lot of business on credit or abroad, you may find it more convenient to use bills of exchange for payment and to extend credit. They are more easily negotiated than cheques and notes and the right to future payment can be expressed more flexibly and is more saleable for immediate cash.

Historically and presently the advantage of financing through bills of exchange is that the seller can be paid when he ships the goods but the buyer does not pay for them until he receives them or even until he has sold them elsewhere. This is why the period (or tenor) of the bill was usually (and often still is) at least three months, to allow for the time of the average shipment overseas. A bank or finance house stands as intermediary for payment, charging a commission for advancing the money during the period of transit by discounting the payment. Through whom the bill can be negotiated and the further amount of the discount depend on the credit-standing of the parties to the bill.

Extensive documentary financing should be entered into only with the guidance of an expert financial adviser or merchant bank. International and national finance has local ground rules which are a trap for the unwary. Trading internationally has various dangers: you may find that currency is in a suddenly blocked account and must be invested in the

* *Ferson Contractors* v *Ferris* (1981)

country where the currency is held, and the yield on the investment may also be blocked.

The following sections offer a brief guide through the commercial credit facilities which may be available to you for larger-scale finance, all of which are based on the negotiating of a bill of exchange. Facilities listed under 'overseas payments' are also available for domestic financing, with appropriate modifications in the rate of interest and the insurance cover.

Bills of exchange

A bill of exchange is an unconditional order in writing addressed by one person to another, signed by the person giving it, requiring the person to whom it is addressed to pay on demand, or at a fixed or determinable future date, a fixed sum to, or to the order of, a specified person, or to bearer.

These semantic convolutions can best be sorted out by comparison with payment by cheque. The pattern is the same: a drawer is the person who signs the bill, a drawee is the person to whom it is addressed (in a cheque the drawer's paying bank), and a payee. But there are differences:

1. A bill can be drawn on anyone but a cheque only on a bank.
2. A bill can be payable on demand or at a future date; a cheque is only payable on demand.
3. A bill must be presented for payment when it is due, or the drawer and endorsers are discharged. The drawer of a cheque is not discharged for six years, unless, through delay in presentation, his position is prejudiced.
4. Cheques can be crossed but bills can not.
5. A bank which pays bills domiciled with it (that is, pays out on bills from a customer's account) is not legally protected. It is protected, subject to certain conditions, when paying out on cheques. The same distinction applies when a bank collects the proceeds of bills or cheques for its customers.
6. Unless it is payable on demand, a bill is usually 'accepted'. Acceptance is written confirmation that the drawee will meet the bill on the due date. The drawer pays the acceptor a previously agreed percentage of the face value and the acceptance is endorsed on the bill. The acceptor then becomes primarily liable to the

holder and his acceptance makes the bill freely negotiable.

A cheque is not usually accepted, so the drawer is primarily liable. Bills, but only very occasionally cheques, can also be 'backed', when they are endorsed by someone who is neither the drawer nor the acceptor, who is liable to a holder in due course. The bill is backed when sold at a discount for immediate payment. The endorsement increases the discount value because of the additional credit derived from the signatures and successive backers can endorse it throughout its life. Their signature may be on a 'tranche', a slip of paper attached to the bill. Do not lose it. It is your guarantee — or additional guarantee — for payment on the due date.

If all the parties to a bill are trading companies, it is usually referred to as a 'trade bill'. Negotiability and discount value still depend on the credit-standing of the signatories but generally a trade bill is negotiated in a different money market and at a higher rate than a bill with a bank as drawee.

Commission charged for acceptance on inland bills with a bank or finance house as drawee varies from 1 to 2 per cent per annum above the Bank of England minimum lending rate for overdrafts. The 'finest' trade bills may change hands at the same percentage commission but ordinary trade bills can be discounted at anything up to 5 per cent above the minimum lending rate. Commission on foreign bills, however, has to take into account the current and various lending rates of the countries with which you are trading and can fluctuate on a daily or even hourly basis.

The seller's bank may agree to negotiate trade bills (that is, buy them and become the holder in due course) or make an advance on the security of the bill (when they are the holder in due course for the amount advanced). They can then take them for collection by themselves or, if they are foreign bills, collection by their overseas branch or correspondent bank. Inland bills are usually taken for collection, as well as bills covering business abroad.

If the bank buy the bills, they calculate an amount of interest to be deducted from the face value or handle them on a 'charges after payment' basis. Instructions must be given as to the steps to be taken if they are dishonoured and the bank has recourse to the drawee, but generally they look to their own customer, the drawer. When the bank collects the amount payable on the bill, the proceeds are credited to the customer's account after collection charges are deducted.

The bill can be an unqualified order to pay out of a particular fund or account, or a statement of the transaction which gives rise to the debt. Banks usually prefer to hold bills drawn on specific shipments or transactions and the 'clausing' (description) states what is covered. The value given in return for the payment does not appear on the bill and it need not specify, although it can, where it is drawn or payable. If the drawee accepts the bill, he is the acceptor and the bill becomes freely negotiable.

A bill can be payable on demand, at sight or on presentation and is payable on demand if no time is specified. It can also be made payable at a determinable future date, after a fixed period after date or sight, or after a fixed period after the occurrence of a specified event. It cannot be payable on a contingency, so the event must be certain to occur.

The amount can be expressed to include accrued interest or a provision that payment is to be by instalment and, if any instalment is in arrear, the whole amount becomes due.

If the bill is drawn outside the United Kingdom and payable in foreign currency, you can specify the rate of exchange, otherwise it is calculated according to the rate of exchange for sight drafts at the place of payment on the day the bill is payable.

Bills which are drawn and payable within the United Kingdom or drawn or accepted on a United Kingdom resident are inland bills; any other bill is foreign.

The main difference is that, if the bill is dishonoured by non-acceptance or non-payment, a foreign bill must be 'protested', otherwise it is sometimes optional. In addition, inland bills are usually 'sola', which means they are drawn up in only one part. Foreign bills are sometimes, although less often than was once the case, drawn in sets of two or three parts separately numbered but otherwise identical, except that each refers to the others. This is to protect against loss: two parts are sent for acceptance by different mails, the third, if there is a third copy, being retained in the drawer's country. You should accept and endorse only one part, otherwise you could be liable on the two signatures for the one amount.

To collect payment, you should have presented the bill for acceptance, as well as for payment, on the due date. Strictly this is only necessary if the bill is payable after sight — when acceptance fixes its maturity date — if the bill specifically requires it, or if it is payable anywhere except at the place of business or residence of the drawee. In practice, a holder, or holder in due course, should present it to confirm the acceptance, as it secures the drawee's liability and makes it possible to negotiate and discount the bill. If the drawee refuses to accept it the holder has an immediate right of recourse to the drawer.

Acceptance must be written and signed by the drawer on the bill and must state that he will pay the amount payable in cash. It can be accepted before the drawer signs it or when it is overdue after dishonour — either by non-payment or because of a previous refusal to accept — unless it is a bill payable after sight, which is dishonoured if it is not accepted. If the drawee later accepts it, the acceptance is backdated to the first presentment.

Acceptance can be general or qualified. General (unconditional) acceptance affirms the order of the drawer; qualified (conditional) acceptance expressly varies it and can be of only part of the amount. The holder can refuse qualified acceptance, unless it is partial acceptance of the face value, and treat the bill as dishonoured by non-acceptance, when the drawer and any endorser are discharged from liability, but this rarely arises in practice. Partial acceptance of which due notice can only be protested as to the balance.

A bill must be presented for acceptance before it is overdue and, unless it is payable on demand, it must be presented for payment on or before the due date. If it is payable on demand, it may be presented for payment at any time after the date of issue.

Presentment is usually at the acceptor's or drawer's address on the bill or his business or residential address but you can agree to present it by post. All joint acceptors or drawers must be presented with the bill, unless one is authorised to accept for them all. If the acceptor or drawer is bankrupt or dead, you can either treat the bill as dishonoured or have it accepted by the trustee in bankruptcy or their personal representatives. It must, however, be presented, even if you think it will be dishonoured.

The drawer and endorsers are usually discharged from liability if a bill is not presented for payment on the due date but the acceptor remains liable, unless he has stipulated that it must be presented for payment. The drawer can, however, waive presentment.

If the bill is not accepted within a reasonable time, notice of dishonour by non-acceptance can be given to the drawer and endorsers, without presenting it for payment, but if it is not 'noted' or 'protested' you lose your right of recourse against them, unless you are a holder in due course.

Where the bill is dishonoured when presented for payment, you have an immediate right of recourse to the drawer and endorsers. Non-payment of an accepted bill also gives you an immediate right of (legal) action against the drawer as acceptor, without having to protest the bill or give notice of dishonour.

Generally notice of dishonour must be given to all parties to the bill, unless you cannot trace them or notice has been waived. It should be written or made personally as soon as the bill is dishonoured – on the same day or on the working day following dishonour. But it must be received after dishonour, so do not post it until you are sure that the bill has not been met. If notice of dishonour is given by an agent, limited extra time is allowed for communication to pass between agent and principal. A properly addressed and posted notice is assumed to have been delivered, even if it is never received, but you will have to show evidence of posting by, for example, a recorded delivery slip with the name and address of the addressee.

Formal proof of presentation and dishonour is necessary for foreign bills. The bill must be re-presented by a 'notary public' and refusal of acceptance or payment is 'noted' on the bill. A declaration (the 'protest') is then made for the claim in a separate document.

You do not have to note or protest inland bills but it is safest to do both and it is usually done if there are any foreign endorsements. Foreign bills need only be noted and protested once to retain the acceptor's liability, that is, for non-acceptance or, if accepted, for non-payment. But it is best to do it twice, so that the drawer and endorsers also remain liable.

The bill must be noted on the day of dishonour or the following working day and protest should be completed on the following day. Delay is only excused if circumstances beyond your control prevented its being done on time.

Overseas payments

Overseas business is usually done under letters of credit or documentary or acceptance credits issued by a bank or accepting house. Your source of finance lends its name and standing to overcome lack of knowledge of, or confidence in, the buyer or seller or the economic and/or political situation internally or externally. The interest rate varies according to the estimated *per capita* increase of the buying country and its political stability.

Interest rates are, however, currently so volatile that, even if you are selling to countries where political and economic stability is not necessarily a factor, it is impossible to forecast discount rates with any accuracy.

If you import goods, the rate of interest also depends on your own credit-standing and the UK banks' prevailing interest rates. Your bank may want the credit to be partly covered by cash and your account will be debited with the appropriate amount immediately. The bank then issues a letter of credit in favour of your supplier, undertaking to accept his bill drawn on them for a stated figure, provided it is accompanied by the shipping documents (usually the bills of lading, pro forma invoices and insurance policies or certificates). The supplier's bank buys the bill for cash and sends it with the shipping documents to your bank for presentation and acceptance. Your bank will release the documents to you, so that you can take delivery of the goods on arrival.

Commercial letters of credit are usually restricted to a particular intermediate banker and are only negotiable with the buyer's consent, although they can be transferred, divided or assigned. They can be issued to all the issuing bank's correspondents throughout the world. If they are an open invitation to negotiate drafts, accompanied by documents, they are, in effect, addressed to any bank that cares to accept.

Your overseas customer can open irrevocable documentary acceptance credits in their own favour at their (foreign) bank. Their London branch or their bank's correspondent bank take their bills for current shipments on the security of the shipping documents. When they are accepted (and they should be confirmed with your own UK branch) they can be discounted.

Occasionally you may come across revocable credits, which can be modified or cancelled without notice. A change in the credit, however, does not affect your rights, or those of your bank, if you have not been informed.

An importer can also arrange an acceptance credit with an acceptance house or bank. They accept bills drawn on them, subject to certain conditions. You draw the bills before you pay your overseas supplier and, when the bills are accepted by the accepting house or bank, the proceeds are remitted to your supplier. The accepting house or bank may, however, want you to pay them directly, before you import the goods.

The proceeds are then sent to the bank's overseas agents, who pay your supplier when he hands over the shipping documents. Your overseas supplier may also have an arrangement with his London bank to draw bills on the security of the shipping documents, which are forwarded to be released to you against payment.

Acceptance credits are often made on a revolving basis. When the original drafts mature, new drafts are drawn up to an agreed maximum for as long as the facility is open. Usually this kind of arrangement is conditional on any security's being insured and on the security exceeding the total amount of acceptance outstanding under the credit.

Overseas customers may have a documentary credit with their bank's London branch to negotiate bills drawn by you on them, accompanied by the shipping documents. The bills are presented to the London branch, which buys and forwards them to the customer's country, where they are surrendered in exchange for cash or against acceptance of the bills.

An importer can make an arrangement under which his overseas supplier draws sight or time bills on him. The sight bill is sent to London with the shipping documents and presented to the importer for payment in cash against delivery of the documents. With a time bill the importer has to arrange a credit with a foreign branch or correspondent of his own bank. His bank's London office authorises them to negotiate the supplier's bill if it is accompanied by the shipping documents. They buy it at the bank's buying rate of exchange for similar sight drafts in London and send it on to their London office, which presents it to the importer for acceptance. If the importer is a good risk, they will offer D/A terms (documents against acceptance) and the goods can be delivered on arrival. Otherwise the goods are warehoused and insured at the importer's expense and the bill is paid at maturity or he may be able to take earlier delivery by paying it off at a premium.

Raw materials are sometimes bought by bank loan or advance through a London accepting house by acceptance credit. Drafts are accepted under the credit up to a specified amount drawn upon them by a manufacturer, usually payable three months after date. The manufacturer has to put them in funds at or before the maturity date by way of cash or fresh bills and, once they are drawn and accepted, they can be discounted.

Government participation and the exporter

The so-called 'export drive' sponsored by successive governments since the second World War has spawned some creative and flexible government financial schemes. The Market Entry Scheme is part loan to the manufacturer, part guarantee against loss, while the Export Credit Guarantee Schemes are a form of credit insurance, enabling the exporter to finance export business at advantageous rates.

The Market Entry Scheme is designed to help the small to medium-sized manufacturing business open up new markets. The Scheme contributes 50 per cent of certain overhead costs on ventures of between £20,000 and £125,000 but the government will not make a capital investment. The venture must be confined to a single project in a single new market but the government will not underwrite an isolated transaction. The exporter pays 3 per cent of the Scheme's 50 per cent contribution for an agreed period, as a premium for a guarantee that the loan is not repayable and the Scheme shares the loss if the venture fails. For each year of the agreed period to a maximum of five years, or until the Scheme has recovered its contributions with a commercial rate of interest, the exporter pays a levy on sales receipts of approximately 2.5 per cent above the weighted average of the UK clearing banks' base rate. While the exporter is not unduly restricted in his exploitation of the new market, he must give notice of any significant changes he wishes to make and he can withdraw from the Scheme on six months' notice on certain conditions. If expenses fall below certain levels, government can terminate the agreement and no further contribution or levy is payable, but in some circumstances the levy on sales continues even if the venture is effectively abandoned.

For tax purposes, the Scheme's contributions are treated as reducing the costs of the venture and the premium for the guarantee and the levy payments are allowable reductions.

Further information about the Scheme can be obtained from the British Overseas Trade Board (BOTB) or the export sections of the Department of Industry in London and from the Department's regional offices.

The Export Credits Guarantee Department (ECGD) offers credit insurance by way of guarantees direct to an exporter or to his financing bank. The cover includes the creditworthiness of the buyer, transfer risk (to cover exchange transfer problems) and political risks.

The Department usually wants to insure all export business, although they will sometimes cover exports to a selected market. Usually they will issue a supplementary unconditional guarantee of finance which is made available to your bank and the bank will lend at special rates against the security of the guarantees. The cover applies when the bank buys 'without recourse' bills (which means they cannot turn to you for payment) or promissory notes received by you for deferred instalments of the price of the goods and a separate guarantee is issued for each contract. The bank buys unconditionally guaranteed payment and you retain only a contingent liability to reimburse the Department for anything paid to the bank which is not payable under the credit insurance policy.

Transactions requiring credit of six months or less can be arranged under the Comprehensive Short Term Guarantee Scheme, usually on the exporter's undertaking to insure his whole export turnover for at least 12 months. Longer-term credit can be covered for individual contracts or continuous business with the exporter's overseas distributors and dealers under the Supplemental Extended Terms Guarantee.

Insurance for buyer credit is also available for transactions of over £1,000,000, with the exception of exports within the EEC, at special fixed rates. This is a guarantee on a direct loan to your overseas buyer and the bank has recourse to you in case of non-payment. Finance is provided at fixed preferential rates for up to 85 per cent of the value of the contract and repayable on terms appropriate to the size of the contract. Your bank pays out from the loan taken out on behalf of the buyer, including, in suitable cases, progress payments prior to delivery, in accordance with the terms of your contract. The buyer repays the loan by instalments under the terms of his own agreement with the bank.

Lines of credit on the export of capital goods can be arranged to ensure payment on cash terms on contracts for a minimum of £10,000 for, usually, 80 or 85 per cent of the value of the contract repayable over two to five years.

Trade within the EEC

Different arrangements apply to ECGD insurance and guarantees covering exports to the member States of the EEC on credit transactions covering two years or more. Unconditional guarantees are available and the rate is the rate set by the financing bank.

Foreign bank financing

Cover on loans through foreign banks can also be arranged through the ECGD if the bank is registered as a company in the UK but finance for foreign currency contracts is not refinanced by the Department.

ECGD bank guarantees and insurance arrangements are flexible and you will obtain a better rate on your finance which, together with the price for the risk covered, more than compensates for the price of the insurance, but you will have to carry between 5 and 10 per cent of the risk yourself. You may, however, be able to negotiate advantageous lending rates with your own bank or finance house and decide that you do not wish to pay the price of insurance cover through the Department.

You should therefore take expert advice first from your own bank and there are several government services which give information to exporters, including the British Overseas Trade Board, which offers a wide range of export services, and the Central Office of Information, which arranges publicity overseas. You can obtain information from the Department of Trade in London or at one of their regional offices and full details of their services are published in their *Export Handbook*, obtainable from the Department.

Credit insurance on overseas purchases with foreign insurers

If you are buying abroad there is a similar scheme to the ECGD's supervised by the Berne Union, an international association of credit insurers. Buyer credit guarantees with the supplying country can be arranged under the scheme or under one set up by a government outside the Union, but any arrangements should be thoroughly investigated.

STATUTORY REFERENCES

Bank of England (Time of Noting) Act 1917

Bills of Exchange Act 1882

Cheques Act 1957

Companies Act 1948

European Communities Act 1972

Export Guarantees and Overseas Investment Act 1978

Partnership Act 1890

11
Intellectual Property: Patents, Copyrights and Trademarks

'Intellectual property' is a rather high-flown term referring to anyone who manufactures or markets, directly or under licence, a product or process which depends for its profitability and/or marketability on the fact that it is unique, because it is new or its marketing strength depends on its name.

The law protecting 'uniqueness' is covered by patent law, giving temporary protection to technological inventions, registered designs, which protect the appearance of mass-produced articles, copyright, which gives longer-term rights in literary, artistic and musical creations, and trademarks, which are protected as long as they are used in trade. You can also stop competitors disparaging your products maliciously or 'passing off' their goods or business activities in such a way as to lead their customers to mistake them as your own and prevent the commercial exploitation, without consent, of information given in confidence.

Protection given by the different areas of law varies but each is principally concerned with stopping competitors exploiting your product or process without consent. Generally, enforcement of your rights is similar and often you will want to base your claim on more than one method to restrain the activities of competitors and licensees.

You are warned at the outset, however, that this is a very complex area. If you want to protect a right which you know and can prove is your own, you should seek specialist advice in the context of this very general view of the legal rights to which you may be able to lay claim.

EEC law

Claims to rights in intellectual property protect a trader against rival enterprises which would otherwise sell goods or services in competition. Internationally, such protection leads to the restriction of goods moving from one area to another. The assertion of a private right can therefore effectively impose an embargo on distribution and marketing which is contrary to the expressed aims of the EEC, which looks to the promotion of trade, without the interposition of financial or legal barriers. You can therefore only protect industrial and commercial property under UK law to the extent that the exercise of your rights does not amount to a quantitative restriction on imports within member states.*

Unification or harmonisation of intellectual property law in the EEC has had a difficult time and the European Court of Justice and the European Commission have to some extent anticipated EEC legislation in their interpretation of situations which they see as jeopardising the free movement of goods between member States and the establishment of a system to prevent distortion of inter-state trade. The provisions on free movement of goods do not apply when you are trading with a State outside the EEC but once you have marketed or manufactured a product abroad, you cannot restrict imports into a member state.† Otherwise, however, trademark rights in a member State can be used to exclude imports from outside the EEC,‡ but, if you are trading internationally, your agreements should be professionally drafted.

Patent protection

Patents protect articles which are in some way superior to previous similar products or are manufactured by a superior process. Your rights can extend to improved articles or processes which are superior for the same reasons as that on which your patent is based, and your patent can be wide enough and be a sufficient advance on earlier ideas to give a complete monopoly. For example, the patent on the transistor initially gave its inventor a complete monopoly on the market. However, if your patent is, or is thought to be, valid, competitors will usually have to do their own design and research work rather than copy your patented product.

The effectiveness of patent protection depends on how new and important your product is and for how long you need the protection. Novelty decides whether you can get the patent and

---

* *Deutsche Grammophon* (1971) ECR 487
† *Terrapin/Terranova* (1976) ECR 1039, Cassis de Dijon
‡ *EMI* v *CBS* (1976) ECR 811

how wide a monopoly it will cover. The product's importance will decide whether competitors will try to avoid your monopoly or whether they will run the risk of legal action. The length of time you are protected may be decisive as to the practicability of competitors doing the design and research work necessary to sidestep your patent.

You will therefore need a substantial and very wide patent, based on a major invention, to build up a new and substantial market, as an ordinary patent is likely to be avoided by competitors long before your business is properly established. However, where you are marketing a new line of goods which are not of major importance, a comparatively narrowly based patent may be sufficient, as your competitors will find it relatively simple to produce something different which is not likely to attract patent proceedings. If your product, though more streamlined or effective, is very similar to a previous line, you will be unlikely to be able to obtain sufficient patent protection.

Licensing patents

If your patent is valid, manufacture, importation, sale or use of the patented article or of the articles made by your patented process or machine are only lawful with your consent, which is usually given under licence. With some important exceptions you can make any terms you wish for use of your patent. Permission to use and sell yourself is implied when you license the manufacture of your product but there are express limitations on your rights. Anyone buying the article knowing of the conditions must comply with them or risk infringing your patent and not every condition is lawful.

By granting an exclusive licence you limit inter-product competition. This is seen by the European Commission as a distortion of competition under the Treaty of Rome, if the licence affects a significant share of the relevant market, or the licensee has undertaken not to sell outside his allotted territory.

The European Commission is formulating a draft block exemption that will set out the conditions under which licences will be permitted. Exclusive rights to manufacture within a territory are currently allowed if the exploitation is not already established by the time the licence was granted.* The licensee

* *Bronbemaling* v *Heidemaatschappij Beheer* (1975) 2 CMLR D 67

must, however, show an element of risk, for example the cost of completing development of the product or the cost of service facilities, especially if they would also be available to a later licensee.* There are various other restrictions and concessions. Again, you are reminded that inter-EEC dealing in patents is a complicated matter and you should take expert advice to ensure that you can fully exploit your patent while complying with EEC requirements.

British law also has restrictions on some terms in licensing agreements. A licensor cannot usually force a licensee to buy his unpatented materials, but you can agree preferential terms on unpatented goods, provided you comply with EEC rules. The licensee cannot be stopped from ending the licence once the original patents have expired although you can require him to stop manufacturing if he does, again provided that EEC rules are observed.

Copyright and EEC law

Once you have exported or marketed your copyright in a member state of the Common Market, you cannot exploit it exclusively in the United Kingdom or anywhere else.†

Copyright protection

Most new industrial designs are copyright, either through the initial drawings or the prototype model on which they are based. Any copy is an infringement of the copyright, which exists as soon as pen is put to paper or the model takes shape, without the requirement of registration or any legal formalities. Others working in the same field and coming up with the same ideas will have their own copyright, which may be for an almost identical design, although your copyright stops exact copying. If your product is distinctive, because, for example, it is of high-quality workmanship and you market it on that basis, copyright gives you sufficient protection from inferior copies.

Computer programs

Computer programs in a written or diagrammatic form which have been produced with sufficient effort, skill and judgement

---

* *Davidson Rubbers Agreements* (1972) CMLR D 52
† GEMA Cases 55 and 77/80, 20 Jan 1981 and *Polydor Ltd & RSO Records* v
  Harlequin (1980) 2 CMLR 413

have copyright protection,* owned by the person who devised the program and who can stop copies being made or used without his consent. Each successive stage probably involves are, however, problems when the program is put into a form readable by the computer, on punched cards or tape, although this might reduce the program to 'writing' or 'some other material form' which should also be copyright. However, until computer programs are given specific copyright protection or a system of registration of copyright like that in the USA is introduced, their most effective legal protection is under the provisions of an individual contract and as confidential information.

Registered designs

You can also protect designs by registration, but it is expensive and must be done before anyone is shown the product, except in the strictest confidence. Registration is worth while if your design is an almost inevitable development in an existing field. Your design is then, unlike a copyright, infringed by anyone using the same design, even if it was created entirely without reference to your product.

Periods of protection

Patents last for 20 years from the date when the full specification of your invention is filed with the Patent Office, but the patent is not fully effective until the Patent Office publishes the specification, which is usually a considerable time after application. Patenting easily produced and short-lived goods may therefore be useless, as the patent may no longer be important by the time it becomes effective. Delay in publication may be advantageous as the invention can be kept secret until publication.

Copyright in 'artistic' works arises on creation and, with some exceptions, lasts generally for the life of the creator plus 50 years, but use of a copyright work as an industrial design lasts only for 15 years after the product made to that design is first marketed.

Registered designs are not protected until completion of the registration procedure, which can take up to three months.

---

* *Northern Office Micro Computers (Pty)* v *Rosenstein* (1982) FSR 124

Registration lasts for five years from the date of application and can be extended on payment of the fee for two further five-year periods.

Taking action against competitors

In theory, when patents or registered designs are infringed your rights are legally protected, and it makes no difference whether the product is copied or independently produced. You must, however, first decide whether your patent or design registration is valid and whether the monopoly it gives you is wide enough to have been infringed. It is irrelevant that the infringer was not aware of your rights.

In copyright proceedings the infringer must be shown to have copied, either directly or indirectly, from your copyright work.

New products in this technological age are often likely to infringe patent or design rights. Infringement of designs can be avoided by a proper search of the Design Registry, but an innocent infringement of patent, particularly in an industry where there is a good deal of technical research and development, is more difficult to avoid. You must have a thorough knowledge of existing patents and research in your field and should carry out frequent and careful searches. These are difficult and expensive and should, if possible, be carried out by a patent agent.

Confidential information

Information may be protected against breach of confidence, including, in addition to trade and technological secrets, commercial records, marketing, professional and managerial procedures and information about personal relationships.

Technical ideas which can be put to commercial use can quickly become public, either when marketed or through discussions with associates and potential investors. Patents, if the invention is sufficiently described in the specification filed at the Patent Office, protect monopolies but obtaining undertakings to keep information confidential is another method of protection. It is, however, only possible aginst those who receive information directly or, in some cases, indirectly, from the inventor. You can also cover a central invention with patents and protect the information gained in production by confidence undertakings. The courts are reluctant to impose obligations on ex-employees to stop them using their knowledge and skill but, in other areas, some security is possible.

As with copyright protection action in breach of confidence proceedings can only be taken if the information derives from the plaintiff but the action does not depend on the particular way of using the material and is only concerned with exploitation of the information. For example, a summary of a written work is a breach of copyright only if there is substantial reproduction of the protected work, but there may be a breach of contract or of implied obligations if advantage is taken of confidential information.

Unfair competition

Unlike most European countries we have no general law forbidding unfair competition, although there are some rules which forbid the running of a business in such a way as to take a competitor's trade. British law protects business goodwill (which, in law, is that characteristic of a business which renders it permanent and distinguishes an established business from a new business), and you must not mislead customers into mistaking your goods for someone else's or confusing your business with another's. It is irrelevant whether other traders or the general public are misled and whether the deception is mistaken, accidental or fraudulent. The deception is called 'passing off' and if you suffer consequential financial loss you can sue for compensation and obtain an injunction against continuance of the deception. Full trials of passing off cases are rare, however, as individual witnesses who can swear they were actually deceived may be very difficult to produce, and proof usually depends on showing that circumstances are such that customers were certain to have been deceived. This is not easy and is the most important reason for registration of trademarks, which substitutes an action for infringement of your mark.

Trademarks

When you have full (Part A) registration of your trademark, imitation of the mark or your brandname or badge can rarely occur without infringement of registration, but full registration is not always possible or easy as you have to show use of a new and distinctive mark. Registration protects goods even if you have no established market and you cannot bring an action for infringement of an unregistered mark.*

You will only succeed in a passing off action, however, if you are already marketing established lines of goods. Passing off actions are more frequent, because trademarks are often not fully or validly registered and passing off can arise when trademark protection is impossible, for example, where the name of a new company is misleadingly similar to an old one or where packaging is deceptively similar to an established line.

Part A trademark protection gives complete protection as no one can use your mark to advertise their goods, even comparatively, for example, to state that their goods are as good as your's at half the price in an advertisement whether it is true or not. Even with Part A registration, however, you cannot stop a non-visual use of your mark, for example, if a competitor makes the same comment, truthfully, in a shop or the reference is in a voice-over on a TV or filmed advertisement.

Part B protection is less effective but it is more valuable than relying on a passing off action. For Part B infringement you do not have to prove that your goods are known to the public but, as in a passing off action (although not with Part A protection), there is a full defence if it is shown that, although your mark was used, it was not used in a way likely to mislead the public.

A mark registered in Part B can, after substantial goodwill has attached to it, be registered in Part A.

It is usually a straightforward matter to decide if a trademark has been infringed and a search of the Trade Mark Registry will show whether you can safely use a new mark. Infringement is often accidental and usually stops when the infringer is notified, but if you do not register your mark you may find yourself involved in unnecessary litigation by way of a passing off action, quite apart from the extra cost of relabelling your goods and business documentation if you lose the action.

A good deal of litigation arises, however, where the law cannot help, for example, where your trademark is spoilt when a competitor's mark is not sufficiently close to yours to be mistaken for it but close enough for the public not to bother to prefer your brand over his.

---

* *Henry Denny & Sons* v *United Biscuits (UK)* (1981) FSR 114

Foreign marks

The right to registration of a mark depends on distinctiveness in this country and you cannot own an unregistered mark unless it is limited to your business goodwill. Even if a foreign mark is not established in this country, the courts will generally stop a British trader registering a mark belonging to a foreign business.

EEC law and trademarks

EEC trademark law is still in a state of flux. It seems, however, that the owner of a mark in one member State can only stop imports coming in under the same mark from another member State if the goods were wrongfully put on the market of the exporting state, or if they were legitimately marketed but without the consent of the owner of the mark in the importing country. In addition, there must not be a legal, financial, technical or economic link between the two owners. These restrictions only apply to trading between member States and trademark rights can be enforced against imports from outside the EEC.

You cannot stop marked goods sold in the EEC from being resold, even if the marks in the two countries are in different ownership. An agreement between the two owners to keep out of each other's territory is probably invalid as tending to restrict competition and the free flow of goods.

Certification trademarks

A certification trademark indicates that the owner has certified the goods as reaching a certain standard. Before the mark is registered, a set of regulations governing its use and the standards to be complied with must be approved by the Department of Trade and anyone whose goods reach the required standard can use the mark. Regulations can be inspected at the Patent Office.

Certification marks can only be registered in Part A and must be distinctive in the same way as other Part A marks. Infringers are sued in the same way as Part A trademark infringers. Using the mark on the wrong goods is likely to be an offence under the Trade Descriptions Act.

Ownership of the mark can only be transferred with the consent of the Department of Trade and marks are usually owned by trade associations or other similar non-profit making bodies. The regulations can require inspection by the owner of the mark, but usually a manufacturer is authorised to apply the mark to his own goods, under proper control by the owner. Authorised users are not registered at the Trade Mark Registry but the owner keeps his own register.

Passing off

Passing off covers a considerable range of activities from straightforward cases of dishonest trading, when a different and cheaper brand of goods is supplied to a customer, instead of a named brand, to cases which are very near to infringement of a trademark.

Passing off actions are often concerned with business names, because, although they must usually be registered, registration gives no right to stop others using the name. Most cases of passing off, however, involve the application of a distinctive badge or sign by a trader to his merchandise, which implies that they are someone else's goods with which the customer is familiar and which he associates with certain qualities. The mark may be an ordinary trademark, which, for some reason, is not registered and is therefore not within the Trade Mark Act, or the name of a business or of someone associated with it. It can also be a special package or appearance and must be something which, because of use, serves to distinguish the goods of a particular trader or group of traders. In addition, there must be a copy which, deliberately or accidentally, is close enough to the genuine article to deceive, mislead or at least confuse the customer. Success in an action may often turn on what customers are involved and whether, and in what form, the name goes on the goods.

There can be passing off even if there is no trade or business, where, for example, professional institutions or societies sue people who falsely pretend to a qualification. There usually, however, has to be some business connection and a real likelihood of a plaintiff suffering damage to some sort of business interest.

Proceedings can also be instituted against a manufacturer selling second-hand goods as new, lower priced goods as better quality or spoilt goods as sound.

Slander of goods

This is another sort of unfair competition and it has also been described as slander of title, trade libel and injurious falsehood and consists of injury to someone else's business by making a false statement to a third party from some indirect or dishonest motive. The plaintiff must be able to prove real financial loss or the real risk of it. The statement must be false and a true statement, however harmful and disparaging, is not actionable.

Remedies

Although the various rights are enforced by similar actions, the cost and complexity of litigation varies widely in the different areas of law. Actions for infringement of patent, however, are by far the most lengthy, complicated and costly and often an infringement will cease to be commercially important before the case comes to trial. Copyright, trademark and passing off actions can be brought to trial within a few months and cost far less. Actions for infringement of industrial designs vary in cost and complexity, depending on the conduct of the action and how the case is approached.

An interlocutory (or pre-trial) injunction, ordering a defendant not to continue or to embark on a course of action until the trial, is a fast and relatively cheap method of dealing with infringement available to the plaintiff in proceedings related to intellectual property. Trademark infringements, many infringements of copyright and cases of passing off (especially where the defendant may have been dishonest) are often most effectively dealt with in this manner, but the plaintiff must give a cross-undertaking to compensate the defendant in damages. This means that he must be prepared and able to pay the defendant for the financial effect on his business of an injunction, which, because of the delays in a patent case, may be considerable.

After trial the plaintiff may be awarded a final (continuing) injunction and, in addition, delivery up or destruction by the defendant, of infringing articles or documents and damages.

The measure of damages in the various actions is similar and a plaintiff will usually be compensated for any monetary damage he has actually suffered that can fairly be attributed to the defendant's action. There are additional bases, including the costs a trademark owner may incur for advertising to restore his position, compensation for any reduction in prices forced on a copyright or patent owner while waiting for the issue to be tried, and for damage to goodwill caused by passing off or slander of goods. A copyright owner can also claim damages for conversion, which means he can claim compensation based on his ownership of work sold or destroyed by, or as a result of, infringement.

Criminal law

You should ensure that your trademark is not a false trades description within the Trade Descriptions Acts (see page 153). Even if you are using someone else's mark with the owner's consent, it must not give a 'false indication, direct or indirect . . . of the person by whom the goods are manufactured or produced'. An additional problem with trademarks is that the use of a certification trademark by an unauthorised user or one which is not used in accordance with the rules is an offence under the Acts.

Restrictive practices and the EEC

An agreement or restrictive trade practice which affects, or might influence, the pattern of trade between member states may contravene EEC Treaty provisions.*

Restrictive trade practices

Producers and suppliers of goods and services in the UK who carry on business must notify and register agreements under which at least two of them undertake to restrict their conduct in one or more of the ways listed in the Restrictive Trade Practices Act 1976.

The Act is concerned particularly with prices and charges, terms and conditions of supply, the quantities, descriptions or area for the supply of goods and the scale and extent of services, the persons to or by whom goods or services are to be supplied and, in the case of goods, their processes of manufacture.

Patent, registered design and copyright licences are not registrable under the Act if the only restrictions concern the invention, the articles for which the design is registered or the subject matter of the copyright. For example, if the agreement is to charge standard prices or to use a patented invention only on certain types of goods, although such provisions would

---

* *Heintz Van Landweyck Sarl* v *European Commission* (1980) ECR 3125

normally call for registration, the agreement is exempt if it does not also agree prices on non-patented goods or services.

As soon as the agreement is between more than two parties, however, for example, where each party grants an interest to one or more of the others, the agreement is registrable if at least two of them accept statutory restrictions.

If information is exchanged the agreement may be exempt where the information is related to the production of goods or services. The information must relate to manufacturing processes in an agreement for the supply of goods, and the restrictions must be confined to the kinds of goods to be subject to the processes. Agreements for the supply of services are exempt if the information relates to techniques or processes to be applied in the services, and the restrictions only concern the form or manner in which they are to be supplied.

Trademark licences are exempt agreements if the restrictions only relate to the description of the goods that are to bear the mark or the processes of manufacture to be applied to them.

If you are in doubt about whether or not your agreement is registrable, you should consult the booklet available from the Office of Fair Trading and further information may also be available from your trade association.

STATUTORY REFERENCES

Competition Act 1980

Copyright Act 1956

Defamation Act 1952

Design Copyrights Act 1968

European Communities Act 1972

Fair Trading Act 1973

Patents Act 1977

Registered Designs Act 1949

Resale Prices Act 1976

Restrictive Trade Practices Act 1976

Trade Descriptions Act 1968

Trade Marks Act 1938

12
Litigation

Starting an action

Litigation is a last resort, only undertaken after you have made
every effort at settlement and if you can reasonably expect to
obtain compensation from a defeated opponent. In a substantial
or complicated matter, you should take legal advice at an early
stage, so that your 'letters before action' set out only the
relevant details of your claim, precisely what you are seeking,
and the reasons why you are entitled in law to succeed.

You can take your own case before any court, from the local
county or magistrates court to the House of Lords. Procedure
in small civil claims has recently been simplified to enable
someone without legal knowledge or professional assistance to
put his own case. Substantial and complicated claims, however,
may involve a longer and more difficult fight and you are more
likely to face expensive and expert opposition for which you
will have to pay if you lose. Do it yourself litigation is therefore
best confined to small claims in the county court, disputes
which can be referred to arbitration and straightforward claims
for debt.*

This chapter takes you through only the basics of criminal
litigation. The emphasis is on civil litigation in the county court,
in which taking action yourself is a reasonable option. High
Court civil litigation follows a similar procedural pattern but the
experienced legal practitioner is best equipped to deal with
the finer points of pleading and advocacy and the stricter
enforcement of the rules of court.

The criminal courts

Crime is the business of the magistrates and crown courts

---

* That is, arbitration in the county court. Arbitration before the specialised
  commercial courts referred to in Chapter 9 is best left to experts.

and it is no crime if you do not pay your debts or carry on business at a loss, unless fraud is involved. You can, however, face a criminal prosecution if your business activities adversely affect the health and safety of your employees or the general public or, for instance, for offences under the consumer protection and licensing legislation and both the business and private motorist must conform with road traffic legislation.

Law and order are public matters, so prosecutions are usually left to the police or the authorities responsible under the general law, for example, local authorities suing for outstanding rates. Private action can be taken but the case is usually better left in the more experienced hands of the police solicitors. If they refuse to take action, you may want to take the case to court yourself but you should take legal advice before starting a private fight in the criminal courts, where financial compensation — if it is available — is usually far lower than in the civil courts.

Organisation and personnel
Prosecution in the magistrates court is based on an information which is put before the magistrate and which states that someone has, or is suspected of having, committed an offence. The magistrate issues a summons requiring the accused person to appear before his court to answer the information, or issues a warrant to arrest him and bring him before the court, in which case the information must be sworn on oath. Usually the summons or warrant relates to an offence committed within the county or borough in which the magistrate has jurisdiction but it may be issued in the area in which the accused person, or someone with whom he is charged, is resident, or in a court designated by statute.

A warrant for arrest can only be obtained for offences in specified circumstances, which include offences punishable with imprisonment and those which are tried by jury in the crown court. If you are arrested, you must demand immediate access to a solicitor, although prompt compliance with your request may not always be forthcoming. If you are faced with criminal prosecution, whatever the circumstances, you should immediately seek legal advice, as conviction, even for a minor charge, may have very serious repercussions. For instance, conviction for a road traffic offence which is linked to personal or property damage is admissible in proceedings in the civil courts. The offence is thereby proved and is very persuasive evidence for the court's consideration in deciding liability in a claim for damages.

Costs in criminal proceedings

The court may order the costs of an innocent party's defence to be paid by a private prosecutor. In a police prosecution the defendant will only recover costs if the case was clearly untenable and he was patently innocent. Private or public, however, the innocent defendant — unless he is fully legally aided — pays part of the costs of his defence and this can cost anything from one or two hundred to many thousands of pounds, depending on the seriousness of the offence and the length of the hearing.

Civil actions

Commercial litigation is conducted in the civil courts. The county court and the High Court deal with private disputes, including property and partnership disputes, claims related to the sale of goods, claims for wages or salary outside the employment legislation and compensation for damage to property and to the person.

The large majority of claims are settled without going to trial, either by agreement or because there is no defence or the claim is not contested. The few that are tried often involve a dispute as to the facts, rather than the law, and the court makes its decision on the basis of which version it believes to be correct.

The county court

The county court deals with some claims of up to £30,000 but the £5000 limit on contractual and tort claims usually applies to commercial disputes. Contractual claims cover both written and unwritten agreements where there is a direct agreement between the parties. Claims in tort include claims for damage caused by negligence, such as a claim for compensation for personal injury or property damage caused in an industrial or road accident.

The county court also deals with landlord and tenant disputes relating to residential and business premises where the rateable value does not exceed £1000 and £5000 respectively. This covers nearly all residential property in the major urban areas and the majority of rented premises used by a small business.

Once you are over the county court limits, the High Court takes over, with heavier costs on the litigating parties. On tactical grounds your solicitor may in some circumstances advise you to take action in the High Court on a claim within the county court limits. The procedural changes which came into force on 1 September 1982 now make this a less attractive option, particularly as you may only be able to claim costs against your defendant on the lower, county court, scale.

Organisation and personnel

The county court office will help you in issuing the summons or originating application which starts the action and in filling out the printed form of defence to proceedings taken against you and the various other forms which are used during the action. Your case will be dealt with by a judge, a recorder or a registrar. The registrar deals with procedural matters and the steps which must be taken through the court before the trial. He also acts as an assistant judge and tries most small claims and you can appeal from his decision to the judge.

Court fees

Court fees are additional to the legal costs of the bringing or defending the action. You pay from £4 to £33 to start an action, depending on how much and what you are claiming. The solicitors' fixed costs on issue of the summons vary from £6 to £39, depending on the amount and the claim. The losing defendant pays between £6 and £49 on judgement but pays no other court fees unless he is putting forward a money claim — a counter-claim — which exceeds the amount you are claiming from him. On a successful claim you may also have to pay up to £25 to enforce judgement against the defendant.

Costs in the county court

The county court has a sliding scale. On a money claim of between £25 and £100, you may be able to recover the court fees, witness expenses and up to £40 plus the costs incurred as a result of your opponent's unreasonable conduct. On a claim of up to £25, however, you may only be able to recover costs if the case is complicated; costs may also be awarded if the claim is for damages exceeding £5 for personal injury.

If the defendant in a default action does not put in a defence within 14 days of service or admits your claim, you can ask for judgement, plus costs and interest to the date of judgement, provided you have included this in your particulars of claim.

For claims other than money or where the costs on the summons are not paid into court or the full amount is paid at a later stage, you are entitled to extra costs. You may also be awarded extra costs when the defendant asks for time to pay, although usually only the fixed costs on the summons are awarded on instalment 'orders and hire purchase and moneylenders' claims.

You can apply to the registrar to assess your costs, listing charges and payments for his consideration or have your costs 'taxed'. A losing defendant can ask for the plaintiff's costs to be taxed when he is billed at the end of the action and a winning plaintiff can submit his own solicitor's bill for taxing if he thinks his charges are unduly high.

Assessed costs

Assessed costs are calculated on a fixed scale which is usually far less than a solicitor is entitled to on 'taxation'.

'Taxing' the bill

On taxation, a detailed bill is sent to the defendant and the parties or their solicitors attend before the registrar. The registrar goes through the bill item by item deciding what and how much may be allowed. The defendant can query any item and the total is claimed by a court order served on the defendant.

Scales of costs

The amount allowed for the various items on the bill depends on the scale fixed by the county court rules or decided when judgement is given. There are four scales of charges and the scale depends on the amount recovered, although in some circumstances the court will award costs on a higher or lower scale. Costs allowed on the various items and steps in the action increase from Scale 1 to 3 in proportion to the amount involved, although in the lowest scale they may be far lower than the real cost of the work done. Even in a small claim costs can exceed the amount claimed and taxed costs do not include the costs incurred before starting litigation. You must therefore carefully consider an offer of reasonable settlement in the context of the possible costs of litigation, whatever the ostensible strength of your claim.

The costs of a defended action

The sum of money to which each scale of costs applies is as follows:

Claims over £25 to £100 — lower scale;
Claims over £100 to £500 — Scale 1;
Claims over £500 to £3000 — Scale 2;
Claims over £3000 — Scale 3.

It is very difficult to estimate the cost of a fully defended action, as so much depends on the conduct of the litigation and the manner in which the case is put before the court. Taxed and allowable legal costs of an action on Scale 1 will probably not be less than about £200; costs on the higher scales are much heavier and can be anything from several hundred to several thousand pounds.

Cutting the costs of your defence

The choice is not always fight or submit to judgement. Partial admission of a claim may bring an action within a lower scale of costs. For instance, in an action for payment of a bill for repairs you may be able to admit part of the amount claimed and dispute the balance. Alternatively, there may be a split liability. For instance, in an action for damages for personal injury, the plaintiff may be partly to blame for the accident in which he was injured. You should then pay into court a proportion of the amount claimed, based on a realistic assessment of your liability, plus an appropriate amount for the costs, which will be calculated for you by the court office. It can be paid at any time before judgement but the trial judge is not told of the payment until after judgement and before he makes the order for costs. The plaintiff, however, must be notified promptly and must decide whether it is worth his while to accept your payment or take further action.

The choice is not easy. If judgement is for more than the amount paid into court, you still pay the plaintiff's costs. If judgement is for the same or a lesser sum, however, you usually only have to pay his costs to the date of payment and the plaintiff pays both sides' costs incurred after that date.

If you cannot make a payment into court, you may be able to agree settlement on an instalment basis.

Legal aid

The legal aid fund pays part or all of the cost of legal advice and assistance — not litigation — under the Green Form Scheme if your disposable capital does not exceed £650 and your disposable weekly income is not more than £93. Disposable capital covers liquid assets and property apart from your residence; disposable income is income less tax and national insurance contributions and certain other deductions for maintenance of dependants. There is a sliding scale and at the upper limits you may have to pay part of the costs yourself.

Legal aid in criminal proceedings is also based on means but is only granted to defend a serious charge and if it is 'in the interests of justice' that the grant should be made; the defendant's contribution is decided by the court.

The capital and income limits for legal aid in civil litigation are presently £2725 and £4440 per annum respectively. On capital of £1310 and annual income of £1850 you will have to make a contribution to costs, which increases until you reach the limits which disqualify you from legal aid. The computations are similar to those under the Green Form Scheme but the calculations and your maximum contribution are assessed by the Supplementary Benefits Commission,* who require fully documented evidence of your resources. You must have a reasonable case and may have to pay over part of your winnings to the legal aid fund. A director or partner acting on his own behalf is eligible for legal aid but it is not available to a limited company. The privately funded party facing a legally aided litigant can have a long and expensive fight with little to show at the end of the day except a heavy bill of costs, as the legally aided loser can usually pay only a small proportion of the winner's costs and compensation.

Which court?

Local county courts are listed under 'Courts' in the telephone directory. You can bring the action in the court serving the area where your defendant lives or carries on business or where your cause of action — that is, the circumstances giving rise to the claim — arose. When you sue on a contract, the cause of action arises where the contract is concluded, that is, at the

* **Through the DHSS.**

place where an offer is accepted. It is not always clear who
makes the offer and where or when it is accepted. The legal
rules are set out at page 149 but if your choice is wrong, the
case can be transferred to another court — at extra cost.

Trial or arbitration

Arbitrations are heard in private and are less complicated and
formal than trials in open court.* The purpose of arbitration is
to enable a dispute to be resolved in an informal atmosphere,
dispensing as far as possible with the formal rules of procedure
and evidence. If the claim does not exceed £500, however, you
can only claim the fixed costs on the summons, the cost of
enforcing the award (decision) and any costs incurred by your
opponent's unreasonable conduct. Generally the registrar acts
as arbitrator but larger claims may go before a judge or anyone
else that the parties agree to appoint and who consents to act.
An outside arbitrator receives an extra fee which must be paid
into court by the parties before the case is dealt with, so it is
usually best to accept the experienced nominee of the court,
unless specialised knowledge is required.

If the claim does not exceed £500, either party can ask for
arbitration and the registrar will also consider it on receipt of
the defence. The registrar will consider objections and if he is
satisfied that there is a question of fraud or the dispute is
unsuitable for arbitration, he will order a full trial. Disputes
likely to be considered unsuitable include personal injury
claims, issues of public importance, which could influence or
affect the rights of persons not party to the proceedings, and
difficult questions of law or issues of fact.

The request for arbitration can be made when you take out
the summons at the start of the action or when the defendant
completes his form of defence. An objection to the defendant's
request must be sent to the court within 14 days of receipt of
the defence and he can lodge his objection at any time before
the pre-trial review.

A late request can be made by either party at the pre-trial
review, when the registrar may himself suggest arbitration as a
suitable method of disposing of a larger claim and objections
can be referred for the judge's decision. Both parties can make a

---

* Arbitration is sometimes called the 'small claims court'.

special application for arbitration after the pre-trial review, at any time before the trial.

The terms of arbitration are decided at the pre-trial review. These may include a direction to dispense with the rules of evidence, so that, for instance 'hearsay' evidence (see below) would be allowed, or the registrar might allow the arbitrator to obtain reports from experts of his own choosing or limit the costs payable by the losing party.

The hearing is less formal than a trial and usually evidence is given seated at table, rather than in the witness box and the arbitrator may dispense with sworn evidence. The decision — the 'award' — may be given at the hearing or by a later written decision and it is enforceable in the same way as a judgement given in open court.

The loser in arbitration has different rights of appeal from a party whose case is tried in open court. Broadly, you can appeal only if the arbitration was improperly conducted or the award contains an apparent error, for example, it was inconsistent with the proved facts. An appeal should not be considered without taking legal advice.

Time limits

The final letter before action should set a time limit for acceptance of your terms of settlement, failing which you will institute proceedings without further notice or put the matter in the hands of your solicitor.

Once embarked on litigation, time limits are very important, both for delivery of the pleadings and for attendance at court. For instance, the court does not tell you if the defence and other pleadings are delivered on time or at all and you should ask for acknowledgement of safe receipt when you serve documents on your opponent. The court will usually allow an extension of time if there is a reasonable explanation for delay but you may win an action simply because your opponent deliberately and persistently fails to deal with the claim.

There are also time limits for objections to arbitration and various other steps in the action and missing a hearing may mean that you have to re-issue proceedings. Dates can however be changed and to save costs, you should, if possible, obtain your opponent's consent to any change before applying to the court.

The parties

The plaintiff or applicant is the person who starts the action and the person sued is the defendant or respondent; if several people are involved, there may be several plaintiffs and defendants and before starting the action you must ensure you are suing the right party.

Usually you will be dealing with one of two kinds of claim, a dispute about an agreement or a claim for compensation for damages caused by a wrongful or unlawful act. In most cases it is not difficult to identify your opponent. In a contractual dispute relating to an agreement, for instance, where the business buys faulty equipment, the contract of sale is between the business and the supplier, who are respectively the plaintiff and the defendant. A claim for compensation for damage caused in a road accident falls into the latter category. You can sue the driver but you may have an alternative claim against the car owner or the driver's employer if the car was being used for their purposes at the time of the accident. You can only collect compensation once, however, and if your claim is against more than one defendant in, for example, a multiple car accident, the defendants pay in proportion to their liability.

Names and addresses

Proceedings must be served on the defendant, that is, filed with the court and delivered to him, so the summons must have the correct name and address or, if he has instructed a solicitor, his name and the address (the address for service) of his solicitor.

Companies

Court documents must be served on a limited company's registered office, which may not be the office with which you have been dealing. The address should be on business documentation and, if not, it is on file at the London Search Room of the Companies Registration Office.

Partnerships

The firm's name and the address to which documents must be sent are on business documentation and must now be filed at the Companies Registration Office.

Business and trading names

You can take action against someone trading in a name other than his own by naming him or his business as the defendant and serving proceedings on him at his principal place of business or at his residence.

Suing management personally

The names of directors and of partners in a firm with up to 20 partners are on business documentation and filed at the Companies Registration Office. Partners' names and addresses must be disclosed to the court if you sue them personally or in the name of the partnership and you can serve them personally or at their principal place of business.

Particulars of claim

The court and the defendant must have written details of your claim. These are called the 'particulars of claim' and should be a concise chronological statement of the facts which support your claim, stating why you are taking action and how much you are claiming.

The technical name for the particulars of claim — in the High Court, the 'statement of claim' — and the defence and other documentation which formally set out the case and pass between the parties are the pleadings. The county court rules are not strict as to their form, although in some actions, such as hire purchase and mortgage proceedings, they must contain specified information.

The name of the court heads the particulars of claim and the plaint number is inserted on issue of the summons. The plaintiff's and defendant's names are set out below, followed by a concise statement setting out the facts of the claim and the sum of money or other remedy sought.

In a straightforward claim for debt you can simply state: 'I claim £X the price of goods delivered to Y on . . .', but usually the pleadings refer to the plaintiff and defendant to read: 'the plaintiff claims £X etc . . .'. Other claims require more details. For instance, a claim for damages sustained in a road accident should give the date and place of the accident, set out the circumstances in which it occurred, show that the defendant was responsible and that as a result of his actions, you suffered pain, injury, loss and damage. If you are also suing his employer, you must state that he was 'acting in the course of his employment'; the claim for damages must give details of out-of-pocket expenses and loss of earnings — 'the plaintiff claims damages limited to £X' is an additional head of damages which covers only the compensation, which is left for the assessment of the court; the limitation is put on the money claim to put the action within the appropriate county court scale.

You can amend your pleadings at any time before the pre-trial review or, if there is none, before the trial, but if you leave it until the pre-trial review, you will need the registrar's consent. The court can also order amendment and the amended pleading must be served on your opponent.

The particulars of claim can be handwritten but must be legible and a copy must be filed with the court and served on each defendant. The forms in Appendix 4 are examples of fairly straightforward claims and may be helpful as showing what must be pleaded.

The request

The first step in the action is to fill in a 'request' form available from the county court office, on which you give the information that the court requires for the summons or originating application. The court staff will help you complete the form and tell you whether you need a default or fixed date summons or an originating application.

The court fee

The court fee is paid when you complete the request and varies with the claim.

Service of proceedings

The request and copies of the particulars of claim or originating application are sent to the court together with the fee. The summons is then served on the defendant or respondent. It can be served personally or by post but it is worth paying the additional fee of £4 for service through the court, as it is difficult for your opponent to prove he did not receive proceedings delivered to his proper address by the court bailiff.

Documents should be taken to the court office or sent with a stamped self-addressed envelope for the court's reply.*

The plaint note

The court prepares the summons for service and sends you the plaint note which is marked with the plaint number of your action and to which all documentation connected with the case should refer.

Types of summons

Proceedings in the county court start by summons or originating application. A default summons is used in an action to recover a sum of money, for instance, the price of goods sold or the cost of repairs, and can be for a specific sum or for an amount to be assessed. A fixed date summons is used in all other actions unless you are seeking an order, when you start off with an originating application. The court notifies you when proceedings are issued and the steps which follow depend upon whether you start off by default or fixed date summons or by originating application.

Judgement in default actions

No date is fixed for the parties to attend court in a default action and if the defendant makes no payment or admission or the defence or counter-claim is not delivered within 14 days of service of the summons, you can apply for judgement to be entered against the defendant. The application is made in person or by post to the court on a printed form. You must also send your plaint note and can ask for payment by instalments or immediately and the court will notify the defendant that judgement has been obtained. In an action for money secured by a mortgage you can only obtain judgement in default with the consent of the court.

Admission in default actions

The defendant receives a form with the summons which can be completed to admit the claim, or to defend it and/or make a

---

* If you are unable to trace the defendant, it may be worth employing an enquiry agent or process server to search him out and serve him with proceedings.

counter-claim against you. If he admits it but wants time to pay he must give details of his means and set out an offer for payment which must be accepted or rejected through the court office within 14 days of receipt. If you reject the offer, the court fixes an appointment before the registrar, who decides how payment is to be made.

Disposal

The hearing before the registrar is called the 'disposal'. It is informal and if no one is at court or an adjournment has been requested, the action may be adjourned or even struck out, when you will have to apply to the court to have it restored. The defendant can be heard in your absence but you may want to question him as to his means.

Unliquidated claims

If you have not quantified your claim, judgement will be 'interlocutory', which means it is given on an interim basis, pending assessment of the amount by the registrar.

The defence

If the claim is not admitted, the defendant must deliver his defence to the court within 14 days of service and a copy will be sent to you. The printed form sent with the summons is basically a questionnaire which allows the defendant to deny the claim or admit it with reservations and/or an assertion that the circumstances of the claim give rise to a (counter-)claim against you, which may exceed your claim. Alternatively, he may have a 'set-off' stating in, for instance, a money claim for storage charges, when the claim should be reduced because goods have been lost or damaged.

The defendant may, however, deliver a defence which follows a similar pattern to your chronological particulars of claim.

On receipt of the defence, the court arranges a preliminary hearing — the pre-trial review — or fixes a date for trial.

Summary judgement in a claim for debt

If you are claiming more than £500 and you think there is no real defence to all or part of the claim, you may be able to obtain 'summary judgement', even if the defendant has filed a defence. Application must be made to the court, supported by an affidavit setting out the facts and stating that in your belief there is no defence to your claim. The application and affidavit are served on the defendant, together with copies of any exhibits referred to in your affidavit, for instance, invoices in a claim for payment for goods delivered. If there is in fact no defence to the claim, you will obtain judgement but you must set out the facts clearly and put all relevant documentation before the court and if you are wrong your defendant will be permitted to defend the case.

Fixed date summons

A fixed date summons fixes the date — the return day — when the parties must attend court and will usually be for the pre-trial review. The date is also on your plaint note. If the defendant admits part or all of your claim within 14 days you can apply for judgement for that amount on the return day. Admission, defence, counter-claim and set-off must be delivered within 14 days of service but the defendant can simply dispute the claim on the return day and deliver the defence before the trial. He will then, however, usually have to pay any extra costs incurred by the plaintiff consequent on his delay.

Originating application

Originating applications are used for actions taken under various statutory provisions, including an application for a new business tenancy or relating to tenant's improvements to business premises and some actions under the Companies Acts, the Consumer Credit Act, and the Fair Trading Act; summary proceedings against squatters are also started by originating application.

As applicant — not plaintiff — your application must set out the details specified by the Rules and it is served on your defendant — called the respondent — together with a notice of hearing, which will be the pre-trial review or the hearing of the action. In some proceedings the respondent is only required to attend on the fixed date to contest the application but in other proceedings he must file an answer within 14 days; thereafter the proceedings follow the same pattern as an action commenced by fixed date summons.

The pre-trial review

The review is usually in private and is an informal discussion between the registrar and the parties and sometimes the dispute can be settled in the light of the discussion.

If the defendant does not attend, you may be able to obtain judgement, although you may have to prove your case by putting the evidence before the registrar, so you should bring all relevant documentation to court.

When both parties attend but no defence has been filed, the registrar may ask the defendant about the claim and if both parties' pleadings have been filed, he may ask them to be clarified. This is the time to ask for further information and the registrar may make general suggestions as to the sort of evidence you need to prove your claim, for instance, whether you should obtain expert oral or written evidence. There are, however, limits to his advice, as he may eventually hear the case.

Directions for trial

If you are going to trial the registrar will give directions for preparing for the hearing, which may include amendment of the pleadings to give fuller details of each side's case.

Production of documents

You do not have to give advance and detailed warning of your evidence but the registrar may include in his directions an order to produce some or all of the relevant documentation before the trial. There are certain rules and exceptions and your oral and written offers of settlement before and during the action are excluded if made 'without prejudice' and cannot be put before the court unless you choose yourself to put them in evidence. Generally all relevant documentation must be disclosed and available for inspection before the trial but the registrar may allow exchange of photocopies or direct that they be listed for inspection by arrangement within a fixed time.

Agreeing the cost of repairs and agreeing evidence

Agreement before the trial saves the expense of bringing witnesses to the hearing. For instance, in a claim for damage to property, you may be able to agree plans and photographs of the property and the cost of necessary repairs, saving time wasted in argument as to their accuracy, leaving only the issue of liability to be tried by the court.

Fixing the date of trial

If the case is not disposed of at the pre-trial review, a date is fixed for trial or arbitration, but if you are using an outside arbitrator the date may have to be separately arranged.

Notice of hearing

The court notifies the parties of the date of trial and if you want it heard by a judge, you must make a written request to the court within three days of receipt of the notice.

Preparing your case

The decision depends on the evidence put before the court. It is up to the plaintiff to prove his claim, not for the defendant to disprove it and the court weighs the evidence of both sides and decides whether, on a balance of probabilities, the plaintiff has proved his case; it is only in criminal proceedings that the case must be proved beyond reasonable doubt.

Witnesses

Often the plaintiff and the defendant are the main or the only witnesses. Their versions of the dispute may be very different but they may be equally true. No one has total recall and two people may have an entirely different recollection of the same events, so that independent witnesses who saw or heard what happened and can confirm your story are vital.

Anyone can be a witness, including your spouse and children but a child under the age of 14 will have to satisfy the court that he understands that he must tell the truth before he can give evidence.

Witnesses must attend the trial, to give evidence on oath, so that they can be questioned by your opponent and the court (unless the case was referred to arbitration with an order that written statements might be allowed). You can compel a reluctant witness to come to court by serving him with a witness summons, obtainable from the court office on production of your plaint note and payment of a fee for service by the bailiff. Only in exceptional circumstances is a witness excused from attending court but forcing a witness to give evidence on your behalf may elicit unexpected evidence which could jeopardise your case and it is not recommended. Expenses, including travel expenses and something for loss of time at work, must be paid to witnesses brought to court by court order. Your voluntary witnesses are also entitled to expenses and, if you win, all or part of the cost is usually the defendant's expense.

Expert witnesses
A claim for faulty goods or work may need the support of the evidence of an expert in the field who can give his opinion of the defective goods or work and the cost of making good. No special qualifications are necessary unless you are dealing with a specialised claim. You can ask the defendant to accept the expert's report to save the expense of bringing him to court. If he wants a separate report, you must allow him to inspect the goods or work.

Other evidence

All letters, estimates, contracts, agreements, bills, invoices, receipts, bank statements, cancelled cheques and notes of telephone calls should be brought to court, as you may wish to refer to them during the hearing. This material should, of course, have been referred to in correspondence between the parties prior to litigation but you may have to take the defendant through the documentation during cross-examination and some will usually have been given to him on discovery. If the dispute involves faulty goods they should, if possible, be brought to the hearing. If this is not possible, for instance where they cannot be moved, you can ask at the pre-trial review or at the trial for inspection by the court and arrangements will be made for an inspection in the presence of both parties.

The trial

Courts are open to the public and anyone can listen to your case and if you are litigating in person, it is useful to spend some of the waiting time at court watching other cases. You can bring someone with you to help you conduct your case, even if only to help handle your papers.

Giving evidence

Your evidence should be given slowly and — if possible —

212 Law for the Small Business

dispassionately. The judge or registrar will be taking a longhand note and will appreciate a collected approach. You can only give evidence of what you have seen and heard and cannot repeat something said to you by someone else — hearsay evidence — as the speaker must be there to be questioned. You can, however, say that you did or said something 'as a result of what a named person told you' and can quote your opponent and witnesses because they are in court to be questioned.

After giving evidence, witnesses may be questioned by the other side and by the court and they can afterwards qualify or explain anything said when they are re-examined by you or your solicitor, on your behalf.

Judgement

Usually judgement is given immediately after the evidence is concluded, although both parties may in addition sum up their cases. In a difficult case judgement may be reserved, when you will be sent notice of the date it will be given.

Costs and expenses

If you win the action, you can ask for an order that the defendant pay your costs in addition to the judgement debt. This will include the cost of bringing the proceedings, the court fees and witnesses' and other expenses which the court accepts were reasonably necessary in the preparation of the case.

Right of appeal

There may be a right of appeal against what you think is a wrong decision. The court office will let you know if there are any time limits within which it must be lodged and explain the procedure but you should take legal advice before you take action.

Defending an action

The summons or notice of originating application is served personally or by post, together with, where appropriate, the particulars of the plaintiff's claim, or his originating application and the form of admission, defence and counter-claim.

A default summons should be dealt with within 14 days of service, otherwise the plaintiff can apply for judgement without further notice. The return day for hearing on a fixed date summons is usually for a pre-trial review. You can simply appear on the date and admit or dispute the claim but if you dispute it, the registrar may order you to file a defence and make you responsible for any of the plaintiff's costs which are due to your delay. Specified information must be contained in the answer to an originating application for a new business tenancy — to be filed within 14 days of service — but in other proceedings commenced by originating application you are usually only required to attend court on the fixed date.

Transfer to another court

If you do not live or carry on business in the district of the court in which the summons issued, you can ask for the action to be transferred to your local court. You must have a possible defence and give reasons for the request and the registrar may transfer it if he thinks it would be cheaper and more convenient if it were transferred or it might cause you hardship to travel to court; if in doubt, he will hear both parties before making his decision.

Admission in a default action

Payment of the amount claimed plus the fixed costs on the summons ends the action and you are not liable for further costs unless the registrar otherwise directs.

Method of payment

Payment to court must be in cash or by banker's draft, giro draft, postal order or cheque made payable to Her Majesty's Paymaster General and crossed; cheques are only accepted if supported by a current and valid cheque card. Giro and bank drafts and postal orders are sent through the post at your risk but the Post Office will refund the money on a lost postal order on presentation of the counterfoil.

Payment by instalments

You can offer to pay by instalments, giving brief details of your income and expenses. If your offer is not accepted, a date is fixed for 'disposal' when the registrar will consider your proposals. You must attend court if you are asked to give evidence of your means, otherwise you can arrange for someone else to attend on your behalf.

The defence

A simple denial of liability is not sufficient and you must give valid reasons for defending the action. This can be done on the printed form but in a complicated case and if the plaintiff has set out his case in the form of particulars of claim it is usually easier to set out your case in a similar form to the particulars. The examples in Appendix 4 show some defences and how you must deal with each point raised by the plaintiff.

You may find that you cannot dispute some points raised by the plaintiff but do dispute others. For instance, in a contractual dispute, you might agree — and therefore admit in your defence — that the contract described was concluded and that it contained the terms specified but deny you were in breach of the term which the plaintiff alleges gives rise to his claim.

Counter-claim

A counter-claim is really a separate claim by the defendant against the plaintiff; it is usually but not necessarily connected with the plaintiff's action although the registrar may decide that it should be tried separately if it requires bringing in a great deal of additional evidence and would delay the action. An example of a permitted counter-claim is where you deny, or only partially admit, responsibility for a road accident and counter-claim that the plaintiff was fully or partly to blame.

Set-off

A claim for set-off relates to a money claim when you have already paid part of the sum claimed by the plaintiff or a debt for services rendered by you to the plaintiff which is directly related to the claim.

Third party proceedings

Your partial defence may be that you are only partly liable to the plaintiff and that a third party should be joined to the action. For instance, you may be a joint guarantor under the terms of a guarantee given on a business debt. To join your co-guarantor in the action, you must issue a 'third-party notice'. The form is obtainable at the county court office and the reason for issuing the notice must be stated. An example of the grounds for joining a co-guarantor is given in Appendix 4 and you will see that it must show the basis of the plaintiff's claim and the reason why the third party should be joined to the action.

In a fixed date action or a default action when a date has been fixed for hearing, you need the consent of the court before issuing the notice and proceedings must be filed with the court and served on the parties. If you need the court's consent, the action is stayed — that is, the main action stops short — until your application for consent is heard, when you will be given directions as to service and as to the further conduct of the case. If no consent is necessary, your third party is sent the notice as if it were an ordinary summons, together with a copy of the original summons and other pleadings and thereafter has the rights of a defendant to the action.

Setting aside judgement

The summons does not have to be served personally on the defendant so judgement could be obtained without your having received any notice of the proceedings. If so, you should immediately ask the court for details of the claim, producing the order for the judgement debt if you have received it. Judgement will be set aside if the proceedings were not properly served. If you did not defend the action or attend court after proper service, however, it will be set aside only if you have a reasonable defence and a reasonable explanation for the delay and you may have to pay the plaintiff's costs consequent on your failure to respond to the summons.

Applications during proceedings

Both parties can ask for certain orders permitting them to take action or directing their opponent to do, or to stop doing, something pending the full hearing. For instance, you may want specific documents which your opponent has not disclosed, or access to his premises, or even to stop him carrying on business altogether under the existing name (in a passing-off action) until the case is heard.

These applications are called 'interlocutory matters' and, in an urgent case, can be made 'ex parte' (that is, without notice to the other side, for instance, for an injunction) as well as 'inter parties' or 'on notice' (with notice to the other side).

They also include applications to postpone or adjourn the hearing, for leave to issue a third-party notice and to set aside judgement. Unless there is something in the Rules or under statute which calls for a special procedure, the notice must be in writing and served on your opponent and filed with the court. The court office will tell you if there are any time limits which apply in giving notice and for an urgent application you will usually have to swear an affidavit in support of the application.

Some interlocutory relief, such as the grant of an injunction to stop carrying on business, has very heavy financial repercussions, so the court may require an undertaking to cover damages accruing until the full hearing of the case. An injunction, like some other remedies, such as a declaration of the rights of the parties under a contract, cannot be granted in the county court unless it is linked to a (money) claim for damages.

STATUTORY REFERENCES

Companies Act 1981

County Courts Act 1959

The County Court (Forms) Rules 1982

The County Court Rules 1981

Hire Purchase Act 1965

Law Reform (Miscellaneous Provisions) Act 1934

Legal Aid Act 1974

Legal Aid (Assessment of Resources) Regulations 1960

13
Collecting Your Debts

Business may be ticking over efficiently and sales increasing but delay in payment can have a disastrous impact on profits, particularly when interest rates are high. Stringent and effective credit control, backed up by efficient debt collection with, if necessary, a speedy resort to law, can help prevent bad or extended debts.

Records

Customers looking for credit should supply the full name and address of their business as well as the names and addresses of the proprietors and you should ensure that the information on their documentation complies with the Companies Acts. A search at the Companies Registration Office will give you brief, if occasionally out-of-date, details of a limited company's shareholders, the last published accounts and the secured charges on the business. If the business is using a trading name, credit should, if possible, be given to a named individual. A credit reference is useful but is in no way a confirmation of creditworthiness and banks, like any other referee, can disclaim liability for statements about their customers. Your best insurance is a personal guarantee from the debtor and, if possible, a third party, if the amount is substantial.

Terms and conditions of payment

Formal quotations, estimates and acknowledgements of orders, invoices and delivery notes should set out the specific terms of payment, including the due date, with possibly an interest clause if payment is delayed. The terms can include a right to retain title to the goods until payment but this and any clause which restricts your liability for defective goods, should be professionally drawn.

Often terms and conditions are printed on the reverse of documents and are almost illegible. If you have to rely on them in court, you will have to show that they are clear, specific and have been understood. You should therefore ensure that they are pointed out to customers, and repair and replacement arrangements should also be agreed. A separate agreement signed by both parties is useful as, except in very special circumstances, a signed document is sufficient in law to show knowledge of, and agreement to, its contents.

Internal procedures

Both top and bottom limits should be put on credit. Retailers should insist on the production of a banker's card and the number should be written on the back of the cheque by the payee, not the customer. The card only guarantees payment by the bank to the face value of the card, usually £50, and the cheque must be linked to only one invoice up to the stated limit; the bank is entitled to repudiate liability altogether when the transaction exceeds the limit and payment is by more than one cheque, each within the limit.

A top limit should be put on a running account beyond which the account will not be extended until settlement of the outstanding balance and you should fix a cut-off point for the institution of legal proceedings. Small amounts should be dealt with promptly, preferably by cash or cheque (even if post-dated) on delivery, as the costs of legal collection can exceed the amount of the debt.

Weekly or monthly balances should be kept and when you fix a point at which you cease supplying goods and look for payment, letters of demand should be carefully worded, setting a time limit for payment. You should have a standard procedure culminating in a standard 'letter before (legal) action' which can be acted upon by taking proceedings personally or through your solicitor. Interest can be computed and included in an early letter but it is not necessary to supply a separate invoice, and even if you have no interest clause, further interest can be claimed in your writ or summons.

Taking legal action

Some large organisations threaten and take legal action for small amounts on the basis that a 50 per cent recovery rate is justified where internal procedures are efficient and legal costs minimal. It is worth asking your solicitor to draft the final letter before action on a fixed fee basis, even if you do not want him to conduct the case, as a solicitor's letter may bring results when a personal demand might be ignored. But he cannot work on a 'contingency fee' basis, collecting payment only if you win your case. The final letter is the debtor's last opportunity to offer payment and nothing further should be supplied, even for cash.

Do it yourself debt collection through the courts

The procedure for debt collection, through both the High Court and the county court, is very straightforward. If the debtor delivers no defence to your claim, you can enter judgement after 14 days of service of proceedings. If the debtor delivers a defence which is clearly untenable, you may still be able to obtain judgement quickly if you are taking action through the High Court or claiming at least £500 in the county court. You must then apply to the court, filing an affidavit setting out the facts and stating that, in your belief, notwithstanding the defence, there is no defence to your action. A date of hearing will be fixed and the application, a copy of the affidavit and any exhibits to which you have referred (such as supporting invoices) are filed with the court and sent to the defendant/debtor and he will only be allowed to dispute your claim if there is an arguable case which the court thinks should be heard. It is therefore worth going it alone if the claim is clear-cut but you should instruct a solicitor if the facts are in dispute or you are claiming a substantial sum.

Instructing your solicitor

Your solicitor only needs the facts and the documentation, including a full statement of account and relevant correspondence. You should also let him know if there is a potential defence, such as a complaint received from the debtor.

If you are continuously referring debts to a solicitor, you can have a standard referral procedure, with a regular monthly or quarterly summary of outstanding matters, to ensure nothing is missed and settlement by payment of amounts recovered, less his costs to date. A schedule of debts collected, interest covered, VAT and costs incurred and recovered is also useful. Direct payments from the debtor should be notified to your solicitor.

Collecting debts after litigation

Obtaining judgement may be only the first round in a continuing fight. Your credit references should have given you some idea as to the real value of the victory and you may already have obtained an order detaining or preserving the defendant's property before litigation. The order can cover related documentation and, if necessary, allow you access to the defendant's premises to search for it. If the action is related to a specific fund, the court can order it to be paid into court or order perishable property to be sold.

Execution of judgements and orders

Once you have your judgement or order, you can enlist the court's aid to enforce it and the process of enforcement is called execution. The same principles apply whether the defendant puts up an active fight or permits you passively to defeat him by legal process, whether the judgement debt is on your claim or counter-claim, you are a third or subsequent party to proceedings or only claiming for costs.

What is enforceable through the courts

Any judgement which requires payment of money or directs the transfer, delivery or recovery of possession of money or property, can be enforced and a High Court money judgement is enforceable through the county court, whatever the amount. You cannot enforce a statute-barred debt or a judgement on which a stay of execution has been obtained.

You can also enforce orders requiring someone to do, or stop doing, something after the time for compliance (if any) has expired. Some orders under the Companies Acts and awards made by an Industrial Tribunal (after registration) and the Restrictive Practices Court are also enforceable.

Judgements for debt and damages made by the High Court of Scotland and Northern Ireland can be registered in England and have the same effect as an English High Court judgement, the added cost of registration becoming part of the judgement debt. The enforcement of foreign judgements, including EEC judgements, should be left to your solicitor, as should enforcing a UK judgement abroad, where you need advice not only as to the procedural steps but also on the cost and efficacy of collection.

Enforcement of High Court judgements and orders

Generally you can apply directly to the court for execution and it is effective from the date of the order, usually the day it is made. In some cases, however, a writ of execution must be sealed and you must then first enter judgement, unless you choose another method of enforcement, for instance, a garnishee order. Some kinds of enforcement proceedings require the consent (leave) of the court and personal service on the defendant — now your judgement debtor. If you are seeking money payment or the delivery up or transfer of property under an unconditional order, you do not have to make a formal demand before enforcing judgement but it is safer to do so, as judgement may be set aside. When judgement is for payment by instalments, you cannot issue execution until an instalment has been missed.

Procedural steps before enforcing High Court judgements

In some High Court enforcement proceedings you must take a further procedural step before issuing execution which usually entails obtaining the consent of the court to issue a writ of execution. Leave is not required, however, for attachment of earnings or debts, for a charging order or for bankruptcy or winding up proceedings although they do not take effect automatically and you will have to make some application to the court as part of the process of enforcement. Sequestration and — usually — possession of premises require leave but you do not need leave before issuing execution against a garnishee under an order absolute.

Mandatory and prohibition orders

A judgement or order requiring someone to do something other than pay over money specifies a time within which it must be done. An injunction ordering the defendant to stop doing something takes effect immediately — which may mean within a reasonable time. Once the time limit has elapsed, you may be able to enforce the order by sequestration or committal (to prison) but usually the order must be served personally on the defendant.

Partnerships

Judgement against the firm is enforceable against partnership property and the property of a partner, provided he was party to the action. Leave of the court is required before enforcement action can be taken in the High Court by the firm against a partner and between firms which have partners in common; in the county court, except in a default action, you cannot proceed against a partner who does not file a defence to the action or appear at the pre-trial review.

Arbitration awards

Leave of the court is required before enforcement of an award and, once given, judgement is entered in the terms of the award.*

Judgement after discharge of a bankrupt

If a condition of discharge was the bankrupt's consent to judgement for the balance of provable debts outstanding, leave is required before execution and you must show that assets towards payment of the debt have been acquired.

Stay of execution

A stay — that is, the delay imposed by the court in enforcing judgement — is automatic during the first 14 days after entry of a county court money judgement unless the order states the contrary. An order for winding up prevents execution on judgements against a company.

In some cases you can apply to have the stay removed but the court has wide powers to stay execution in some cases, particularly for possession of mortgaged property. You should therefore try to obtain an order which states that you have 'liberty to apply for removal of the stay'. In an order for instalment payments, a default provision should be included to require payment of the whole sum if an instalment is missed.

Choosing your remedy

Before litigation you should not only consider the possibility of winning but the probability of collecting your winnings. The choice of the most fruitful method of enforcement is a tactical decision, made in the light of information about the financial

---

* This refers to disputes resolved under the Arbitration Act 1979, not to county court arbitration.

condition of the defendant, what assets are available, and where and how they are invested.

Information as to the debtor's assets may be obtainable through searches carried out at the Companies Registration Office, the Land Charges Registry, the register of bills of sale at the Central Office of the Royal Courts of Justice and the Register of Deeds and Arrangements. An enquiry agent may be useful and Hire Purchase Information Limited may have details of property purchased under a hire purchase agreement and one of the motoring associations may have details of the debtor's car bought on hire purchase. A search of registered land requires the consent of the registered proprietor but a creditor on a money judgement can apply to the court for an order authorising inspection.

You should also search the registers of bankruptcy notices, receiving orders and petitions at the Thomas More Building of the Royal Courts of Justice, as if your debtor is bankrupt or his company is in the process of being wound up, execution is ineffective. The county court has a register of unsatisfied judgements and you may decide enforcement is not worth while if there are substantial amounts already outstanding.

Discovery in aid of execution

Discovery in aid of execution is a procedure in the High Court and the county court by which a defendant to a money judgement — which includes a garnishee against whom you have obtained an order absolute — is summoned before an officer of the court for an oral examination as to his property and means. The debtor can be represented and, if he fails to attend and does not answer proper questions, he can be committed. A further examination can be ordered if you have additional information as to his means or if his circumstances change.

Remedies pursued through the sheriff

The High Court writs of fieri facias (fi fa), possession, delivery, assistance and the writs issued in their support are sealed at the Central Office in London or the local district registry. They then go to the county sheriff or London deputy of the appropriate bailiwick when the period for compliance or for an application for setting aside or varying judgement has elapsed. The terms of the writ and your (lawful) instructions must be followed and the sheriff must check where and what goods are available. The goods can then be seized and sold, unless the debtor is in arrears with rent or taxes.

A landlord distraining for rent (that is, taking goods in default of payment of arrears of rent) has the first right to the goods; then comes the collector of taxes, who has a claim for back tax to a maximum of one year, plus his costs. Otherwise, the sheriff can levy execution on the goods on the premises, unless the landlord has already distrained. If the sheriff moves first, the landlord's rights are usually barred, unless he is levying under a High Court judgement, when he can claim up to a year's rent.

Bankruptcy and winding up

The right to seizure may also be deferred if notice is received of a bankruptcy petition or of a petition or meeting for winding up the debtor company. Your rights are postponed and you rank as an unsecured creditor if, before execution is completed, a receiving order is made against the debtor or the debtor company receives a winding up order or passes a resolution for winding up.

Walking possession

When execution is on stock in trade, all the stock is usually seized under a 'walking possession' agreement but a retailer is usually permitted to continue trading. However, seizure should only be over an appropriate amount of stock and this should be replenished when the officer of the court ('the man in possession') visits or the proceeds of sale are handed to the sheriff.

Completion of execution against goods

Execution against goods is completed by seizure and sale or by payment. The sheriff must then withdraw from possession. You should let him know if you receive payment on account but if you direct him to withdraw while negotiating and you are not paid in full, you must re-issue the writ and may lose priority.

Third party claims

If a third party claims the goods or the money pending or during execution, the sheriff will notify you and application can be made to the court to sort out the claims of the parties.

High Court writs of execution

The writs of fieri facias (fi fa), possession, delivery and assistance cover money, property and costs.

Fi fa enforces a High Court money judgement for the recovery, or payment, of money, except for money already paid into court. If the property is in more than one county, you can issue concurrent writs. The debtor's goods can be seized. Goods, for this purpose, include cash, cheques, leasehold premises, tenant's fixtures and some growing crops but among the exclusions are real estate and the debtor's clothes, bedding and tools of his trade to a limit of £50. In the case of land, the writ should be registered under the Land Charges Act or, if the title is unregistered, a caution should be entered at the Land Registry to protect your rights against a purchaser. The sheriff can enter the premises to seize the goods, turning a handle, lifting a latch or pushing a door (gently) but he may not enter forcibly.* In default of payment the goods can be sold, usually by auction, unless the court authorises a private sale.

A writ of possession orders the debtor to give up possession of land. You need leave of the court before issuing enforcement proceedings and you cannot obtain possession against a business tenant who has delivered the statutory notice asking for a new tenancy. You do not need leave if you are proceeding under some kinds of mortgage or if you are acting against squatters. A fi fa claim can be included in the writ or you can apply for a separate writ for damages and costs. You or your representative must attend on execution to identify the premises and in this case the sheriff can enter forcibly.

A writ of delivery enforces a judgement for delivery of goods and can also give the debtor the option of paying their assessed value. You can, however, issue a separate writ of fi fa for the value plus damages, or otherwise enforce a payment clause but the debtor always has the option of handing over the goods.

A writ of specific delivery is appropriate if goods have intrinsic value. You can apply for delivery within a specific period enforced by order for committal but you will need leave, unless the judgement gives the alternative of paying the assessed value.

A writ of assistance is useful if you cannot reach the debtor or the goods are locked up. The writ can, in addition, empower

---

* *Southam* v *Smout* (1964) 1 QB 308

the sheriff to restore goods to your possession or to make good your possession of land.

County court warrants

Enforcement by warrant in the county court is for the most part analogous with enforcement proceedings by writ of execution in the High Court. Statistically most enforcement proceedings are taken in the county court and the vast majority for amounts of less than £100, most of which are for a straightforward warrant of execution on the debtor's goods. However, High Court enforcement through the sheriff is often more fruitful than county court enforcement through the bailiff, as the bailiff's powers of entry are more restricted.

Warrants in the county court include warrants of execution, possession, delivery and attachment.

A warrant of execution is enforceable against goods and if the goods are in several districts, you can issue concurrent warrants in the appropriate courts. Separate warrants can issue for the debt and the costs, when costs are to be taxed and payment is not made before the costs become due. On default on an instalment order, execution can issue for the whole or part of the judgement debt. Costs of the warrant are allowable against the debtor unless the court orders otherwise and there is a fee for keeping possession but not for 'walking possession'. You should inform the court if you come to an arrangement with the debtor or withdraw from possession but the warrant will then be suspended and if it is re-issued your priority dates from the time of re-issue.

A warrant of possession enforces a judgement or order for recovery or delivery of possession of land and can be issued on the day after the defendant has been ordered to vacate. If no date is specified, it can be issued 14 days after judgement and an order against squatters can be issued any time after the order is made.

In some circumstances the court can suspend an order for possession for arrears of rent or under a mortgage. The order can be re-suspended and if the debtor pays the arrears plus costs the warrant must be cancelled.

Delivery of goods is enforced by warrant of delivery and can also be enforced by attachment. If the value is assessed, you can execute for the value, and the judgement can also give the option to retain the goods pending payment.

Injunctions and orders are enforced by warrant of attachment. Enforcement against a company is against the directors or other officers but leave of the court is required before issue of the warrant.

Other High Court and county court remedies

If your debtor has disobeyed an existing order of the High Court, you may be able to apply for sequestration. This orders the sequestrators to sequestrate the property until the contemnor has purged his contempt or — in simpler terms — your nominated commissioners (one of whom is usually a sheriff's officer) to segregate and hold your debtor's property until he obeys the order. You need the leave of the court and, if land is involved, the writ should be registered under the Land Charges Act or a caution entered in the Land Register. There is no authority to sell land, although the court may order the sale of goods or authorise payment of money in the hands of the sequestrators.

Committal to prison

A further alternative when an existing court order is ignored is committal to prison. In the case of a money judgement, however, the debtor must have, or have had since judgement, means to pay the debt and the debtor is usually committed only if the order has been persistently and wilfully disobeyed.

Charging order on land

A charging order is used to enforce a money judgement and the order puts a charge on the land to secure payment. The order must refer to a specific sum and can only be used if the debtor owns the land. The charge should be registered at the Land Registry or under the Land Charges Act but, if you are enforcing against a company, it does not need to be registered under the Companies Acts.

Charging order on securities

On a judgement for a fixed amount a charging order on securities can be made on a limited company's shares and debentures and can include dividends and interest payable. You can also obtain a 'stop notice' or injunction, which effectively invalidates dealings.

Charging the interest of a partner

A charging order against a partner charges his interest in partnership property, plus his share of profits, with payment of the judgement debt plus interest. By the same or a subsequent order, you can appoint a receiver of the share of profits and any other money coming to him from the firm and obtain an order for accounts and enquiries and other orders and directions. The partner or his partners can redeem or purchase the charge if a sale is ordered.

Attachment of earnings

Attachment of earnings is available in the county court whatever the amount of the debt but it can, of course, only be used against someone in employment. You need an identifiable employer — which means anyone who pays 'earnings' to the debtor, as a principal. 'Earnings' include wages or salary, fees, bonus, commission, overtime pay and any other payment under a contract of service and pensions, annuities for past services, periodical payments and compensation for loss of office. The debtor must give the court details of his employment and of his current and anticipated earnings, resources and needs. The employer may also be required to file a detailed statement of the debtor's earnings.

The order directs the employer to make periodical deductions from pay and pay them over to the court; the penalty for non-compliance is a fine. The debtor must notify the court of termination of employment and the order then lapses but revives when directed to a new employer.

The county court has an index of debtors satisfying judgements under attachment orders and you can search the index on written request.

Attachment of debts

The High Court garnishee order and county court summons attach to a debt and order the garnishee — the debtor — to appear and show cause why he should not pay the debt. The county court limit does not apply and proceedings are taken in the court in which you could have sued the debtor.

Any unconditional debt can be garnished provided it accrues solely to the debtor and even if it is not immediately payable. Current bank accounts can also be attached and, on conditions, deposit accounts. A third party claimant can be ordered to attend the hearing to put forward his claim but, unless attachment is completed by payment before the date of a receiving order or before notice of a petition or of an available act of bankruptcy, you will lose your priority. Similar provisions apply when you are proceeding against a debtor company.

Equitable execution

If you cannot use any other method of enforcement, the court may allow the appointment of a receiver. The order covers the proceeds of sale of land, or a share of rents and property held jointly or subject to a lien or trust. It can include an injunction ancillary or incidental to the appointment if there is a possibility that the debtor might dispose of the property. In the High Court the receiver must usually give security to account for what he receives and to ensure that he deals with the property as the court directs. On smaller amounts or in the county court, he may have to give undertakings to the court or you may be made personally responsible for his actions.

The appointment stops the debtor from receiving the proceeds of sale or dealing with the property or money to the prejudice of creditor's rights. It does not, however, give you the rights of a secured creditor, so if it is made against land, it should be registered as a charge or a caution should be entered on the Land Register.

Bankruptcy and winding up

Non-compliance with a judgement or order is only one of a number of possible acts of bankruptcy or grounds for a petition for winding up a company. A business may, of course, be unable to pay its debts where no judgement has been obtained but in practice, service of a bankruptcy notice or a demand under the Companies Act often leads to payment of the amount due.

STATUTORY REFERENCES

Administration of Justice Acts 1956, 1965, 1970 and 1973

Arbitration Act 1979

Attachment of Earnings Act 1971

Bankruptcy Act 1914

Companies Act 1948

County Courts Act 1959

Debtors Act 1869, 1878

Judicature Act 1925

Land Charges Act 1972

Land Registration Act 1925

Law Reform (Miscellaneous Provisions) Act 1934

Partnership Act 1890

Taxes Management Act 1970

County Court Rules 1981

Rules of the Supreme Court 1982

14
Bankruptcy and Liquidation

Profit patterns fluctuate and projections are not always accurate. Before embarking on the sea of private enterprise, you should give some thought to what happens if you run aground.

Sole trader

Your financial commitment is complete. If things go wrong you will only have yourself to blame, and your creditors will take the same view. You are personally accountable for all business debts and obligations and if you cannot meet your commitments, the creditors are entitled to seize not only your stock in trade and equipment used in the business, but also your personal possessions.

All you can retain are the tools of your trade and necessary clothing and bedding for yourself and your family. You may also be entitled to retain property held on trust for someone else and rights and monies payable under third party insurance policies. Property held by your spouse is safe, unless transferred by you with an intent to defraud creditors or within three months of the presentation of the petition in bankruptcy. A gift of property to your spouse is only safe if made more than two years before the bankruptcy but, if it was made within 10 years of the bankruptcy, you must be able to show that you were solvent at the time of the transfer.

Bankruptcy procedure

The procedure not only inquires into the reasons for your insolvency and secures fair and equal distribution of available distribution of available property to your creditors but also frees you from your debts enabling you to make a fresh start when you are discharged by the court.

If the business is insolvent — that is, you cannot meet debts as and when they fall due — either you or one of your creditors, who is owed at least £200, outstanding for more than three months after delivery of a formal demand or who is owed a debt under a court order, can petition the court to take over administration of your affairs and the distribution of your estate (your liquidated assets).

You cannot be put into bankruptcy unless you have committed an 'act of bankruptcy', which means you have given presumptive evidence of insolvency, although you may in fact not be insolvent. Acts of bankruptcy are set out in the 1914 Bankruptcy Act and include transferring your property to a trustee or transferring anything to a creditor which gives him preference over other creditors.

The bankruptcy petition asks the court for a receiving order to be made in respect of your estate and the grant protects you and your estate from legal proceedings but puts control in the hands of the Official Receiver, an official of the court. You must then submit to a preliminary examination by the Official Receiver and prepare a full statement of your affairs, listing your assets and liabilities, which is sent to your creditors. Generally there will be a public examination and you will have to disclose how you managed your affairs and describe the circumstances and causes of the bankruptcy.

The public examination is followed by a first meeting of creditors when they can question you on your statement and a scheme of arrangement or composition, under which you undertake to pay them off proportionately, may be agreed. You are not, however, legally bankrupt until the court makes an order of adjudication, which vests your property in the Official Receiver or when the receiver is appointed your trustee in bankruptcy.

If necessary all your property will be realised and, subject to certain priorities among the creditors, dividends of a proportionate part of their claim will be paid to the creditors whose proofs for debts have been admitted by the trustee. 'Proof' simply means giving sufficient and acceptable evidence of the debt's existence.

Finally you will be given an order of discharge, which frees you of all provable debts, with some exceptions, and from any legal disabilities which attach to a bankrupt.

However, even if you are insolvent you can reach agreement with your creditors by arranging your affairs for their benefit. Administration of the arrangement is entrusted to a trustee and the arrangement must benefit three or more creditors.

Alternatively, you can agree a composition — a contract by which they agree to accept a proportion of their claim in complete discharge of their debts — with your creditors.

A petition in bankruptcy and the receiving order can be registered against your property and are binding on the purchaser of a property with unregistered title who is not aware of an act of bankruptcy. If the property has registered title, the petition and order can be registered and prevent registration of later dealings with the land, but both methods stop dealings other than through the Official Receiver or trustee in bankruptcy. Deeds of arrangements with creditors can also be registered.

Partnerships

Partners also have a complete financial commitment to the business and a partnership is more easily and quickly killed off than a company. Like marriage, the tie is broken by death or dissolution; unlike marriage, it ends if one partner becomes bankrupt and you can simply end it all by mutual agreement.

Dissolution by mutual agreement

In theory dissolution by mutual agreement presupposes an ease of disentangling the partnerhsip relationship that, in practice, seldom exists. A partner wishing to withdraw may assert his entitlement to the return of his capital contribution at a time when the business has no available cash and cannot raise sufficient by way of a loan to pay him off. In addition, the business may have suffered a net capital loss, so that his entitlement to the return of his capital is proportionately reduced.

Your Partnership Agreement should therefore contain specific provisions as to dissolution, possibly a period of notice before withdrawal and certainly the taking of an account upon which the splitting up of partnership assets can be based.

Automatic dissolution

The partnership is automatically dissolved if your business activities become illegal — if, for example, you run a pub and the licence is withdrawn — and in any of the following situations the partnership is ended unless your Agreement specifically states that it shall continue:

1. On completion of the undertaking, or at the end of the

fixed period for which the partnership was formed.

2. On the bankruptcy or death of a partner and, if you did not specify a fixed period for the duration of the partnership, when a partner gives notice. No period of notice is necessary unless it is specified and, once given, it can only be withdrawn with the consent of all the partners. The resignation takes effect immediately, or on the date specified in the notice. (To avoid a sale, your Agreement should state that a retiring or deceased partner's share shall pass to the continuing partners at a price to be ascertained by reference to the last balance sheet.)

3. If a partner's share is charged by the court for a personal debt (although the other partners can redeem or purchase it and continue in business).

Other contingencies leading to dissolution can, of course, also be put in your Agreement.

Dissolution by request through law or arbitration

You can apply to the High Court for dissolution if you are carrying on business at a loss or because a partner cannot, or will not, keep to your Partnership Agreement and the business is suffering as a result. You can also make an application on the basis that it would be 'just and equitable' for the court to make the order. The court, however, takes its own (objective) view, and its opinion of what is just and equitable may not be the same as yours.

A creditor of the partnership can also ask the court for dissolution if he is claiming a debt outstanding under a court order or he is owed at least £200, which has been outstanding for more than three months after he has delivered a formal demand.

If you have an arbitration clause in your Agreement, you do not have to make application to the court and the arbitrator can dissolve the partnership on the same grounds as the court. You can, however, still apply to the court in some circumstances and you may have to do so for advice on the liquidation and administration of the assets.

If you are defrauded by a potential partner during pre-partnership negotiations, the Partnership Agreement is rescinded. The partnership is dissolved and you are entitled to damages for deceit and a lien (or right of retention for the price) on surplus partnership assets equal to what you paid for your share, plus interest and costs. This is in addition to your general indemnity against partnership debts and reimbursement for anything already paid towards its liabilities, plus interest and your ordinary rights at dissolution.

Unless a fixed term partnership is prematurely terminated by death, the court or the arbitrator can also order repayment of part of any premium that has been paid.

Dissolution

Your responsibilities and liabilities continue until the partnership is wound up, but, if the dissolution is caused by the bankruptcy or death of a partner, only the solvent or surviving partners remain committed.

Land belonging to the partnership can be sold by the surviving partners of a deceased partner, but, if it was originally purchased before 1926, the deceased partner's personal representatives should join in the conveyance.

If a partner has become bankrupt, his trustee in bankruptcy must be a party to the conveyance.

Surviving partners can mortgage partnership property to secure a partnership debt and the mortgage has priority over the deceased partner's estate's lien on the surplus assets for his share in the business. Since this means that the mortgage must be paid off before his estate can claim his share, you will have to come to some arrangement with the personal representatives before you mortgage the property.

When you apply to the court for dissolution, you must ask for the appointment of a receiver or a receiver and manager. Normally an immediate decree of dissolution is made, with a direction to take the 'usual accounts and inquiries' — that is, those necessary to complete the winding up of the business. The court usually only takes control away from the partners and appoints a receiver if it is considering winding up the business. If one of two partners is insolvent, the other is usually appointed manager, without salary, for a fixed period. He is personally liable in any transactions he completes, although he is entitled to an indemnity out of partnership assets, in priority to the other creditors.

The receiver's job is to take in the income and pay necessary outgoings but a manager carries on the business. Not surprisingly, the appointment of a receiver practically brings business to a standstill. If you want to continue in business, it is best to appoint a receiver and manager. He can appoint a partner as sub-manager, with obvious advantages to the carrying on of the business but the other partners must consent to his appointment, unless the business is a personal one.

On dissolution one partner can sue in the partnership's name to get in the assets, which are distributed between the partners after all the liabilities have been met. Often an important (although intangible) asset is the partnership's goodwill (its connections and reputation). This must be sold on dissolution, unless you have agreed otherwise or it is a very personal connection which is assumed to stay with the partner. If it is sold the partners can still continue in the same field of business but they cannot solicit new business with the partnership's existing connections. If you agree not to sell the goodwill because it is so closely related to the partners that it is unsaleable, each partner can continue to canvass old customers in the partnership's name.

If all the property is sold and the partnership is dissolved completely, a general account must be made up. It is usually based on the last balance sheet, which is taken down to the date of dissolution and kept open until winding up is completed. If no balance sheets have been prepared, accounts must be taken from the beginning of the partnership. The account is taken according to the partnership's usual practice. This may be important when a retiring partner claims the value of his share as at the date of his retirement and there is an insufficient allowance for bad debts, so make sure your bad debt allowance is realistic.

If you continue in business while paying for the share of a retiring or deceased partner, that agreement is substituted for the final account and distribution of assets. You should, however, agree a formal settlement of accounts to protect yourself against possible later claims.

If you are an executor of a deceased partner it is best to apply to the court for the appointment of a manager, or even a receiver, to avoid any allegation of conflict of interest. An option to purchase the share, exercised in strict accordance with its terms, limits your liability to what is contained in the option agreement.

Unless you have agreed otherwise, losses, including capital losses, are paid first out of profits, then out of capital and then by the partners. Your contribution to losses is in the same proportion as your entitlement to a share of the profits.

Assets, including capital contributions to make up losses or deficiencies, must first be applied to pay off the preferential debts of the business, then other debts and liabilities, then proportionately to pay off any advances made by the partners. Any balance remaining is divided between the partners.

Insolvency

The law and procedure applying to sole traders also applies to the partnership and the partners and variations where only the business or one of the partners is bankrupt are dealt with below. A bankruptcy petition filed against the partnership, however, is effective against each partner as well as the business, but the adjudication order is made against the partners individually, not in the name of the partnership. When the petition is filed in the partnership name, registration against title to property is also effective against each partner.

Creditors of the business who hold a security belonging to one of the partners can prove in the partnership's bankruptcy without valuing their security. The same applies if the security for a bankrupt partner's personal debt belongs to the partnership.

Partners are entitled to repayment of advances to the business before the costs of winding up are paid. Anything left is divided between the partners in proportion to their initial capital contribution. If the assets do not cover the costs, you must pay them in the same proportion as you bear general losses.

If not only the partnership but also one or all of your partners are insolvent the situation is more complicated. There are then two claims: first, those between the creditors of the partnership and the creditors of the partner where all the partners are bankrupt; and, second, those between the creditors of the bankrupt partner and the solvent co-partners.

Generally, if all the partners are bankrupt, partnership creditors can claim against the partnership assets and the balance remaining unpaid can be claimed from the partners after they have paid their personal creditors. If any surplus remains from the partnership assets after the creditors are paid, it is divided between the partners according to their entitlement to shares of profits in the Partnership Agreement.

There are, however, several exceptions to this general rule:

1. If there are no joint partnership assets, the creditors can

claim equally against each partner's property.

2. If any partner has defrauded an outsider and the partnership is liable, the partners involved in the fraud can be made personally liable, but only if a claim is not made against partnership assets.

3. Claims can be made against both the partnership and the partners where a debt is based on a contract with the partnership and the individual partners.

4. A creditor of the partnership who has put a partner into bankruptcy can usually still claim as a creditor with the other creditors of the bankrupt partner.

5. The partnership's trustee in bankruptcy can prove for the value of partnership assets dishonestly obtained by a partner against that partner's assets and, if the partnership was involved in the fraud, the trustee can claim against partnership assets.

6. If a partner is in business on his own account and is a trade debtor or creditor of the partnership, the respective trustees in bankruptcy can prove as if the two businesses were entirely unconnected.

If you stand solvently alone among your partners' insolvent estates, the situation again changes. You can carry on business by keeping up to date with current liabilities but you cannot claim against partnership assets, or against the assets of your partners, in competition with the partnership creditors (who are, of course, your own creditors). If all the partnership creditors have been paid in full or your co-partners are insolvent and you are obviously going to be the only person responsible for business debts, you can prove against your co-partner's separate estates.

However, there are again exceptions to the general rule and you can prove against your co-partners' estates if you are claiming because a bankrupt partner has defrauded you. You can also prove if you have been discharged from liability for partnership debts and have become a creditor of the partnership, but this situation rarely arises.

A lender to the partnership can be in the same position as a partner. If the loan was made in return for a share of the profits, or the interest on the loan fluctuates depending on the profits, he cannot prove against the partnership or the partners' estates until all partnership liabilities are met. He should therefore obtain a collateral and separate security for the loan. He will still be paid off after lenders secured on partnership assets, but dissolution and the fact that there are no profits will not affect his security.

Limited partnership

Death and bankruptcy of the limited partner do not lead to dissolution of a limited partnership and the limited partner has no liability to the partnership beyond his original capital contribution, unless he has lost the protection of limited liability by becoming involved in the management of the business.

The general partners wind up the business if the partnership is dissolved, unless the court directs otherwise. The procedure is more complicated than in an unlimited partnership but only the general partners are liable for partnership debts and obligations. If they are bankrupt, partnership debts are provable in their own bankruptcies, even if the partnership itself is not made bankrupt. The only permitted involvement of the limited partner, however, comes at the end of the partnership relationship, when he can participate in any meetings called as a result of the dissolution.

Companies

A company takes longer to die and the wound can be self-inflicted or ordered by the court. The company can decide to stop trading and go into voluntary liquidation, or the court can supervise winding up or order a compulsory liquidation.

Winding up

The wheels can be set in motion by the company, a shareholder, a creditor, the Official Receiver or the Department of Trade. A shareholder (or contributory) can, however, only ask the court for a winding up if he has held shares since incorporation or for at least six out of the 18 months before the liquidation, unless he holds them because of the death of a former shareholder who fulfilled the requirement.

Compulsory liquidation

The company can be put into compulsory liquidation by the court in several situations:

1. On a shareholder's petition, when the number of shareholders has fallen below the permitted number of two.
2. If the company has not started trading within a year of incorporation, or has suspended trading for 12 months.
3. If the company cannot pay its debts (which is proved if a petitioning creditor has been owed at least £200 for more than three months after a formal demand or he has not received payment of a debt under a court order).
4. If the company passes a special resolution requesting compulsory liquidation.
5. If the court considers it would be 'just and equitable' to wind up the company. (This includes a fraud on minority shareholders.)
6. If the Department of Trade makes the request after an investigation into the company's affairs made on the application of at least 200 or one-tenth of the shareholders.
7. On a petition under the Companies Act 1981 presented by a director or seller of shares to the company for capital, on the basis that it cannot pay its debts or that it is just and equitable for the company to be wound up.

The court can also order a compulsory liquidation if the company is not pursuing the business activities set out in the Memorandum or there is mismanagement or deadlock on the board. It will not, however, make the order unless it is satisfied that voluntary or supervised liquidation is not in the interest of the creditors or shareholders.

If the court orders compulsory liquidation the Official Receiver becomes provisional liquidator, but, if you think the liquidator should have a special knowledge of the business, you can apply to the court for a special manager instead.

The liquidator has full responsibility for the company's affairs and his appointment is published in the *London Gazette*. All employees are dismissed and the directors' powers cease. If a receiver is appointed by the debenture-holders, however, the directors may still be able to act for the company, provided the debenture-holders' interests are not prejudiced.*

A director and the company secretary must, within 14 days

---

*Newhart Developments Ltd v Co-operative Commercial Bank Ltd (1978) 2 WLR 636

of the order, submit a statement of affairs to the Official Receiver giving details of the company's assets and liabilities and a list of creditors. The Official Receiver reports to the court and to meetings of creditors and shareholders. They decide whether a liquidator should be appointed to run the business and whether he should run it with or without the help of a committee of creditors and shareholders.

The order to dissolve the company is not made until its affairs are completely wound up. It can be revoked within two years, if, for example, more assets have been discovered which are available for distribution.

Voluntary liquidation

The company puts itself into voluntary liquidation by passing a resolution at a general meeting of the shareholders. Seven days' notice must now be given of the meeting at which the resolution voluntarily to wind up is to be proposed and a notice of a creditors' meeting to be held on the same day or the day after the shareholders' meeting must be sent on the same date.

The shareholders' decision to wind up can be made by ordinary resolution if the company was formed for a specific undertaking or fixed period, otherwise a special resolution must be passed. An extraordinary resolution is necessary if the company is insolvent.

If a majority of the directors file a declaration of solvency at least five weeks before the resolution, the liquidation is a members' (or shareholders') voluntary liquidation. The declaration must set out the company's assets and liabilities and state that the company will be able to pay its debts within at most 12 months. A copy is filed with the registrar before the general meeting which appoints the liquidator.

If no declaration is made or the liquidator disagrees with its conclusion, it becomes a creditors' voluntary liquidation and separate meetings of creditors and shareholders must be called. Both meetings nominate a liquidator but the creditors' choice takes precedence. The creditors can also appoint a committee of inspection, on which the shareholders are represented, to supervise the liquidator.

The advantage of a voluntary liquidation is that, although the company's employees are dismissed if the company is insolvent, the directors' powers continue. This is only the case, however, if their powers are confirmed in a general meeting of shareholders, and approved by the liquidator in a shareholders' liquidation or approved by the committee of inspection in a creditors' liquidation.

The directors prefer a members' liquidation, because the liquidator is not appointed or supervised by the creditors. In the latter case, if the declaration of solvency is inaccurate or fraudulent, the directors can be fined or imprisoned. If the company's debts are not paid off or provided for in full by the end of the specified period, they must show that they had reasonable grounds for making the declaration.

A voluntary liquidation can be made into a compulsory liquidation in the same way as a compulsory liquidation is initiated and the court may instead decide on an order for supervision. Even in a voluntary liquidation, the creditors can apply to the court to settle any major problems. In any liquidation the court has wide powers if called in to investigate the company and in some circumstances — if, for example, fraud is suspected — it can hold an investigation in open court.

Fines and penalties

If the company has been trading with an intent to defraud creditors or anyone else, or incurring debts without a reasonable prospect of repayment, anyone involved may be prosecuted and disqualified from participating directly or indirectly in the management of a company for a maximum of 15 years. Conviction for an indictable offence (which, broadly, means a serious offence triable by jury in the Crown Court) related to the promotion, formation, management or liquidation of a company or with the receivership or management of its property and for persistent failure to file accounts and records, can also lead to disqualification for the same period. Disqualification for only five years, however, is the penalty for someone who has been a director of two companies, both of which have gone into insolvent liquidation during a five-year period and whose actions have unfitted him for management.

Fraudulent trading also brings a personal liability for all the company's debts. Payment may be in discharge of particular debts or go to the liquidator as part of the general assets available for distribution. If management has appropriated the assets, the court can order restoration or repayment of an equivalent amount plus interest.

When the company has bought or redeemed shares with its

own capital within a year of the winding up and the total assets and contributions do not meet its debts and liabilities, including the cost and expenses of winding up, you may be jointly and severally liable with the shareholder who sold the shares for making up the deficiency to the extent of the payment. Anyone contributing to the company's assets can apply to court for an order directing the payment.

Any transaction entered into by the company within six months of liquidation which gives a creditor an advantage over the other creditors and the shareholders will be set aside as a fraudulent preference. The debt can still be proved in the liquidation but any security held is void and the creditor will rank as an unsecured creditor when it comes to distribution of the assets. This is, however, a complicated area and expert advice should be sought by both the creditor and the company if such an allegation is made.

Liquidation

The liquidator collects the assets, pays the expenses of the liquidation and the company's debts and liabilities and distributes any balance remaining between the shareholders. The creditors have a claim on the assets as soon as the liquidation starts and the court can stop legal action being taken against the company at any time to safeguard the creditors' interests.

Assets and shares cannot be sold in a compulsory liquidation or one supervised by the court without the court's consent. No one can sue the company without the permission of the court and the court makes the dissolution order. In a voluntary liquidation, shares cannot be sold or the status of the shareholders altered without the consent of the liquidator. If the court decides to intervene it may appoint an additional liquidator.

Shareholders are only liable for any balance remaining unpaid on their shares, unless it is an unlimited liability company, in which case they are liable for all the company's debts. Shareholders also have unlimited liability for the debts of a limited liability company wound up within three years of re-registration, if it was previously registered with unlimited liability.

If the company has carried on trading for more than six months after the number of shareholders has been reduced, to their knowledge, to less than the permitted minimum of two, the sole shareholder is personally liable for all the company's debts incurred during that period. If the company has altered a director's limited liability to unlimited by special resolution, he is responsible for all the company's debts, unless the shareholders owe something on their shares. Apart from current shareholders, anyone who has held shares within 12 months of the date of the winding up (a contributory) can also be called upon if his shares were not fully paid up and the liquidation does not produce sufficient money to meet the company's obligations.

Available assets must be applied against the company's liability. All debts, present or future, certain or contingent (including claims for damages) are provable, unless the company is insolvent, when some debts which are not settled in amount cannot be proved.

A secured creditor has a choice: he can realise his security and prove for the balance; value it and prove for the balance after deduction of the valuation; or surrender it and prove for the whole amount.

Preferential debts

Preferential debts take the first slice of the assets, after the costs of the liquidation. They are paid proportionately and consist of 12 months' rates and taxes, national insurance contributions, accrued holiday pay and four months' wages and salary due to employees (including directors but excluding the managing director), to a maximum of £1040. Most amounts payable to employees under the employment legislation are also preferential debts but the employer can apply for these to be paid partly or wholly from the Redundancy Fund. Employees can prove for any balance still outstanding together with the ordinary (unsecured) creditors.

Secured creditors under fixed charges have the next claim on the assets. They have priority over the claims of debenture-holders under floating charges and can be paid out of the proceeds of any assets which are subject to a floating charge. In special circumstances debenture-holders secured by a floating charge may have a prior claim to creditors secured by a fixed charge.

The remaining assets are divided between the unsecured creditors. Any surplus is divided among shareholders, in accordance with their rights under the Memorandum and Articles of Association.

When the liquidator has finished winding up the company, he

must call a final meeting of creditors and shareholders and submit accounts and reports. The company is officially dissolved three months from that date if a report of the meeting is published in the *London Gazette* and the report and accounts are filed with the registrar.

STATUTORY REFERENCES

Bankruptcy Act 1914	Insolvency Act 1976
Bankruptcy Rules 1952	Law of Property Act 1925
Companies Acts 1948 to 1981	Limited Partnership Act 1907
Deeds of Arrangement Act 1914	Partnership Act 1890
Employment Protection (Consolidation) Act 1978	

15
Takeovers and Mergers

Business is good, profits are high and management is efficient: these are the right reasons to look about you and see if you can find a larger stage on which to display your talents.

The sole trader and expansion

Having got so far alone, you may feel the need for financial support or additional expertise. The route to expansion can be by way of taking on investors, partners or launching yourself, with or without new associates, as a limited company, a decision based on the factors discussed in earlier chapters, in the context of the nature of your business activity and tax and other financial considerations.

Partnership mergers

Expanding your partnership is also a personal arrangement and most partnerships, with the exception of some professional partnerships, are limited by law to 20 partners.

If you take in new partners or amalgamate with another firm you must change your partnership name. Registration or re-registration is effected through the Registrar of Companies.

You should also amend your Partnership Agreement to reflect your extended liability for your new partners. The tax aspect of the merger is also a factor, as the business is taxed as if you had stopped trading and started again as soon as you take on new partners, unless you elect for continuance.

Incoming partners should confirm the partnership's mandate with the bank and they should be joined as co-sureties to the partners' bank guarantee. You should also consider whether their liability should be extended to cover contracts with the partnership's existing creditors — by replacing the original contracts which include them — and if they should share in existing book debts.

Full disclosure must be made of the partnership's financial

position to your new partners and your books and accounts must be open for inspection.

Company takeovers

Company amalgamations are closely regulated under the Companies Acts. Public companies must, in addition, comply with the Stock Exchange regulations and the requirements of the Department of Trade, the City code, the Takeover Panel and the Monopolies and Mergers Commission. Nevertheless, whatever the existing methods of supervision, the unacceptable face of capitalism has found its most prominent features in the City and, while more safeguards are promised to protect the rights of minority shareholders, they will mainly affect public companies.

The mechanics are the same for both private and public companies, however, and any arrangement you are contemplating should only be entered into after you have taken proper legal and financial advice.

Share for share and part cash offers

You can make an outright bid for a company's undertaking in return for shares, which are distributed to the selling company's shareholders in accordance with their rights. A company has no implied power to sell its business, but power to sell the undertaking and the assets is usually included in the objects clause of the Memorandum. This kind of takeover involves no cash, but you can also make an offer extended generally to all the selling company's shareholders for cash and only partly for your own shares. The offer is usually conditional on the acceptance of at least three-quarters of the shareholders, holding not less than 90 per cent of the shares. This is because you are usually bound, and entitled, to acquire the remaining 10 per cent on the same terms, unless the court orders otherwise on a shareholder's application.

The provisions relating to mergers and reconstructions which involve a new issue of shares at a premium after 4 February 1981 are set out at page 45.

As a private company you can confirm your bid to a particular class of shares, for example, the ordinary but not the preference shares or only sufficient of the voting shares to gain control, provided your company already holds nine-tenths of that class of share. If acceptances exceed the offer, you must take shares, *pro rata*, from all the accepting shareholders.

The straightforward exchange of shares between the buying and the selling company, when you are not looking for further capital, is usually done by sending an offer to the selling company's directors proposing an issue of a specified number of your shares to their shareholders. A majority resolution of the selling company's shareholders is sufficient agreement, the selling company's shares are cancelled, except for any your company is to hold, and the selling company's shareholders receive your shares in payment for their's. They can be paid in cash instead of in your company's shares if the reserve created by the cancellation of their shares is capitalised. This is then applied to pay up further shares in the selling company, which are issued to you in place of the cancelled shares. The court, the creditors and the shareholders must then, however, all approve the arrangement. The result is the same as a share for share takeover completed by compulsory acquisition (described in the preceding paragraph) but the majority necessary to approve the takeover is smaller.

You can also acquire a controlling interest in another company by simply making an offer to shareholders above the listed price of the shares, but below what you consider to be the underlying value of the assets. The two companies remain legally (and actually) distinct, although it is in most respects a merger.

Taking over while raising capital

If you are seeking more capital, you must proceed by way of a winding up of the selling company, putting pressure on existing shareholders to make a further contribution of capital. A new company is formed and the selling company, in return for shares in the new company, sells its undertaking through its liquidator, with each shareholder of the selling company receiving shares in compensation. The selling company's shareholders can, however, be given partly paid-up shares in return for the fully paid-up shares they previously held and must either undertake a fresh liability for calls or give up their rights to the new shares.

This method requires the selling company to pass a resolution to put itself into voluntary liquidation and a special resolution authorises the liquidator to transfer all, or part, of its business to your company, in return for cash or cash and shares (either fully or partly paid-up) which become the assets in their liquidation. If their directors make the statutory declaration of solvency, it will be a members' voluntary liquidation; otherwise the liquidator needs the approval of the court or of the committee of inspection in what will be the creditors' voluntary liquidation.

Consent by the shareholders or creditors may be general or confined to a specific sale which is part of a general scheme of reconstruction. The resolution authorising the sale should be put to the meeting at the same time as the winding up resolution, so that, if the first is not carried, the winding up need go no further. The company may otherwise find itself in liquidation without any arrangement for selling the business.

The selling company's creditors and shareholders are paid in the liquidation without any variation of their rights and they can petition for the winding up to be conducted or supervised by the court. If they do so, however, the consent of the court must be given to the transaction. Any shareholder can stop the merger if he is dissatisfied with the terms of the offer by giving written notice to the liquidator within seven days of the resolution.

A large number of dissenting shareholders can make life difficult as they are entitled to the value of their shares, based not on market value but on a proportionate part of the value of the company's assets, to be determined, if necessary, by arbitration. They cannot, however, be deprived of their right to dissent, either directly or indirectly.

Varying shareholders' and creditors' rights

If the rights of shareholders or creditors are to be varied the selling company must pass an extraordinary resolution, which needs the approval of three-quarters of the shareholders or creditors (in number and in value). Objections must be made within 21 days to the court, which can amend, vary, confirm or overrule the scheme.

A selling company trying to come to an arrangement with its own shareholders or creditors to sell out must make application to the court. When there is no question of the company's being wound up completely, the shareholders or creditors apply to the court to call meetings of the groups affected. If the company is already in liquidation, the liquidator must make the application. Notice of the meetings is sent to shareholders and creditors, with a statement explaining the effect of the arrangement and setting out the interests of directors. If the debenture-holders are affected, the trustees named in the debentures must also set out their interests.

The arrangement must be approved by a majority at the meetings, representing three-quarters of the shares or debts affected. It must also be approved by the court, which confirms that the proper procedure has been carried out and that minority shareholders have been fairly treated. The court also gives directions for carrying out the scheme. These include ordering a transfer of all or part of the selling company's assets and liabilities to your company (excluding any service contracts), the disposal of the shares and dissolution of the selling company without proceeding any further with the liquidation.

The court can order compensation for dissenting shareholders under any of these schemes of arrangement.

Directors' compensation for loss of office

Payment or compensation for loss of office must be disclosed and approved by the shareholders of the selling company, otherwise the directors are liable to prosecution and anything received belongs to the shareholders, even if payment was made within one year before, or two years after, the offer.

If the directors receive more for their shares than other shareholders, the excess is considered to be compensation, unless the bid is only for *de facto* control by the acquisition of less than one-third of the voting shares. The directors are not then accountable to the shareholders, although they may be liable to the company, which ultimately benefits the buying company rather than the shareholders of the selling company.

A genuine payment for premature determination of the directors' service contracts or as a pension for past services is allowed and, if the directors are to continue to work for your company, they can keep anything they receive as a result of the merger. Directors are then, in effect, rewarded for persuading their shareholders to sell out, but only if they do not benefit themselves at the expense of the shareholders, they company or the creditors.

STATUTORY REFERENCES

Companies Acts 1948 to 1980	Insolvency Act 1976
Companies Bill 1981	Partnership Act 1890
Income and Corporation Taxes Act 1970 (as amended)	Registration of Business Names Act 1916

Useful Addresses

Advisory, Conciliation and Arbitration Service (ACAS)

Head Office:
Cleland House
Page Street
London SW1P 4ND

London and South East Region:
Clifton House
83-117 Euston Road
London NW1 2RB

South West Region:
16 Park Place
Clifton
Bristol BS8 1JP

Midlands Region:
Alpha Tower
Suffolk Street
Queensway
Birmingham B1 1TZ

Nottingham sub-office:
72 Houndsgate
Nottingham NG1 6BA

Northern Region:
Westgate House
Westgate Road
Newcastle-upon-Tyne NE1 1TJ

Yorkshire and Humberside Region:
Commerce House
St Albans Place
Leeds LS2 8HH

North West Region:
Boulton House
17-21 Chorlton Street
Manchester M1 3HY

Merseyside sub-office:
2nd Floor
27 Leece Street
Liverpool L1 2TS

Wales:
Phase 1
Ty Glas Road
Llanishen
Cardiff CF4 5PH

Association of British Chambers of Commerce
6 Dean Farrar Street
London SW1

Association of Independent Businesses
Europe House
World Trade Centre
London E1 9AA

British Institute of Management
Management House
Parker Street
London WC2B 5PT

British Overseas Trade Board (BOTB)
1 Victoria Street
London SW1H 0ET

Central Office of Information
Hercules Road
London SE1

Community of St Helens Trust
PO Box 36
St Helens
Merseyside

Confederation of British Industry (CBI)
Centre Point
New Oxford Street
London WC1

Co-operatives Production Federation
30 Wandsworth Bridge Road
London SW6

Council for Small Industries in Rural Areas (CoSIRA)
Queen's House
141 Castle Street
Salisbury
Wiltshire SP1 3TP

Department of Employment
8 St James's Square
London SW1Y 4JB

Department of Industry: Small Firms Division

Head Office:
Abell House
John Islip Street
London SW1P 4LN

London and South Eastern Region:
6 Bulstrode Street
London W1

South Western Region:
Colston Centre
Colston Avenue
Bristol BS1 4UB

Northern Region:
22 Newgate Shopping Centre
Newcastle upon Tyne NE1 5RH

North West Region:
320-5 Royal Exchange
Manchester M2 7AH

Merseyside sub-office:
1 Old Hall Street
Liverpool L3 9HJ

Yorkshire and Humberside Region:
1 Park Row
City Square
Leeds LS1 5NR

East Midlands Region:
48-50 Maid Marian Way
Nottingham NG1 6GF

West Midlands Region:
Ladywood House
Stephenson Street
Birmingham B2 4DT

Eastern Region:
24 Brooklands Avenue
Cambridge CB2 2BU

Wales:
16 St David's House
Wood Street
Cardiff CF1 1ER

Scotland:
57 Bothwell Street
Glasgow G2 6TU

Northern Ireland:
Department of Commerce
Chichester House
64 Chichester Street
Belfast BT1 4JX

Department of Trade
Export Division
Export House
50 Ludgate Hill
London EC4M 7HU

Development Board for Rural Wales
Ladywell House
Newtown
Powys SY16 1JB

Enterprise North
Durham University Business School
Mill Hill Lane
Durham DH1 3HB

Equipment Leasing Association
18 Upper Grosvenor Street
London W1X 9PB

Executive Stand-by Ltd
310 Chester Road
Hartford
Northwich CW8 2AB

Export Credits Guarantee Department
Information Section
Aldermanbury House
London EC2 2EL

Finance Houses Association
18 Upper Grosvenor Street
London W1

Forum of Private Business
Ruskin Rooms
Drury Lane
Knutsford
Cheshire

Foundation for Alternatives
10 Grenfell Road
Beaconsfield
Bucks

Highlands and Islands Development Board
Bridge House
Bank Street
Inverness IV1 1QR

Hire Purchase Information Ltd
Greencoat House
Francis Street
London SW1

Industrial and Commercial Finance Corporation (ICFC)
91 Waterloo Road
London SE1 8XP

Industrial Common Ownership Movement
31 Hare Street
Woolwich
London SE18 6JN

Institute of Directors
116 Pall Mall
London SW1

Institute of Small Businesses
1 Whitehall Place
London SW1A 2HD

London Chamber of Commerce
69 Cannon Street
London EC4 5AB
Business Registry offers advice,
certificate of registration, and
search facilities.

London Enterprise Agency (LENTA)
69 Cannon Street
London EC4 5AB

Market Entry Guarantee Scheme
MEGS Unit
Export House
50 Ludgate Hill
London EC4M 7HU

National Federation of Self-employed and Small Businesses
32 St Anne's Road West
Lytham St Anne's
Lancashire
and
45 Russell Square
London WC1

National Research Development Corporation
Kingsgate House
66-74 Victoria Street
London SW1 6SL

National Union of Small Shopkeepers
Western Buildings
Theatre Square
Nottingham NG1 6LH

Northern Ireland Development Agency
Maryfield
100 Belfast Road
Hollywood
Co Down

Northern Ireland Local Enterprise Development Unit
17 The Diamond
Londonderry

Office of Fair Trading
Field House
Breams Buildings
London EC4

Register of Deeds and Arrangements
2-14 Bunhill Row
London EC1

Registrar of Companies
Companies House
Crown Way
Maindy
Cardiff CF4

Scottish Co-Operatives Development Committee
100 Morrison Street
Glasgow G5 8LP

Scottish Development Agency
Small Businesses Division
102 Telford Road
Edinburgh EH4 2NP

Trade Marks Registry
Patent Office
25 Southampton Buildings
London WC2A 1AY

Union of Independent Companies
71 Fleet Street
London EC4

Welsh Development Agency
Small Business Unit
Treforest Industrial Estate
Pontypridd
Mid-Glamorgan CF37 5UT

Further Reading

Free publications

The Small Firms Service publishes a series of booklets on all aspects of running a small business. These are available from their information centres (see Appendix 1 for addresses).

Starting in Business and *Employer's Guide to PAYE*, published by the Inland Revenue and available from all local branches

The Rights of Employees: A Guide for Employers and *Small Firms Employment Subsidy (and Amendment)*, published by the Department of Employment. Available from job centres, employment and unemployment benefit offices

The Hotel and Catering Industrial Training Board publishes a series of information sheets and booklets on aspects of the hotel and catering industry. These are available from Information Department, PO Box 18, Central Square, Wembley, Middlesex HA9 7AP

The Pitfalls of Managing a Small Business and How to Avoid Them, Dun & Bradstreet Ltd, PO Box 17, 26-32 Clifton Street, London EC2 2LY

Home study kits

The Small Business Kit, published by the National Extension College, Cambridge. Provides comprehensive advice and information on how to assess business ideas, raise money, find premises, sell products/services and control finances. Available from the National Extension College, 18 Brooklands Avenue, Cambridge CB2 2HN

Self-help training packs relating to the hotel and catering industry may be obtained from the Hotel and Catering Industrial Training Board, PO Box 18, Central Square, Wembley, Middlesex HA9 7AP

Reference books

The Complete Guide to Managing Your Business, published by Eaglemoss: London and updated bi-monthly. Available from Managing Your Business Ltd, 87 Elystan Street, London SW3 (Price £44.50)

Croner's Reference Book for the Self-employed and Smaller Businesses and *Croner's Reference Book for Employers*, published by Croner Publications Ltd: New Malden and updated monthly. Available from Croner, 46-50 Coombe Road, New Malden, Surrey KT3 4QL (Price £22.10 and £27.60 respectively)

Financial Management Handbook, published by Kluwer Publishing Ltd:
London and updated bi-annually. Available from Kluwer, 1 Harlequin
Avenue, Great West Road, Brentford, Middlesex TW8 9EW (Price from
£57.50)

Know Your Business (1978), published by British Institute of
Management: London. Available from Publications Sales, BIM,
Management House, Parker Street, London WC2B 5PT (Price £6.40 for
members; £8.00 for non-members)

Money for Business and *Money for Export* (1978), published by Bank of
England. Available from Bulletin Group, Economic Intelligence
Department, Bank of England, London EC2R 8AH (Price free of charge
and £2 respectively)

Sources of Finance for Small Businesses. Available from Small Business
Guardian, 119 Farringdon Road, London EC1R 3ER

Update: Employment Law. Journal of employment case law, edited by
Richard Clayton and published by Stewart Williams International Ltd,
Carlton Chambers, Station Road, Bromley, Kent

Other books

Bates, J (1971) *The Financing of Small Business* Sweet and Maxwell:
 London
Chandler, P A (1981) *An A-Z of Employment and Safety Law* Kogan
 Page: London
Clarke, P (1972) *Small Businesses: How They Survive and Succeed* David
 and Charles: Newton Abbot
Douglas, P (1974) *Run Your Own Business* Dent: London
Edwards, R (1979) *Running Your Own Business* Ward Lock: London
Elliot, A (1976) *Your Business: The Right Way to Run It* Elliot Right Way
 Books: London
Fiber, A (1975) *Be Your Own Boss* Management Books: London
Golzen, G (1982) *Working for Yourself: The Daily Telegraph Guide to
 Self-employment* Kogan Page: London
Hazel, A C and Reid, A S (1978) *Managing the Survival of Smaller
 Companies* Business Books: London
Jenner, P (1979) *Your Business Problems Solved* David and Charles:
 Newton Abbot
Knightley, M *Bees Business Guides* Malcolm Stewart Books: London
Mason, M (1980) *Creating Your Own Work* Gresham Books: London
Peters, M A (1978) *Basic Business Management* Jordans: Bristol
Price, A St J (1979) *Buying a Shop* Kogan Page: London
Ryan, J M (1979) *It Can Be Done* Scope Books: Newbury
Sproxton, A (1979) *Starting and Running A Small Business* United
 Writers: St Ives
Stanworth, J and Curran, J (1973) *Management Motivation in the Smaller
 Business* Gower Press: London
Taylor, A (1975) *Starting Your Own Business* Moore: Elland, Yorkshire
Townshend, R (1971) *Up the Organisation* Coronet Books: London
Wood, E G (1972) *Bigger Profits for the Smaller Firm* Business Books:
 London

Appendix 3
Glossary

acceptance (of a bill of exchange): when the drawer of a bill writes his signature across it, with or without the word 'accepted', thereby undertaking to pay the bill when due.

accommodation bill: bill of exchange signed by the drawer, acceptor or endorser, without receiving value, in order to lend his name and credit-standing to some other person.

act of God: accident or incident which happens independently of human intervention (ie as a result of natural causes, such as storm or earthquake) and against which no foresight or prudence can provide.

annual accounts: financial records of a business prepared by your accountant for the Inland Revenue.

arbitration: determination of disputes by the decision of one or more persons called arbitrators, often in commercial matters.

arrangement (deed of): arrangement by which someone unable to pay his debts can pay his creditors privately, by agreement or in the bankruptcy court, in discharge of his liabilities by partial payment or composition.

Articles of Association: rules establishing how a company must be run, drawn up when the company is formed and representing a contract between the company and its shareholders. Standard Articles are now used by most new small companies.

asset: property owned by a business or an individual; liquid assets are those which can very quickly be realised into cash.

attachment (of debts): used in the High Court when a judgement for the payment of money has been obtained against a debtor to whom money is owing with another person (the garnishee); the person who has obtained the judgement can obtain an order that all debts owing or accruing from that person (the garnishee) to the judgement debtor shall be 'attached' to satisfy the judgement debt. The order then binds the debt in the hands of the garnishee. An order nisi is first made, which is served on the garnishee and if he does not pay, the order is made absolute and execution can be issued.

audit: process of checking the accuracy of financial records by an independent third party (auditor), who states whether in his view they are accurate.

balance sheet: record of business assets and liabilities at a specific date, usually the end of the financial year.

banker's draft: draft or order for payment of money drawn by a bank on its head office.

bankruptcy: when an individual, sole trader or partnership cannot pay its bills or is declared insolvent; its property is thereafter administered for the benefit of the proven creditors.

beneficiary: person for whose benefit property is held by a trustee or executor.

bill of exchange: negotiable instrument containing an unconditional order to pay at a future date.

bill of lading: document signed and delivered by the master of a ship to the shipper when goods are shipped.

bond: contract under seal to pay a sum of money or a sealed writing acknowledging a present or future debt.

business name: name under which a business is carried on which must, in some circumstances, be registered.

capital: total resources of an individual or company including property, cash, equipment and goods.

carrier: someone who receives goods in order to carry them from one place to another for hire, either under a special contract or as a 'common carrier'.

casual: employee who does not work for you regularly. He is normally paid net but can be paid gross by prior arrangement with the Inland Revenue. Complete and accurate records of payments to casual employees, including their names and addresses, must be kept.

charge by way of legal mortgage: charge by deed expressed to be by way of legal mortgage, the effect of which is the same as a mortgage.

charging order: an order that any stock of fund standing in the name of, or the property of, a judgement debtor, shall be charged with the payment of a judgement debt in favour of the judgement creditor. It can be enforced by action for sale after six months.

chattel: any property except freehold land, including leaseholds.

cheque: bill of exchange drawn on a bank, payable on demand.

common carrier: someone who undertakes for hire to transport goods from place to place. He is an insurer of goods entrusted to him and therefore liable for their loss or injury in the absence of a special agreement or statutory exemption, unless the loss or injury is caused by act of God or the Queen's enemies.

composition: arrangement between two or more people for the payment by one to the others of money in satisfaction of an obligation to pay a sum differing in amount or mode of payment. For example, a debtor can propose a composition (or a scheme of arrangement) to his creditors in satisfaction of his liabilities as an alternative to bankruptcy.

contract: agreement enforceable in law. An essential feature is an exchange of promises, express or implied, by the parties to do or forbear from doing certain specified acts.

copyright: exclusive right to print or otherwise copy original artistic, literary and musical works and to prevent all others from so doing.

counterclaim: claim by a defendant who alleges he has a claim or is entitled to any relief or remedy against a plaintiff in an action brought against him by the plaintiff.

credit sale agreement: agreement for the sale of goods under which the purchase price is payable by instalments.

damages: compensation or indemnity for loss suffered which can be claimed in law.

debenture: legal document specifying the terms of a loan.

deed: a writing or instrument on paper or parchment, signed, sealed and delivered, to prove and testify the parties' agreement.

distress (for rent): the act of taking goods out of the possession of a tenant to compel payment of rent.

dividend: share of profits paid to shareholders by a company.

employee: person working for you on a regular or casual basis, usually on the basis of an agreed contract of employment.

endorsement: a writing on the back of an instrument, consisting of the signature of the person to whom the instrument is payable, which transfers bills of exchange, bills of lading, cheques, etc.

execution (of judgement): act of completing or carrying into effect a judgement of the court, effected by writs of execution, orders and notices, compelling the defendant to do or pay what has been adjudged; (of deeds): by signing, sealing and delivering them to the parties as their own acts and deeds, in the presence of witnesses.

finance company: company lending larger amounts for longer periods than is usually the practice of the clearing banks.

financial year: period covered by your profit and loss account, ie the business's accounting year.

fixed cost: expense or overhead which does not vary with the level of production.

fraudulent preference: payment, conveyance or other advantage given by a debtor to a creditor within three months before his bankruptcy, with a view to giving the creditor a preference over other creditors.

guarantee: a promise to answer for the debt or default of someone else.

guarantor: someone who binds himself by a guarantee or who promises to answer for another's debt or liability; a surety.

garnishee: a debtor in whose hands a debt has been attached (that is, the debtor has been warned only to pay his debt to a person who has obtained judgement against the debtor's own creditor).

garnishee order: the order served on a garnishee attaching a debt in his hands.

hire purchase agreement: agreement under which the buyer can buy the goods or under which the property in the goods will or may pass to the buyer.

holder in due course: someone who takes a bill of exchange for value, complete and regular on its face, before it is overdue and without notice of dishonour or of defect in title.

indemnity: collateral contract or security undertaking to make good a loss that someone has suffered as a result of the act or default of another.

injunction: order or decree of the court by which a party to an action is required to do, or refrain from doing, a particular thing.

insolvency: situation in which a person or business is not able to pay his (or its) bills. Insolvency does not constitute bankruptcy, as the insolvent may have assets which can eventually be realised to pay his bills while the bankrupt is deemed not to have such assets.

joint and several obligation: obligation entered into by two or more persons, jointly and severally, so that each is liable severally and all liable jointly; a creditor can sue one or more severally (separately) or all jointly.

judgement creditor: someone in whose favour a judgement (of the court) for a sum of money is given against a judgement debtor.

judgement debtor: someone against whom judgement is given (by the court) for a sum of money and for which his property is liable to be taken in execution at the instance of the judgement creditor.

liability: debt or obligation.

licence: authority to do something which would otherwise be inoperative, wrongful or illegal; right to enter and occupy land, which gives no interest in the land and is revocable with or without notice.

lien: right to hold the property of another as security for the performance of an obligation.

liquidation: legal process of closing down a bankrupt company and selling its assets to pay debts.

liquidity: extent of the cash assets of a company or its ability to realise other assets in cash.

loan capital: finance lent to a company for a specified period at a fixed rate of interest, normally secured, which gives no 'share' in the profits or control in the running of the company.

misrepresentation: statement or conduct which conveys a false or wrong impression.

national insurance: state-run scheme under which all employees, employers and self-employed people pay a percentage of their earnings to the government in return for payments during periods of unemployment and/or sickness.

negligence: action or omission actionable by someone suffering damage in consequence of the defendant's breach of duty to take care to refrain from injuring him.

negotiable instrument: instrument, the transfer of which to a transferee, who takes in good faith and for value, passes a good title free from any defect or equities affecting the title of the transferor. The most important kinds of negotiable instruments are cheques, promissory notes and bills of exchange.

overhead: cost which does not vary according to the level of production.

partnership: business association in which the partners are formally and personally responsible for the debts they incur.

passing off: pretence by one person that his goods are those of another.

patent: exclusive privilege, protected by law, to make or sell an invention or new product for a specified period.

PAYE: pay as you earn; method of collecting tax from employees at source. Employers must debit the necessary amount of income tax and national insurance from their employees' salaries and forward it to the Inland Revenue.

power of attorney: formal instrument by which one person empowers another to represent him or act in his stead for certain purposes, usually in the form of a deed poll and attested by two witnesses.

premium: sum payable in advance of, or over and above, the consideration for an agreement.

prima facie (case): a case in which there is some evidence to support the charge or allegation made and which will stand unless displaced.

profit and loss account: record of profits before tax, showing the tax due and profits after tax. Depending on the business, it shows other factors affecting profits, including allowances and amounts brought forward from the previous financial year and to be carried forward to the next financial year.

promissory note: unconditional written promise to pay.

proof (of a debt): establishing the existence of a debt owing from a bankrupt's estate.

receiver: person appointed by the court to receive the rents and profits of real estate or get in personal property affected by proceedings, in lieu of the person then having the control of the property in order to protect it until the rights of the parties have been ascertained.

receiving order: order made by the court on presentation of a bankruptcy petition for the protection of the debtor's estate making the Official Receiver the interim receiver of the property of the debtor and restraining all legal proceedings against the bankrupt in respect of provable debts.

registered office: the office of the company which is registered with the Registrar of Companies.

seal: formal expression of consent to a written instrument by attaching to it wax or some other material impressed with a device; a deed must also be signed or marked, as sealing alone is not sufficient.

Schedule D (cases 1 and 2): the Inland Revenue Schedule which defines the tax allowances available to self-employed persons.

Schedule E: Inland Revenue Schedule which defines the tax allowances available to employed persons, including directors.

secured creditor: person whose debt is guaranteed, for example, by a charge on business premises as collateral in a transaction.

self-employed person: someone working on his own in a freelance capacity or in his own business, under the control, direction, or supervison of an employer, who supplies his own equipment and organises his own work as to hours, etc.

slander of title: false and malicious statement about a person, his property or his business, inflicting harm on his personal reputation, his title to property or his business or generally on his material interests, including slander of goods, which is a false and malicious depreciation of the quality of the plaintiff's goods.

specific performance (decree of): order of the court when damages would not be adequate compensation for the breach of an agreement, compelling the defendant to perform what he has agreed to do.

statute: Act of Parliament.

statute-barred (debt): where the right of action is barred because the time limit for taking action has elapsed.

stay of execution: the suspension of the operation of a judgement or order.

stay of proceedings: the suspension of proceedings in an action, which may be temporary, until something further is done or ordered to be done.

stock: finished goods, goods in course of production and raw materials in store.

strict liability: automatic liability, independent of fault on the part of a defendant.

subpoena: writ issued in proceedings requiring the person to whom it is directed to be present at a specified time and place and for a specified purpose under a penalty.

summons: document issued from the office of the court calling upon the person to whom it is directed to attend before a judge or officer of the court.

surety: person who binds himself, usually by deed, to satisfy the obligation of another person, if the latter fails to do so; guarantor.

tender: offer, for instance by a debtor to a creditor, of the exact amount of the debt or by a trader as a first step in the course of pre-contractual negotiations.

tort: civil wrong consisting of an act or omission injuring someone, intentionally or not, not being the breach of a duty arising out of a contract or personal relationship.

trustee in bankruptcy: person in whom the property of a bankrupt is vested in trust for the creditors whose duty is to discover, realise and distribute it among the creditors.

undue preference: where an insolvent debtor, within the three months preceding his bankruptcy, pays a creditor in full.

unenforceable: that which cannot be proceeded for, or sued upon, in the courts.

vicarious liability: where someone is responsible for the acts for another (for instance in negligence) even though he did not himself commit the act.

waiver: renouncing or disclaiming a benefit. A person is said to waive an injury or tort or breach of contract when he abandons a legal remedy available to him.

warranty: guarantee or assurance in an agreement with reference to goods which are the subject of a contract of sale but collateral (contingent) to the main purpose of the contract.

winding up: operation of putting an end to the carrying on of a business, by realising the assets and discharging the liabilities, settling the accounts or contributions between the contributories and dividing the surplus assets (if any) between them.

working capital: the amount of business capital which is tied up in normal day-to-day business activities.

writ: document in the Queen's name and under the seal of the Crown, a court or officer of the Crown, commanding the person to whom it is addressed to do or forbear from doing some act.

Draft County Court Pleadings

These draft pleadings are of course only examples but they may be helpful as showing the way in which your case should be presented to your opponent and to the court.

CLAIM IN CONTRACT FOR THE SALE OF GOODS

IN THE . . . .

COUNTY COURT

No of Plaint

BETWEEN   JOHN SMITH   Plaintiff

and

ALFRED BROWN   Defendant

PARTICULARS OF CLAIM

1. On the 1st day of June 1982, the Plaintiff entered into a written contract with the Defendant whereby the Defendant agreed to sell to the Plaintiff a motor vehicle registration No XYZ 323 for £2200.

2. It was an express term of the said contract that the said motor vehicle was in good order and in a roadworthy condition.

3. Further or alternatively it was an implied term of the said contract that the said motor vehicle was of merchantable quality and fit for the purpose for which it was supplied.

4. In breach of the said term the Defendant delivered the said motor car to the Plaintiff with the following defects:
   a. List defects

5. By reason of the said breach the Plaintiff has suffered loss.

PARTICULARS

a. Cost of repairing the said defects	£233
b. Cost of hiring replacement motor vehicle during the period of repair	30
AND the Plaintiff claims	£263

Dated this   day of   1982

To the Registrar   (signature of Litigant in person)
and to the Defendant

DEFENCE TO THE ABOVE CLAIM

IN THE . . . .
COUNTY COURT
No of Plaint

BETWEEN   JOHN SMITH   Plaintiff

and

ALFRED BROWN   Defendant

1. The Defendant admits that on the said date he agreed to sell the said motor vehicle to the Plaintiff at the said price.

2. The Defendant denies paragraph 2 of the Particulars of Claim.

3. The Plaintiff was given and took the opportunity thoroughly to examine the said motor vehicle and the said price was agreed and calculated in accordance with the defects disclosed by such examination.

4. Save as aforesaid the Defendant denies each and every allegation in the Particulars of Claim.

Dated this   day of   1982

To the Registrar   (signature of Litigant in person)
and to the Plaintiff

CLAIM IN CONTRACT FOR THE SALE OF GOODS

IN THE. . . . .

COUNTY COURT

No of Plaint

BETWEEN   JOHN SMITH   Plaintiff

and

ALFRED BROWN   Defendant

1. The Plaintiff is and was at all material times a dealer in second-hand furniture.

2. By an oral agreement made between the Plaintiff and the Defendant on or about the 10th day of March 1982, the Defendant agreed to purchase from the Plaintiff a mahogany bookcase for £800, payment to be made by the Defendant to the Plaintiff within seven days of delivery.

3. On the 15th day of March 1982 the Plaintiff delivered the said bookcase to the Defendant but the Defendant refused and still refuses to pay for the said bookcase.

AND the Plaintiff claims £800

Dated this   day of   1982

To the Registrar   (signature of Litigant in person)

and to the Defendant

DEFENCE TO ABOVE CLAIM

IN THE . . . .
COUNTY COURT
No of Plaint

BETWEEN   JOHN SMITH   Plaintiff

and

ALFRED BROWN   Defendant

DEFENCE

1. The Defendant admits paragraph 1 and 2 of the Particulars of Claim.

2. The Defendant denies that the Plaintiff delivered the said bookcase on the said date or at all.

3. In the premises the Defendant denies that he is liable to the Plaintiff in the amount claimed or at all.

Dated this   day of   1982

To the Registrar   (signature of Litigant in person)
and to the Plaintiff

CLAIM IN NEGLIGENCE

IN THE . . . .
COUNTY COURT
No of Plaint

BETWEEN   JOHN SMITH   Plaintiff

and

ALFRED BROWN   Defendant

1. On the 1st day of August 1982 the Plaintiff was lawfully driving his motor van registration No ABC 314X along the Kings Road, Greenbury in the County of Shropshire when the said motor vehicle was struck in the side by a motor vehicle registration No VBF 789M driven by the Defendant.

2. The said collision was caused by the negligence of the Defendant.

PARTICULARS OF NEGLIGENCE

The Defendant was negligent in that he
a. drove too fast
b. failed to keep any or any proper look out
c. failed to keep a safe distance away from the said motor van
d. failed so to steer, slow down or stop the said motor vehicle so as to avoid the said collision.

3. By reason of the matters aforesaid the Plaintiff suffered injury and has suffered loss and damage.

PARTICULARS OF INJURY

List

PARTICULARS OF SPECIAL DAMAGE

List for instance cost of repairs, repairs/replacement to clothing, loss of use of van, loss of earnings etc.

                     (total)   £X

AND the Plaintiff claims damages (ie general damages (see pp 204-5) in addition to above)

Dated this   day of   1982

To the Registrar   (signature of Litigant in person)
and to the Defendant

DEFENCE AND COUNTER-CLAIM TO ABOVE CLAIM

IN THE . . . .

COUNTY COURT

No of Plaint

BETWEEN   JOHN SMITH   Plaintiff

and

ALFRED BROWN   Defendant

1. The Defendant admits that the said collision happened at the said place and on the said date.
2. The Defendant denies that the said collision was caused as alleged in the Particulars of Claim or otherwise by his negligence.
3. Further or alternatively, the said collision was caused wholly or in part by the negligence of the Plaintiff.

PARTICULARS OF NEGLIGENCE

The Plaintiff was negligent in that he
a. drove too fast
b. drove on the wrong side of the road, etc according to the facts.

4. No admission is made as to the alleged injury, loss and damage. (NB The Defendant cannot deny injury, loss or damage but an 'admission' is too open-ended as it would mean that the Plaintiff not have to prove the injury, etc.)

COUNTERCLAIM

5. The said collision was caused wholly or in part by the negligence of the Plaintiff.

PARTICULARS OF NEGLIGENCE

The particulars under paragraph 3 hereof are repeated.

6. By reason of the Plaintiff's said negligence the Defendant suffered loss and damage.

PARTICULARS OF SPECIAL DAMAGE

details

AND the Defendant counterclaims   £X

Dated this   day of   1982

To the Registrar   (signature of Litigant in person)
and to the Plaintiff

THIRD PARTY NOTICE

IN THE. . . . .

COUNTY COURT

No of Plaint

BETWEEN　　　　　JOHN SMITH　　Plaintiff

　　　　　　　　　and

　　　　　　　　　ALFRED BROWN　Defendant

The form must be completed to ask for a contribution or indemnity from the third party or to show that the Defendant is entitled to claim something against the third party which is directly related to the subject matter of the proceedings or that an issue which affects all three parties (Plaintiff, Defendant and proposed additional party) must be heard before the action can proceed. The Defendant must, however, show a reason for joining someone else to the action. The example given at pp 214-15 above involved a Defendant guarantor to a debt, who wants to join his co-guarantor to the action brought against him by the Plaintiff.

　The grounds of the Defendant's claim therefore being:

　'This action has been brought by the Plaintiff against the Defendant. In it the Plaintiff claims against the Defendant the sum of £1000 the amount of a guarantee given by the Defendant and by you to the Plaintiff for moneys owing to the Plaintiff by one John Smith, as appears from the summons herein a copy whereof is served herewith. The Defendant claims against you contribution to the extent of one half of the Plaintiff's claim on the ground that you are jointly and severally liable with the Defendant to the Plaintiff on the said guarantee.'

The form then sets out the third party's rights in the action and it must be completed in the same way as the other court forms with the date and signature of the litigant in person.

Dated this　　　　　day of　　　　1982

To the Registrar　　　　　　　　(signature of Litigant in person)
and to the Defendant

Index

add: address

ACAS, *see* Advisory, Conciliation and Arbitration Service
ACT (advance corporation tax), 21, 99
accident
  Book, 117
  insurance, 111, 117
  prevention, 77, 80-1, 82-3
  responsibility, 81-2, 83, 84-5
accounting, 18, 51-2
  exemptions, 16, 19
  inflation, 52-3
  periods, 63, 90-1
accounts, 28, 63-6
  abridged, 65
  annual, 63, 256
  profit and loss, 62, 63, 65-6
Administration of Justice Acts, 230
advance corporation tax (ACT), 21, 99
advertising, misleading, 153
Advisory, Conciliation and Arbitration Service (ACAS), 121, 122, 124
  adds, 251
  codes of practice, 129, 136
Animal Boarding Establishments Act *1963*, 86
applications during proceedings, 215-16
arbitration, 8, 143-5, 201-2, 256
  awards, 222
  commercial tribunals, 144
  in settlement of insurance claims, 113
Arbitration Acts
  1950, 38, 160
  1975, 38, 160
  1979, 38, 144, 160, 230
Articles of Association, 15, 35-7,
163, 256
  and directors' responsibilities, 58-9
  increasing capital, 43-4
assets, 45, 47, 52, 256
  loan of, 47-8
  protecting, 12
  rules for valuation, 52, 66
Association of British Chambers of Commerce *add*, 251
Association of Certified and Corporate Accountants, 61
Association of Independent Businesses *add*, 251
attachment of debts, 228-9, 256
attachment of earnings, 228
Attachment of Earnings Act *1971*, 230
audit, annual, 19, 256
auditors, 61-2
average clauses, 110

BOTB, *see* British Overseas Trade Board
balance sheet, 62, 63, 90, 257
Baltic Exchange, 143
Bank of England (Time of Noting) Act *1917*, 180
banker's drafts, 166, 169, 257
Banking Act *1979*, 154, 160
bankruptcy, 222, 224, 231-45, 257
  of partner, 29-30, 31, 237
  procedure, 231-3
  and winding up, 224, 229
Bankruptcy Act *1914*, 230, 232, 245
Bankruptcy Rules *1952*, 245
banks
  accounts, 162-3
  foreign financing, 180